Praise for
HUNGRY BEAUTIFUL ANIMALS

"This compelling read calls us to breathe into our humanity and to understand how our joy increases when we help bring joy to others. We are all connected, and anytime someone experiences kindness, whether human or more than human, our world is made better."

—Gene Baur, resident and cofounder,
Farm Sanctuary

"Halteman is a brilliant writer; the man could make a book about watching grass grown sing. So, imagine what he can do with the topic that is more important to him than anything else in his life other than his family. Quite simply, *Hungry Beautiful Animals* is a spectacular read—profound and also funny, and among the most beautifully constructed books I've ever read. Read this book—you won't be disappointed."

—Bruce Friedrich, president and founder,
Good Food Institute

"Through storytelling, Halteman's *Hungry Beautiful Animals* offers an array of positive reasons to choose vegan, from human rights to personal health, and, importantly, provides a handful of ways to choose vegan. This deeply personal book is not only reader friendly and sprinkled with good humor, but vegan friendly— joyful encouragement to leave meat, dairy, and eggs off the plate."

—Lisa Kemmerer, author of
Animals and World Religions and Eating Earth

"Welcome to Halteman's affirming vision for all of us hungry beautiful animals. Settle into time with an author who believes in our ability to transform moral burdens into gifts of consciousness and lives of abundance. Park feelings of shame, guilt, or blame at the door—they aren't needed here. Instead, in this readable, entertaining, evocative, and joyful book, Halteman offers us vulnerable, questing, caring animals a compass for our compassion and recipes for our individual and collective flourishing."

—Carol J. Adams, author of
The Sexual Politics of Meat

"A visceral argument for the embrace of a joyous vegan lifestyle, advocating that we must alleviate the profound suffering of our fellow travelers on this journey through life, swallowed up in the eternity before and after."

—Christof Koch, author of
Then I Am Myself the World

"This book is remarkable. Halteman invites his readers into an engaging journey of reflection that will leave few unchanged. He sets aside the all-too-common dour and dutiful discussions of this territory in favor of a gentle and winsome invitation to see and feel the attraction of eating differently. I challenge you to read the first few pages with confidence that you'll enjoy Halteman's company until the end."

—David Clough, chair, theology and
applied sciences, University of Aberdeen

"Halteman is a brilliant, incisive thinker and gifted storyteller who writes gorgeous, sharp, vivid prose—page for page and sentence for sentence, not despite but amid sometimes grisly, subtle, and often hilarious observations about being human, his work is a total joy to read. But all of this is second to Halteman's honesty—a rhetorical transparency and open-handedness so complete that his vulnerability in *Hungry Beautiful Animals* is nothing short of incandescent. His willingness to bare the most human of his shortcomings and failures, be they intellectual, spiritual, or personal—without guile, without defensiveness, and without advocating for any brittle or extreme ethical ground—is both inspiring and urgently important. *Hungry Beautiful Animals* is as much a gritty, get-real book about food ethics as it is a rigorous, unpredictable spiritual memoir, and a gentle unfolding of increasingly difficult questions about what it means to be a person engaged in the process of examining their life."

—Bonnie Nadzam, research fellow,
Harvard Animal Law and Policy Program

"*Hungry Beautiful Animals* is the work of a seasoned philosopher and masterful storyteller. It is a deeply honest and intimate but also ebullient book. Halteman doesn't try to argue the reader into anything, but instead uses indirection, humor, and story to make going vegan a salient (and joyful!) option for everyone. By the end, no gap remains between the feeling that one ought to do this and the feeling that one wants to."

—Andrew Chignell, Princeton University

"Veganism is usually motivated by the awareness of disaster—animal cruelty, environmental degradation, avoidable health problems, and needless public health risks, at least. Halteman shows how we can be aware of these tragedies but not let them drag us down—we can respond in uplifting ways that promote meaning, happiness, connection, and love in ourselves and our many communities. He shares how going vegan is not only the appropriate response to many of the world's greatest problems but can help us each become our best selves. Anyone looking to improve the world, and improve themselves, will find great inspiration and wise guidance in this book."

—Nathan Nobis, Morehouse College

"I read *Hungry Beautiful Animals* across three sittings in a single day. So much of what's good about it will be apparent to any reader: its enthusiasm and empathy; its open-heartedness and open-mindedness; its welter (not pejorative!) of funny and helpful stories; its presentation of the complexity of the food system; its idea that because food is so important to so many memories, and because animals are so important to food, animals are sites of nostalgia that a Tofurky for Thanksgiving doesn't really help with; its presentation of vegan commitments as extensions of good ideas we learned in kindergarten; its arguments about shame and change and identity protection; the first sentence of every chapter. I enjoyed reading this sharp, funny, welcoming, helpful, and catholic invitation to going vegan."

—Tyler Doggett, professor of philosophy and graduate faculty of food systems, University of Vermont

HUNGRY BEAUTIFUL ANIMALS

HUNGRY

BEAUTIFUL

ANIMALS

THE JOYFUL CASE FOR
GOING VEGAN

MATTHEW C. HALTEMAN

BASIC BOOKS
New York

Basic Books

Hachette Book Group

1290 Avenue of the Americas, New York, NY 10104

www.basicbooks.com

Printed in the United States of America

First Edition: November 2024

Published by Basic Books, an imprint of Hachette Book Group, Inc. The Basic Books name and logo is a registered trademark of the Hachette Book Group.

The Hachette Speakers Bureau provides a wide range of authors for speaking events. To find out more, go to hachettespeakersbureau.com or email HachetteSpeakers@hbgusa.com.

Basic books may be purchased in bulk for business, educational, or promotional use. For more information, please contact your local bookseller or the Hachette Book Group Special Markets Department at special.markets@hbgusa.com.

The publisher is not responsible for websites (or their content) that are not owned by the publisher.

Print book interior design by Amy Quinn.

Library of Congress Cataloging-in-Publication Data

Names: Halteman, Matthew C., author.

Title: Hungry beautiful animals : the joyful case for going vegan / Matthew C. Halteman.

Description: First edition. | New York : Basic Books, [2024] | Includes bibliographical references and index.

Identifiers: LCCN 2024004291 | ISBN 9781541602052 (hardcover) | ISBN 9781541602069 (ebook)

Subjects: LCSH: Veganism—Moral and ethical aspects. | Meat animals— Moral and ethical aspects.

Classification: LCC TX392 .H25 2024 | DDC 179/.3—dc23/eng/20240314

LC record available at https://lccn.loc.gov/2024004291

ISBNs: 9781541602052 (hardcover), 9781541602069 (ebook)

LSC-C

Printing 1, 2024

For Susan, my partner in love, life, parenting, and advocacy work. Thank you for helping me to see fellow hungry beautiful animals where once I had seen only things.

CONTENTS

Contents

HUNGRY BEAUTIFUL ANIMALS

WE HUMAN BEINGS ARE *HUNGRY* BEAUTIFUL ANImals. We hunger for survival, pleasure, belonging, flourishing, and transcendence, converting food into energy that powers ever-expanding appetites for the meaningful, new, and improved. As feeling creatures, we always already care about the world and find ourselves invested in it, desiring its contents and striving to make them our own. The mere thought of a perfect taco sets our mouths to watering, our fingers to Googling best local options, our minds to canvasing plausible excuses for a longer lunch. We are creatures of powerful hunger, and the adventure of training and fulfilling these desires can draw us toward our best selves or send us careening toward our worst; it can bless the world or curse it.

And we human beings are hungry *beautiful* animals. That we are here at all is a spectacular mystery, a transgression of probability, a gorgeous brute fact in a teeming ocean of mere possibility. That we are here precisely as we *are* is downright breathtaking—big-brained, walking upright, kissed with capacities for creation, cooperation, and love exquisite enough to receive as divine gifts. Who among us has not been rendered gape-jawed by our scientific and artistic ingenuity, moist-eyed by our solidarity in adversity, or warmhearted by those we cherish most or even a stranger in trouble? That we are capable of something more than bare, brute survival, a collective thriving that is lovely to behold, is one of the oldest, most audacious human hopes—the stuff of everything from cave drawings to sacred texts to *Hamilton* to contemporary justice movements. We are achingly beautiful creatures, even and especially when we resolve to do the impossible and fall short.

Yet we human beings are hungry beautiful *animals*. Our desires and our loveliness must make their home together in vulnerable creaturely bodies. We are bounded by breath, blood, bone, belonging, limited perspective and its firstborn, shortsighted selfishness. We are dependent on deep-seated instincts, habits, and herd ways to which we owe our very being and so obey and fear to transgress. We can do very well, but only under conditions that are hospitable to our many frailties and forgiving of our deep vulnerability to harm and death. To survive and thrive, we must learn to live in concert with our fellow earthlings, human and otherwise, respecting and caring for our creaturely limitations and theirs, sharing a world that is all too frequently inhospitable to our efforts.

All hungry beautiful animals must adapt to these inhospitalities to feed the flourishing of fragile bodies. For pigs, elephants, orcas, dogs, and human beings alike, the phrase "hungry beautiful animals" captures our shared predicament in a lovely way, with beauty hanging in the balance between desire and limitation, held in place by a hunger that pushes forward and inviolable animal limits that push back.

But we human beings are the only hungry beautiful animals so far whose adaptive strategies for feeding our hunger and negotiating our creaturely limits have proved mighty enough to challenge the Earth's capacity to continue nourishing vulnerable, dependent creatures at all, including us.

This hunger for more (and ever more convenient and comforting!) food is at the inception of our rise to prominence as a species. In his bestselling book *Sapiens*, historian Yuval Noah Harari describes our earliest ancestors as "a race of cooks" whose domestication of fire vastly expanded the range of safe, convenient, easily digestible foods, freeing humans to spend just one hour a day eating cooked fare while chimpanzees labored away chewing raw foods for up to five.[1]

Three hundred thousand years later, our enduring hunger for ever faster food in ever greater abundance is proving somewhat less liberating. Granted, Spooky Edition Glow-in-the-Dark Oreos are a thing, and air-frying is awesome.[2] But the consequences of raising and consuming eighty billion land animals annually aren't so great.

Climate science warns that we have less than a decade to take radical action to avert the worst effects of climate change. Meanwhile, the most prestigious peer-reviewed research on how to mitigate this coming disaster fingers industrial animal farming as among the biggest contributors to human-caused greenhouse gases and calls eating a plant-based diet "the single biggest way to reduce our environmental impact on the planet."[3] A wide variety of voices—from the Food and Agriculture Organization of the United Nations, to the prestigious journals *Science* and *Nature*, to the EAT-Lancet Commission on Food, Planet, and Health— urgently proclaim in unison that if we want to save the planet, it's well past time to transition away from animal-heavy diets toward plant-based alternatives.[4]

And it's not just our planet that suffers from the excesses of industrial animal agriculture. Nutrition science and epidemiology reveal that our individual and collective health are at stake too. High rates of diet-related diseases like cancer, stroke, diabetes, and heart disease degrade the quality of our lives, hasten our deaths, and swamp our overtaxed healthcare system.[5] COVID-19 is an all-too-vivid harbinger of the pandemic risks posed by bird flu, swine flu, and other zoonotic viruses.[6] Not only are animal products making us sick, but they also threaten our ability to treat illness, as the overuse of antibiotics in confined animal populations is one of the main causes of antimicrobial resistance.[7]

To add insult to injury, the catastrophic practical fallout of our overconsumption of animals is predicated on a moral tragedy. Even as the science of animal behavior confirms that animals are intelligent, emotional, social creatures who care about their lives— indeed, even as record numbers of us experience these truths daily with our beloved pets—our eating habits annually cause the miserable lives and violent deaths of billions just like them.[8]

Let's not forget that the labor required for raising and killing these animals is among the most undesirable and degrading work in the world, described in a recent Oxfam report as grim, dangerous, disproportionately unjust to people already marginalized by racism and/or sexism, and so mercilessly paced that workers resort to wearing diapers for lack of bathroom breaks.[9] The nearly universal consensus of ethics experts is that the modern industrial food system is morally indefensible.[10]

The ugly truth is that our hunger has spawned a food system that is working against our beauty and the hunger and beauty of untold billions of other animals. The resulting lack of balance is making the Earth a much less hospitable place for all of us. Ignoring the increasingly perilous consequences of our collective eating habits is no longer an option for those who wish to avert climate disaster and stand on the right side of history where the lives of our fellow hungry beautiful animals are concerned.

At a minimum, those who care about the viability of life on planet Earth and aspire to live a moral life ought to stand against the scourge of industrial animal agriculture. Those who enjoy the freedom to choose what they eat from a variety of options have excellent reasons to change their diets as a means of expressing and living out their values and hopes for preserving—and improving—life on the planet.

The jury is in. The world needs many more vegans and the most compelling scientific evidence and moral arguments strongly suggest that this global influx of herbivores can't happen soon enough.

And there it is. The v-word. The word that stops the action like a record scratch freeze-frame in a bad '80s movie just before the narrator offers a crestfallen voiceover about how they got into this mess. Want to end a conversation? Work the v-word in there.

Want to sabotage a party? Tell the person with the best jeans that the buffet is vegan. Want to get a person abruptly to stop browsing an incredible new book . . . look, never mind.

If you had told me twenty-five years ago that the new millennium would find me advocating for a vegan world in hopes of wresting creaturely flourishing from the jaws of moral and climate apocalypse, I would have grabbed the nearest side of beef and licked it up and down just to spite you.

Back then, I knew little to nothing about what vegans were actually *for*, and altogether too much about what vegans were *against*—all my favorite foods, my purebred English bulldog, the zoos and aquariums I loved to visit, and of course animal suffering, death, and other unpleasantries that threatened to spoil my dinner, limit my wardrobe, and alienate my friends and family.

I may not be the world's least likely vegan, but the cosmic deck was still well stacked against the decision to change my attitudes and actions toward other creatures. Animal agriculture is deeply rooted in my heritage. My paternal grandfather was an egg farmer. My maternal grandfather was an herbicide chemist. My mom's cousin is an executive at one of America's largest pork producers. I wasn't raised on the farm, but favorite childhood activities included riding tractors, shucking corn, exploring the chicken houses, and playing freeze tag with my cousins behind Great-Grandpop's butcher shed. I owe my existence, my spiritual and moral aspirations, and many of my most cherished experiences to good people in agriculture.[11]

And growing up in the American Midwest, I've spent the lion's share of my life eating and *loving* to eat animal products. I'm the steak-craving high school football player who gorged with fellow linemen on mammoth porterhouses and uncountable infinities of fried shrimp at strip-mall buffets. I'm the knucklehead who posed for photographs at my own wedding with a mouthful of short-rib fangs. I'm the proud amateur dessert chef who delighted friends and family by transfiguring two pounds of mascarpone cheese, a dozen eggs, and a small lake of brandy into the world's most decadent tiramisu.

I'm also a professional philosopher with a strong skeptical streak. It's hard to convince me of anything without compelling evidence, and I've got some well-honed tools at my disposal for warding off ideas I don't like. When a fellow philosopher suggested to me at one fateful conference that my French dip sandwich was practically and morally incompatible with my cherished (and supposedly well-worked-out) views about humankind, other animals, and the environment, my response was aggressively to try to prove him wrong. I went so far as to work up an entire college course on food ethics in hopes of finding ten knock-down, drag-out reasons for him to shut his bunny-kissing mouth so I could continue stuffing mine with fennel-rubbed pork loin.

What I found instead, to my shock, was a compelling combination of empirical evidence and emotional, moral, and spiritual arguments in strong favor of a conclusion I had desperately hoped to avoid: not only did I have every good reason to go vegan myself to benefit my family and me, but I also had urgent cause to inspire others to join me on the journey, given the catastrophic ethical and environmental costs of our collective resistance to changing our suicidal way of life. In the wake of this epiphany and my own decision to go vegan, I've spent the past two decades learning as much as I can from others, writing, and offering courses, public lectures, and workshops—I even cofounded a festival!—to share what I've learned.

So now I'm going to put the climate gun to your head and the ethics knife to your throat and try to bully you into eating plants, right? Maybe if I rub your nose in facts and arguments long enough while yelling "Booooooooo!" in your ear loud enough, you'll slink away from the comforts of familiarity, chastened into considering obligations you dread (temporarily, at least, until you're seduced by the next irresistible waft of whatever favorite food you've been guiltily fantasizing about since the first mention of the v-word)?

Heavens, no! This time-tested recipe for failure is most definitely not on the menu.

One of the most important lessons I've learned over the past twenty years is that shame and blame rarely lead to transformation.[12] My hope, rather, is to woo you, to dazzle you, to inspire you with a vision of a vegan world so grand that no rigid "-ism" with a one-size-fits-all rule book and infinite ways to get disqualified could contain it.

I want to kick shame and blame to the curb and open the road to a gorgeous life of abundance perfectly tuned to delight the hungry beautiful animals we are—a life that satiates our deepest desires, respects our inviolable limits, and makes room for the flourishing of other hungry beautiful animals too. I want to convince you that we're all in this beautiful thing together—not just the edgiest, eco-friendliest, most justice-driven among us, but *everyone* who is hungry to make the most of the gorgeous opportunity to steer a fragile body full of need and desire toward the fullest possible flourishing for all of us. I want to articulate a vision of the vegan life so beautiful that it captures your imagination and compels participation not by the threat of shame, but by the delight of your own irresistible desire to draw nearer to what you love.

Think about someone you richly enjoy, or something you find beautiful, or that favorite holiday dessert you sneak downstairs at two in the morning to pilfer out from under your slumbering family. Do you need an argument for a second round of drinks or another game of one-on-one with your BFF? A reason for lingering past dusk on the cooling sands of a recently deserted beach? A sales pitch to motivate a second round of tiramisu?

You probably don't. If you're like me, products of careful reflection like arguments, reasons, and sales pitches are the farthest thing from your mind in situations like these, because desire is on the job and you are feeling it. The beautiful object of your desire is doing the motivational work, so all that browbeating required to force you toward less welcome things is completely unnecessary.

My teacher in the ways of woo when it comes to gorgeous vegan living that requires no justification but its own beauty is the inimitable Bryant Terry.[13] A celebrated chef, cookbook author, and food justice activist as comfortable cheffing a pop-up in San Francisco as taking the lectern at Yale, Bryant always says, "Start with the visceral, move to the cerebral, and end at the political"—another way of saying "Let's put on some Isaac Hayes, fill the house with the aroma of pomegranate-peach barbecue sauce, and break bread together before we don our thinking caps and conspire to solve the world's problems."

In serving as an advisor for the development of his *Afro-Vegan* cookbook, I was the one who got served a sumptuous plate of his gratitude-drenched, beauty-first approach to vegan living, and it left an indelible impression. Bryant taught me that if you want to get people fired up about making the world a better place— and we must!—invite them first into an experience they love so that the connections between their deepest desires and the better world we must create together can shine forth in the light of beauty.

Imagine for a moment (however far-fetched it may seem now) that the vision of a vegan world moved you to action through deeply felt desire rather than a sense of dreaded obligation—that going vegan felt more like moving in for a second bite of tiramisu than carving out time to clean the house. What would that vision look like? How would it feel to experience it and be carried away by its beauty? How might its wind in your sails change the course of your life in the day to day?

I hope this book will furnish you with an inspiring set of answers to these questions, because let's face it: mass enthusiasm about the pressing need for a new vegan normal is not the current state of play. The sad truth is that most people would rather skydive without a parachute than go vegan. As Farhad Manjoo observes in a fervent plea in the *New York Times* to "Stop Mocking Vegans," "The stereotype of the smug, self-satisfied, annoying vegan has taken deep cultural root," so much so that—according to one study—"vegans are viewed more negatively than atheists" and are "only slightly more tolerated than drug addicts."[14]

It isn't difficult to understand why going vegan is widely perceived as a serious buzzkill. Everyone knows the perceived downsides. For starters, many of the most obvious markers of material success and cultural dominance are straight-up off limits. Say goodbye to lobster, filet mignon, leather upholstery, exotic pets, fur coats, blue suede shoes, and trophy hunting and fishing.

Setting these luxuries aside, vegans face unwelcome prohibitions on even the most homespun cultural and religious identity markers: good riddance to the cherished Thanksgiving turkey, Christmas ham, Eid lamb kebabs, and roasted brisket for Shabbat. From outside, going vegan inevitably looks to many like a recipe for sad, lonely lives of self-deprivation and judgment of others. In the immortal words of the grinning raccoon meme, "I start conversations with 'As a vegan' when I no longer wish to be friends with someone."

To make matters worse, vegans themselves often tacitly assume this life-negating frame of reference and communicate the significance of going vegan as though its spiritual heart were abstaining from particular things that are bad. See this horrific factory farm? That's wrong! Don't support it! See these evil medical experiments on animals? That's heinous! Stop taking those drugs! Look at these bored, listless baboons! For shame! No more zoos!

It's beyond dispute in my view that the need is urgent to direct our moral attention to these and other places that perpetuate animal cruelty.[15] But the incessant drumbeat of bad news, sometimes delivered in what is perceived as a spirit of condescension or even contempt, has a way of burying the lead that there are many great goods that inspire people to go vegan and many advantages (for people, animals, and planet) to making it a way of life.

And the judgmental spirit that can emanate from this negative framing of going vegan isn't just reserved for folks outside the club. Vegans are often even harder on themselves, privately enduring the deep shame of internalizing their own inevitable failures to give up all the things. Cheap chocolate at Halloween. Samples at the grocery store. Free pizza at work. Favorite shoes. Even after every delinquent leather belt has been purged from the closet, the threat of inauthenticity looms behind every flu shot (cultured in egg products!), teaspoon of sugar (refined using bone char!), or glass of wine (clarified with fish bladders!).

If vegans themselves often fall victim to the shame and blame game, it's no wonder that the wider world can scarcely imagine what a fulfilling vegan life might look like. And this *lack of imagination*—this inability to conceive of going vegan as resulting in a true, beautiful, and good life worth living—can haunt us in the very deepest reaches of our lives. The mere entrance into the break room of a vegan friend or colleague can serve to pummel us with defensive questions that ripple across our physical, social, emotional, intellectual, and moral selves: Could I survive a life without cheese? Would my family disown me if I gave up hunting? Aren't human beings more important than animals? Aren't animals a gift from God to use for our comfort and enjoyment? How could I ever run a marathon on a diet of rice and steamed broccoli? Am I supposed to start judging my friends now for eating ribs?

These questions almost always discourage further inquiry and understandably so. The forces of resistance to going vegan stirred by such questions are no joke. Enjoyment of pleasure. Familial loyalty. Human fellow-feeling. Gratitude to the divine. Concern for bodily health. The comforts of friendship. The fear of rejection. These are among the most powerful shaping forces at work within us! Summoning the courage to try to reset these defaults is no small feat. To claim otherwise is to underestimate how deeply encultured our dietary habits and attitudes toward animals really are.

But even if we find the courage to expand our imaginative horizons far enough to envision going vegan as an exciting prospect, yet another problem lies in wait: our faltering wills. It's one thing to imagine oneself choosing the vegan chili over the pastrami sub, or the canvas kicks over the python pumps if the two were floating side by side, equally accessible, in a social vacuum. It's quite another thing to make those choices when the cost is extra prep time, additional expense, lost pleasure, jeering friends, or skeptical family members.

Imagining being happy and fulfilled as a vegan, then, and *willing* the attitudes and actions to make it possible every day, can feel like two very different prospects. Not only do these abilities not come naturally to most people, but they cut deeply against the grain of many comforting and pleasurable things that do. Imagining oneself content never to eat another eggs benny birthday brunch or wear another merino sweater is hard enough. But finding the will to follow through as the grocery bill increases, stylish, well-made clothing becomes harder to source, and you struggle to find delicious dishes at favorite restaurants, well—that may seem impossible to endure!

So our predicament is complex.

We'd be vastly better off, individually and collectively, if going vegan became the new normal. Going vegan has many personal and global benefits and is key to ameliorating catastrophic environmental and ethical problems including climate change, diet-related diseases, global pandemics, antibiotic resistance, worker injustice, and animal cruelty.

But going vegan is unpopular, even infamous. People are generally much more familiar with the downsides than the upsides, both because going vegan is often framed negatively (and sometimes judgmentally) as a reaction to bad news, and because a skeptical world is just waiting to pounce on any perceived inconsistency as confirmation that going vegan is so much holier-than-thou hooey.

Against this backdrop, it's difficult for most people to imagine both *what* would motivate a person to go vegan in the first place and *how*, more concretely, they could do so themselves without compromising aspects of their identities that seem nonnegotiable for happy, healthy living. And even if one has the imaginative bandwidth to aspire to go vegan, there's that pesky problem of finding the will to go through with it in the face of what can feel like insurmountable financial, social, and physical costs.

Making the world safe for a new vegan normal, then, requires solutions to three central problems, which I call the challenges of illumination, imagination, and motivation.

The challenge of illumination is to rescue the decision to go vegan from infamy and misinformation by offering a clear and compelling case for the practical and moral urgency of going vegan based in mainstream scientific and ethical views that most people already accept. But if lighting the path in this way can remove important obstacles to going vegan and demonstrate the resonance of doing so with mainstream beliefs and commitments, it is often not enough to get people excited about taking the journey. It's one thing, after all, to *see* that something is in our best interest and another thing entirely to desire to do it.

Getting energized about the challenge of reimagining our ideal world and enthusiastically embracing all it has to offer is a second step in the process. The challenge of imagination, then, is to cast a vision of a vegan world so true, beautiful, and good that it captures our imaginations and stokes our desire to go vegan not just because we should, but because we aspire to realize the many great goods that we, our neighbors, other animals, and the Earth stand to gain from doing so.

However evocative of a desire for change this reimagination of a vegan world may be, the realities of life on the ground all too often thwart even our best laid and most fervently desired plans. So the challenge of motivation, finally, is to construct an engaging, accessible, inspiring set of strategic tools for finding the will to go and stay vegan even and especially when we can't realize our vegan aspirations as fully as we hope in an imperfect world.

The goal of this book is to show how we can meet these three challenges in such a welcoming and inspiring way that readers of all kinds will come away enlightened about the practical and moral urgency of going vegan, energized about the promise of a vegan world, and emboldened to take whatever concrete steps toward that aspiration their talents, gifts, and circumstances permit.

It's no accident that my strategies for meeting these challenges map nicely onto the ideas of truth, beauty, and goodness—the "transcendentals" that philosophers in traditions as diverse as Hinduism, Neoplatonism, and Christianity took to represent the deepest desires of humankind: the desire to be enlightened by the naked truth of our circumstances rather than duped by the fraud of a fool's paradise; the desire to be elevated by the beauty of captivating creatures and inspiring places instead of degraded by repugnant company and depressing surroundings; and the desire to enjoy the great goodness of flourishing within our limits rather than suffering the maladies of failing to respect them.

I'm inviting you into a vision of the vegan life that runs on desire rather than shame, that makes attraction to what we really want deep down rather than obligation to unappealing expectations the powerhouse of our commitment. And what better way to achieve that result than to structure this vision around the fulfillment of the three deepest human desires?

The three parts of this book are aimed, thus, at meeting the challenges of illumination, imagination, and motivation with a strategy custom-fitted for hungry beautiful animals like us who desire truth, beauty, and goodness above all else.

Part I meets the challenge of illumination by elucidating the practical and moral urgency of establishing a new vegan normal, explaining why this urgency comes as such terrible news to most people, and showing that—despite our collective reluctance—the great promise of going vegan can be framed compellingly in terms of widely shared views and moral commitments that most of us already hold dear. Despite appearances, a vegan world turns out to be something that many of us already deeply desire, even if we haven't explicitly tapped into it yet.

Part II meets the challenge of imagination by drawing on that wellspring of desire to develop a beautiful, holistic vision of what vegans are for, clarifying the many interconnected ways that establishing a new vegan normal could propel the world toward a truer, more beautiful, and altogether better state for human beings, other animals, and the Earth.

Part III meets the challenge of motivation by distilling the general aspirations of the vegan imagination into realistic goals for our specific circumstances, designing a disciplined but malleable regime of daily practices to motivate steady progress toward these goals, and developing a strategy for discerning and delighting in the incremental progress of our transformation rather than lamenting what remains imperfect or undone.

But more important than the goal of this book is the soul of this book—the animating spirit that I hope will sweep you up into the work of *Hungry Beautiful Animals* and abide with you at each step, filling you with a sense of purpose and solidarity much bigger than the sum of the parts.

If you've ever been involved in a sports team or fandom, a religious community or political movement, a determined task force at work, or even a die-hard friend group facing a shared ordeal, you know how crucial it is for the endeavor to have *soul*—for there to be a spirit of unity working among you that transcends your individual frailties and foibles and somehow reveals and mobilizes everyone's best gifts as the challenges mount and the heat rises.[16] There are many ways to think about what soul might be and where it comes from, but I'll just think of it here as a binding, elevating chemistry that unifies willing participants in a common cause, buoying them up to do important work together.

The soul of this book—its elevating chemistry—is the aspiration for each of us to work out our own compelling answer to a simple but transformative question that could render us unstoppable together: What if the world knew as much about the true, beautiful, and good things that vegans are for as they know about the false, ugly, and bad things they're against and what would it look like to channel our unique talents and gifts into catalyzing that cultural awakening? Imagine how the public perception of going vegan might change if we stopped describing this way of life in terms of abstaining from things that are false, ugly, and bad and reimagined it instead in terms of aspiring to a world that is true, beautiful, and good!

As Keeanga-Yamahtta Taylor powerfully observes, "No social movement begins with the question of what is possible; it is typically fueled by imagining what could be."[17] In its most compelling form, the aspiration to go vegan is not about negating life as it is, but rather about imaginatively embracing life as it could be—envisioning a world in which we do not need to exploit, abuse, and oppress others to enjoy an abundant and healthful diet, innovative style, expanded consciousness of the lives of others, genuine interspecies kinship with intelligent, emotional, social creatures, and increased hope for social justice and climate stability.

By giving pride of place to the imagination-capturing power of this positive vision of the vegan life, my hope is to supplant the popular caricatures of vegans as judgmental hipsters, pie-in-the-sky ascetics, and self-denying fad dieters with a much more compelling portrait of going vegan as a reasonable, compassionate, pragmatic, inclusive, and ultimately inspiring journey into being and doing well in an age of unprecedented moral and environmental crisis.

Flipping the script on what it means to go vegan has been my dream for the past decade. For years, the standard negative framing of the vegan life has been a perennial source of deflation in my teaching, writing, and advocacy work. It has been endlessly frustrating to me that a vision of the world grounded in mainstream moral values like wanting to be healthful, well-informed, fair-minded, compassionate, and helpful to those in need is so often communicated and received—sometimes even by folks striving to live out this vision (guilty!)—as a radical, judgmental, exclusionary, and lonely negation of life.

The transformational shift in perspective that results from reimagining the vegan life in view of the true, beautiful, and good things that vegans are for (rather than the false, ugly, and bad things they're against) has been both deeply inspirational and profoundly liberating for me. In my personal life, this vision has moved me away from rigidity, anxiety, and even despair over what I cannot do perfectly, toward freedom, confidence, and even joy in what I'm aspiring to do.

In my teaching and speaking, it has facilitated much more curiosity, enthusiasm, and empowerment among audiences and far less defensiveness, discouragement, and chastened shame. Sharing this abundant vision of the vegan life with you in this book is nothing short of a dream come true, and it's my answer to the above question of what it would look like to channel my unique talents and gifts into catalyzing this cultural awakening. Over the next nine chapters, we'll develop all the tools you need to formulate your own one-of-a-kind answer to this question so that you and the world can receive the transformational gift of your unique contribution to this elevating chemistry!

The destination of this journey is an inviting, empowering, and inclusive understanding of everyday vegan living that abandons the demoralizing goal of *arriving* once and for all at a perfected individual *identity* in favor of inspired but practical *striving* toward a global *aspiration*—to do what one enthusiastically can, within one's limits and always imperfectly, to live toward a truer, more beautiful, better vegan world. Instead of framing our individual efforts to go vegan unrealistically in terms of the achievement of a one-size-fits-all state of being (a "cruelty-free" identity), we'll envision going vegan as a liberating journey of becoming that unfolds uniquely for every person based on what their individual and communal situations inspire and enable them to contribute.

That's why I'm assiduously avoiding using the term "veganism" to describe the vision of the world and accompanying set of practices that I hope to beautify in this book. In my experience, "-isms" often just aren't very inviting. Even when they're inclusive, they're often still perceived as uncompromising and identity focused. No matter how friendly and welcoming vegans themselves may be (and in my experience, they're usually both!), veganism seems to offer little room to deviate from stringent expectations and value judgments that many find alienating even when they're open to moving in a vegan direction.

"Going vegan," by contrast, is an open-ended, ongoing, aspirational activity that takes shape through practicing an evolving set of exercises.[18] One can be at different places along the way of one's journey into going vegan—the beginning, the end, a slump in the middle, a renaissance brought on by a beautiful new cookbook or friend—but the adventure of going vegan lasts a lifetime and this adventure is an action, not an identity. One cannot "be a vegan" in the sense of having mastered the practice or fully instantiated the ideal. One is always still *going vegan*, no matter how long one has been in the game.

By explicitly embracing the language of "going vegan" rather than "adopting veganism," I am advancing an outlook on the vegan life that is progressive and action focused rather than perfectionistic and identity based. I want to create space for anyone who is even remotely intrigued by the vegan vision to adopt the aspiration of "being on the way," even if their day-to-day practices still depart radically from the ideal. Whether one is a level-50 vegan who eats nothing that casts a shadow (like Lisa Simpson) or a person resolving to try a new vegan recipe once a week as a first step, the important thing is that one is going vegan—moving in the direction of that beautiful vision through the practice of concrete disciplines that enable whatever approximation your circumstances will currently tolerate.

But who are you, dear reader, and how do I make sure you can profit from this book?

My aim is to write with such humility, hospitality, and verve that anyone can!

If you're veg-curious but still inclined to see going vegan as so much radical, privileged, plant-based pie in the sky, I hope this book will persuade you that aspiring to go vegan is among the best things going for reasonable, emotionally intelligent, morally centered people of goodwill who want to put their resources and advocacy where their ideals are.

If you're a conflicted carnivore looking for ways to smooth out your cognitive dissonance and motivate yourself to become increasingly herbivorous, I hope this book will help you kick shame and blame to the curb and step out in boldness toward a life of decreased anxiety and increased joy.

If you're a concerned parent looking for insight into why your child is suddenly refusing favorite meals and picketing restaurants, I hope this book can demystify and illuminate these new commitments and clarify their deep resonance with much older family values that you raised them to cherish.

If you're an activist or an entrepreneur wondering how the promise of a new vegan normal might amplify or complicate the causes or enterprises to which you're devoting your life, I hope this book will help you to throttle up your efforts in provocative and compelling ways previously unimagined.

If you're a proud meat producer, angler, hunter, or trapper to whom this vision of a vegan world seems absurd or threatening or both, I hope this book goes some way toward narrowing the gap between us, preferably by shoring up some spaces of common ground despite big differences, but, at the very least, by enabling you better to know and respect your adversary.

And if you're already an aspiring vegan, perhaps suffering as I have under the weight of expectations that can feel impossible to meet, I hope this book helps you understand your vegan aspirations better, strive for them more cheerfully and sustainably, and gain confidence with some compelling strategies for inviting others to the party. Though this book is not principally concerned with "preaching to the choir," I would love to help the choir learn some beautiful new songs that can captivate and delight ever-larger audiences.

Perhaps you even identify with *many* of the above hypothetical personas. I've been five of the six myself, often at the same time, and yes—"proud angler" was one of them. Whoever you are and wherever you happen to be on the journey, please know that this book is rooted in a sincere desire to be radically inclusive and to set a place at this sumptuous table just for you.

As you'll discover in these pages, the state of the world is such that we need everyone at the banquet. The vision is grand enough for everyone to find their special place. And the strategy for success is flexible enough to meet folks where they are. The reimagination of the vegan life that inspired this book is not about arriving at a particular vegan identity as individuals, but rather about striving in solidarity—along whatever paths we happen to be traveling—toward a beautiful vegan world that is deeply desirable for human beings and appreciably better for all hungry beautiful animals and the earthly home that sustains us.

PART I

ILLUMINATION

THE NEED FOR A NEW VEGAN NORMAL

CHAPTER 1

VEGAN OR BUST

A WORLD IN CRISIS

G US HALTEMAN WAS AN ENGLISH BULLDOG. HE PRE-
ferred root vegetables to kibble and ate roughly six pounds
of carrots per week. He despised it when Susan and I went on vacation without him. The merest glimpse of a suitcase elicited a defi-
ant dump in the middle of the dining room where no one could
miss the protest. For years, his veterinary bills were the second
highest line item in our budget after our mortgage, encompassing
a nose job and palate surgery to open his scrunchy airways, lipo-
suction to disburden his stocky joints, and emergency abdominal
surgery to extract an erstwhile hockey puck. His many charms
were so universally compelling that walking him became a daily
time-management crisis, as even the steeliest passersby needed
a minute to melt into a puddle of joy at the sight of him. This
muscle-bound sawmill slept in our bed for almost twelve years, and

his ambitious and varied snoring became so essential to my beauty rest that, upon his death, a dear musician friend had to compose a "Gus Snoring Lullaby" from scattered recordings to help me sleep.[1]

Gus compelled me to see our animal-based food system as an existential threat to life on planet Earth. It's probably more accurate to say that he opened me fully to feeling this disturbing truth. Just "knowing" about it, as we all now reluctantly seem to—reading umpteen apocalyptic articles, viewing this or that horrifying documentary—couldn't render the tragedy of our food system viscerally enough to move me from uncomfortable if tolerable cognitive dissonance to that guts-deep bodily repulsion that propels one involuntarily away from what is vile. There's a self-doubting part of me that wishes the experiential catalyst of my awakening were more objective and reason driven, and much less contingent on something as happenstance as my emotional entanglement with a flatulent, squishy-faced fireplug on legs. But the truth is the truth.

Loving someone as much as I loved Gus made me considerably more curious about the lives of other creatures like him—chickens, pigs, cows, and turkeys no less clever or feeling than the chowderhead snoring in my lap—and directed my attention to the consequences of treating them as we do, not just for the animals themselves, but for us and for the world at large. It's one thing to know in the abstract that bad things happen to large numbers of animals in our food system and that treating them thus is unpleasant for workers and causes a bunch of other climate- and health-related problems. It's another thing entirely to feel deep down disgust for a system that inflicts lives of abject suffering on hundreds of billions of creatures just like Gus, radiating the horrors of their exploitation across the world in the wildfires, floods, and hurricanes of climate change, the health scourges of heart failure, cancer, and pandemic disease, and the psychological and physical degradation of already marginalized workers who must repeatedly harm, kill, and finally hack them to pieces in our names.

My feelings for Gus transformed the endless stream of horrors visited upon the world by our food system from a cable news ticker just beneath the threshold of my serious attention to an intolerable sorrow that has in turns caused me to burst into tears, shake with rage, curse myself and my fellow human beings, shake my fist at the heavens, and eventually devote my life in letters and teaching to trying to be the change I want to see in our eating habits.

"Well, shit," you might be thinking. "Bait and switch much?! What happened to wooing ourselves into doing something in deep resonance with our truest, most beautiful, and best desires? This book is starting to sound like the usual shame and blame fest that inevitably spills forth whenever the v-word is invoked."

I see the worry. My interest in sharing all this terrible news is to grow caring, induce empathy, and attune us to the opportunity costs in truth, beauty, and goodness of our current system—certainly not to wallow in shame and blame. Still, is it really a good idea to begin a journey that aspires to beauty with such a painful first step?

I think so.

There is a reason that fasting comes before feasting, the climb before the summit, and the sweetest victory at the expense of the most formidable opponent. To attempt to behold beauty without first facing the hard truth risks the imagination's escape into a fool's paradise and denies us the vivifying contest that heightens our appreciation of a hard-won outcome. To fully appreciate the holistic beauty of a vegan world requires that we become painfully aware of the pervasive ugliness and destruction of our current practices and the full range of their disastrous effects.

But the promise of heightening our appreciation of the beauty we can expect of a new vegan normal isn't the only reason to start with the hard truth. The reality for creatures like us is that inertia is a powerful force. Finding the gumption to change the status quo requires dissatisfaction and even pain to enter the equation. If it ain't broke, we won't fix it. And it's not just because we're lazy (though sometimes, admittedly, we are). It's because we're wired from deep in our evolutionary history to conserve precious energy by falling back on habit, letting the autopilot of the "old brain" (the parts that evolved first to regulate our most basic survival functions) run the show.

In *Unwinding Anxiety*, renowned addiction psychiatrist and neuroscientist Judson Brewer explains that breaking bad habits requires becoming disgusted with the self-defeating pseudo-comforts of negative behaviors so that our old brain can unlearn these ruts and seek "bigger, better offers" for more sustainable, mindful forms of comfort and security. Becoming disgusted with our bad habits, Brewer explains, demands first that we pay close attention to our negative habit loops so that we can see, and more importantly, feel their ill effects in our lives, impressing upon our old brain that these behaviors are hurting us.[2] Brewer describes, for example, patients who quit smoking by tuning in to the bad experiences habit usually hides—the terrible smell, the social stigma—so that these alienating realities leap out of the habitual background, encouraging the brain to seek a more productive habitual response to anxiety (say, a mindful meditation or breathing exercise).

This chapter is devoted to bringing the pain before the gain, helping us to become conscious of and repulsed by the destruction wreaked by our food system and the eating habits that prop it up. But the pain itself is not the point and we won't wallow in it. In thinking about the role of pain in this chapter (and more broadly, in Part I of this book), let's keep in mind the famed "change formula" popularized by Kathie Dannemiller, the late great innovation expert: $C = D \times V \times F > R$. Change happens, Dannemiller contends, when the combined impact of Dissatisfaction with the way things are now, Vision for what the future could hold, and access to concrete First steps toward that vision is greater than the forces of Resistance to change.[3]

If you prefer spiritually charged language on the importance of feeling pain for motivating change to neuroscientific or corporate consulting lingo, Pope Francis makes the point beautifully in his encyclical on climate matters, *Laudato Si'*: "Our goal is not to amass information or to satisfy curiosity, but rather to become painfully aware, to dare to turn what is happening in the world into our own personal suffering and thus to discover what each of us can do about it."[4] The purpose of cultivating painful awareness here is the very opposite of wallowing in shame and blame. The point is gathering life energy for increased caring that manifests in real acts of reconciliation.

With these insights in mind, think of this chapter as a surgical exercise in becoming painfully aware. The goal is to provide an essential ingredient for change that is catalyzed by the beautiful vision of a new vegan normal advanced in Part II and the concrete strategies for striving toward this vision developed in Part III. We'll get the bad news first in facing the true costs of our hunger for cheap animal products, but it's all for the sake of becoming the most beautiful animals we can be by bringing our desires into lovelier harmony with our limitations.

If you're already a level-50 vegan, my focus on the food system may raise your blood pressure. You might be thinking, "Going vegan is first and foremost about justice for animals. Framing the vegan life as primarily about eating habits is disingenuous and incomplete. We need to take direct aim at the injustice of treating other animals as property to obliterate the very foundation of the pet, clothing, entertainment, and animal research industries too![5] That's not going to happen by getting people jazzed about plant-based sausages, Mr. Meatless Monday."

Too true, level-50 vegan, too true. I share your concern about justice for animals and I agree that going vegan is not just about eating plants. My aspiration throughout this book is to cast a vision of the vegan life that sees food choices as one particularly important and holistic way (among many) to promote truth, beauty, and goodness for *everyone* who can experience them, including and especially the nonhuman animals we so often neglect to consider.

I'll have more to say in Chapters 5 and 6 about how justice for animals—the guiding and worthy aim of the modern vegan movement these past fifty years—gears into the holistic vision of going vegan I advance in this book. For now, let me explain why our animal-based food system is at center stage, especially here in the pain chapter but also throughout the book.

The reason is straightforward. When it comes to going vegan, dietary changes are at once the most urgent concern for most people and the action that would create the biggest collective impact by far. When vegans at the party cause horrified friends and family to scatter like roaches from a tactical flashlight, it's typically their refusal of cocktail sausages rather than their pleather shoes that get them in trouble. And given industrial animal agriculture's outsized influence across a dizzying array of social, commercial, and political institutions and its profound reach into the lives and habitats of every existing earthling from the topsoil to the oceans to the atmosphere, focusing on this system and the standard Western (and increasingly global) diet that sustains it is the clearest and most compelling way to highlight both the urgent need for a vegan world and the incredible promise that going vegan holds out to us.

It can be difficult to grasp the vastness and reach of our food system, especially when our understanding of what is at stake is limited to the parts of it that are routinely sensationalized in advocacy campaigns and on the news: concentrated animal feeding operations (CAFOs or "factory farms") and slaughterhouses. Make no mistake that these places are horrific. The widespread public criticism they receive is well earned. I'll echo and amplify it below. But CAFOs and slaughterhouses are just two sites in a tremendously complex system of intermeshed industries, institutions, and practices that support and sustain one another. To transform this system, we must overcome the tunnel vision that tempts us to scapegoat CAFO farmers and slaughterhouse workers for the sins of an entire system and acknowledge that this system is a whole of interconnected parts.[6]

To understand industrial animal agriculture is to become painfully aware that all of us are already actors in this drama. Some of us are major players and some of us have only bit parts, but the work of turning pigs into bacon and chickens into wings requires many hands, the vast majority of which are not castrating piglets in CAFOs or slitting chicken throats in slaughterhouses. That we often reserve our disgust and disapprobation for those who have little choice but to become the hands that do the dirty work doesn't change the fact of our participation in the system or our potential to be a part of its transformation.

Consider all the hands that must be hard at work before one can raise a fork at the average Western dinner table:

The timber and pulp industries clear forests to create land for grazing and growing grain.

Oil companies produce petroleum for chemical companies to make herbicides, pesticides, and fertilizers to support crop growth.

Feed companies use vast amounts of water, land, and petroleum products to grow grain for animals used for food.

Selective breeding scientists and bioengineers design economically advantageous breeds of animals whose bodies convert grain to product as quickly and profitably as possible.

Pharmaceutical companies make antimicrobial drugs to keep disease under control in confined animal populations otherwise vulnerable to widespread sickness and death.

CAFOs and feedlots house and feed animals until they reach market weight.

Handling companies transport animals from CAFOs and feedlots to slaughterhouses.

Slaughterhouses and processing plants kill and dismember animals for distribution.

Distributing companies supply hotels, universities, and retailers.

Grocery stores and restaurants purchase food for consumer sales.

For all these industries, banks and investors provide capital, law firms and marketing companies provide support services, and lobbying agencies secure favorable legislative conditions.

Lawmakers represent the interests of food industries in their states.

Finally, consumers purchase and eat the food.

Facing the true costs of industrial animal agriculture thus confronts us with the impact of our daily consumer decisions on everyone and everything on the planet. Tempting though it is to fantasize from afar that the horrors of industrial animal agriculture are contained within the darkest corners of the worst CAFOs and slaughterhouses, the grim reality is that the fallout of this vast system marbles our lives and our Earth like the fat in a beef short loin. Every meal is shot through with opportunities to trace the ripple effects of our daily choices across the world.

A traditional breakfast of eggs and bacon raises the question of what life is like for the chickens and pigs who become the food. The drive-thru "value meal" at lunch prompts us to wonder about the hidden labor, environmental, and climate costs of keeping such resource-intensive Mcfoods so "cheap and convenient." The surf-n-turf brunch reveals the hidden path from the feed-lots where cows consume resource-guzzling grain to the runoff of their excrement into our waterways and the resulting devastation of aquatic life. The pizza at midnight gives us pause to reflect on the correlation between our rising blood pressures and ballooning healthcare costs. The cheapness and ubiquity of fast food relative to the expense and scarcity of fresh, nutrient-dense food in economically challenged neighborhoods reveals that lobbyists and legislators have a heavy thumb on the scale of food justice and that "food apartheid" is a more accurate description of the realities on the ground than "food desert."[7] Becoming painfully aware of the ripple effects of our eating habits, though sobering, is undeniably an enlightening starting point as an activity that daily illuminates both the devastating impact of our current food system and the transformative promise of reforming it.[8]

Reassessing our eating habits is an empowering starting point too as an activity over which many of us have a significant degree of control. Few of us can decide overnight to become full-time activists, ecologists, entrepreneurs, biodynamic produce farmers, or even electric car owners. But a great many of us have the power to change our eating habits in ways that can collectively transform our lives and the world at large. And because eating is often a communal activity, the convictions of a few can inspire a great many, as friends and family, teachers and students, businesses and workers, religious leaders and their communities begin to see that eating more intentionally is something they too can find inspiring—as well as delicious, nutritious, and cost-effective.[9]

This choice to focus on our food system has the final advantage of providing an accessible gateway into broader concern for the lives of animals in other sectors. Many of us find it difficult to confront the implications of seeking justice for animals while we're still eating them. But as we grow curious about making plant-based choices for other reasons—perhaps our own health, or the environment, or justice for hungry or oppressed fellow human beings—we may become less resistant to the idea that animals matter too, and more likely to explore other ways to improve their lives.

This combination of factors—that our animal-based food system generates enormous global pain across all sectors of the human, animal, and environmental world, that the vision of its reform is thus gorgeously far-reaching, and that the first steps to pursuing that transformation are both accessible to many and also likely to demystify the idea of animal liberation more broadly—makes focusing on this system a uniquely powerful strategy for illuminating the need for and promise of going vegan. Starting with the pet, clothing, entertainment, and animal research industries (other places where the modern vegan movement is keen for good reason to see transformation take shape) does not offer the same strategic benefits.

The first step in meeting the challenge of illumination, thus, is to become painfully aware of the sordid details of industrial animal agriculture's catastrophic fallout. One does not become painfully aware, though, by reviewing a depressing list of facts that most of us already know on some level. Cultivating painful awareness is a work of emotional education—a task that involves internalizing and allowing oneself to feel the experiences of others in ways that engage curiosity, expand empathy, and elicit action. Let me begin by acknowledging three things that make engaging emotionally with the catastrophic impact of industrial animal agriculture very difficult.

First, there's no groundbreaking new information in this chapter that hasn't been splashed for years across the pages of the likes of the *New York Times*, the *Atlantic*, the *American Conservative*, *National Review*, *Science*, and *Nature*. The bad news reported here is exceedingly well-documented by every sector that's been paying attention, from news organizations to popular magazines to peer-reviewed journals to NGO reports to expert nonfiction. At this point, one can barely turn a page or doomscroll away the wee hours without being bombarded by apocalyptic stories about our food system and the urgent need to transform it.

Second, the ubiquity of apocalyptic news about industrial animal agriculture means that many of us are just plumb exhausted by it. Like those insufferable emails from political candidates who claim that your immediate $15 contribution is the only remaining defense against anarchy, we just can't do it anymore. Yawn. Delete.

Third, there are so many nasty things one can truthfully say about industrial animal agriculture that one simply can't cover them all without going well beyond most people's threshold of tolerance for bad news.

This situation is not exactly a writer's dream. I hope to move you past knowing what everybody "knows" about our broken food system to feeling viscerally that the situation is intolerable. But I can't tell you anything new, you're probably already fatigued by the topic, and unless you're a masochist, I've got very limited time to make my case. Only the world's most compelling curation strategy has a chance in blazes of winning the day.

It was Gus the bulldog who changed the frame for me, so I'm turning to Professor Gus in the clutch to help us out of this pickle. Gus was my companion and teacher throughout my emotional education on these matters. Loving Gus led to a deeper, more holistic love of the world—a love that had little choice but to find the animal-based food status quo repulsive and ultimately intolerable. Undergoing this learning process alongside a unique, irreplaceable, and completely devoted nonhuman friend catalyzed my awakening, enabling a gaggle of noisome facts to become a deeply moving and ultimately life-transforming narrative.

Reconstructing that narrative here will allow me to trace some of the most devastating and revolting effects of our animal-based food system on human beings, animals, and the planet while tempering all that carnage with a loving remembrance of Gus's life from the cradle to the grave. Juxtaposing the details of his birth, daily experiences, and death with analogous experiences undergone by fellow creatures used for food can bring the horrors of industrial animal agriculture into sharp and poignant relief. The story that emerges is one in which my love for a nonhuman friend freed me up finally to recoil from a food system whose exploitation of animals is both disgusting in itself and responsible for spawning repulsive effects in every conceivable direction.

I have chosen the words "recoil," "disgusting," and "repulsive" here rather than, say, "repent," "immoral," or "evil" because the former words reflect more honestly what my experience was like. I suppose I'd be a better philosopher if there had been moral heroism in the offing here—I, resolute, seeing from above the evils of the system, weighing their purchase on my character, electing with honor to repent of the convenience and deliciousness of a flesh diet to walk the narrow path of vegan righteousness. But that isn't how it went. How it went was that I knew everything I should have needed to know to change my eating habits but felt powerless to engage until loving Gus broke my heart and feeling came forth from that wound for the forgotten billions destined to become gristle on the lips of people like me who also need warm, snoring dogs at their feet to fall asleep.

There are good reasons to call this food system morally indefensible. Many, including me, have done so in no uncertain terms. But framing this story as a morality tale, especially here on the outset, has a way of inviting defensive feelings to the table that are unhelpful at this early stage of the emotional education process. If you're like me, being invited to acknowledge that you're an accomplice to something morally indefensible is emotionally more demanding—and more likely to elicit complex, reflective feelings like denial, shame, anger, and hatred—than being invited to experience disgust over aspects of a system that are straightforwardly repulsive.

In me, moral outrage usually explodes into judgment of others, kicking back plenty of shame over all the ways I'm also falling short. But disgust is much simpler. It's like opening an old takeout box and succumbing to a waft of the hairy slime of death where my ziti used to be. There's nothing nuanced to parse here. I'm not an agent in this experience at all. My old brain takes the wheel, as bile floods my throat and nostrils and I stagger backward, repulsed to the core and involuntarily propelled as far from the vile offender as the kitchen island permits.

So my curation strategy for helping you to become painfully aware of the catastrophic fallout of industrial animal agriculture is to wield the elemental forces of Gus and disgust in narrative tandem, hopefully generating enough tension between them to bring forth the painful awareness one must feel to be thrust beyond the inertia of acquiescence to a food system we already "know" is destroying us. All the better for my efforts if every mention of Gus resonates across your experience of a beloved, irreplaceable animal companion of your own by whose bright light your heart warms and your imagination becomes more vivid.

I didn't start out as a dog person. Getting a dog was a spousal concession. The deal was that when we finally left the ranks of no-pets rentals for a house of our own, there'd be a dog on the premises. It didn't matter to Susan which dog. As the resident dog skeptic, I got to choose the breed. I thought bulldogs were adorable, with their giant jowly heads, scrunchy faces, broad low shoulders, and stocky builds. I had read that they didn't need much exercise and were hypoallergenic—two necessities for a person like me who had little interest in dog-walking and (like many dog skeptics) imagined myself deathly allergic.

What I didn't know until the first visit with our no-nonsense veterinarian is that bulldogs are Frankendogs, selectively bred for traits that unsuspecting human beings love but that make life expensive, difficult, and often short for bulldogs. Those broad low shoulders? They make it impossible to mate because the dogs can't mount, and so bulldogs must be artificially inseminated. Those giant jowly heads? They're too big for the birth canal, and so litters must be delivered by cesarean section. Those scrunchy faces? They make it both harder to breathe and easier to get irritating skin and eye infections. And that stocky build? It's a recipe for joint pain, difficulty walking, and obesity—a cruel complement for a short-snouted pup already inclined to be gasping for breath! Looking over her glasses at me like a coach at a player who needs a good talking-to, our vet made no bones about it:

"Giving this fine fellow a good life is going to be precious costly, so I hope you're ready for that."[10]

Living with Gus through the everyday discomforts of enduring these traits and paying extravagantly for the corrective surgeries and medications to ameliorate them brought home the cruelty of selective breeding. The thought that haunted me most once my love for Gus began spilling over into curiosity about the lives of other animals was this: If we're willing to breed this suffering into the animals we love, what horrors must be selectively visited on the expendable billions of animals whose bodies and reproductive products we eat?

I wish I could say I rushed to find out. But Gus had been crowding me out of bed for over a year before I taught my first course in animal ethics and learned that, shockingly but somehow still unsurprisingly, the horrors depend on exactly what kind of food you are being bred to become. If you're a chicken, your breeding puts your legs at risk of breaking under your own weight. If you're a laying hen, that's because you've been designed to lay so many eggs in such a short period of time that your calcium-depleted skeleton is too brittle for continued service. If you're a broiler chicken, your legs might snap under the weight of your outsized breasts, bred as you have been to grow the largest amount of "all white meat" in the shortest possible time.

The indignities inflicted through selective breeding differ from species to species, but the result is the same in every case. Even before they are born, we consign intelligent, feeling creatures to bodies that are designed for the best interests of our sandwiches, roasts, and omelets instead of their creaturely flourishing. Like Gus, these unheralded billions are bred into bodies that are manifestly harmful to them for the sake of human happiness. Unlike Gus, the overwhelming majority of them will never meet a veterinarian paid richly to have their true best interests at heart.

When you love someone, you want what is best for them every day. So compensating for Gus's genetic inheritance was just the beginning. We quickly discovered that our initial plan of leaving him alone on workdays was unkind. Soon, a steady stream of student caregivers knew the joy of reading with his colossal snoring noggin in their laps and the frustration of trying to move him from the street when he abruptly decided to end a walk.

With Gus's help, we learned that dogs crave attention and affection at weird times that aren't always convenient. That if these needs go unmet their anxiety and sadness readily morph into fouled carpet, destroyed pillows, and ravaged kitchen trash. That cheapo dog foods are full of skin and stomach irritants. That dogs love to play with other canines, and to contest for their place in the complex social hierarchies that govern the extended family, the dog park, the groomer's, the veterinarian, and the neighborhood. Most of all, we learned that when a dog eats six pounds of carrots per week, it looks like somebody detonated a giant pumpkin in the backyard unless you're Johnny-on-the-spot with the pooper-scooper. Johnny I am not. But if not always heroic, our efforts to enable Gus to live his best dog's life were heartfelt, concerted, and often costly. So why didn't it bother me more that the animals whose bodies I routinely ate had so few opportunities to exercise their creaturely capacities?

It wasn't because I didn't know what they were up against. I knew, for instance, that mother hens in confinement farms have it about as bad as any creature could. For starters, they never get to gather their young. In hatcheries, their chicks are sorted by sex, and the female chicks are sold to lay eggs while the male chicks—about a quarter billion of them annually—have no value and are thus ground up alive or suffocated in trash bags. I was aware, too, that hens who lay eggs for consumers typically share a small cage with several other hens, lack the room to spread their wings or establish pecking orders, and have the tips of their beaks burned off to keep them from harming cage mates under the stress of confinement. Even when they aren't being actively physically injured by all these procedures of control, confined hens are mercilessly harmed in being denied the opportunity to go outside for fresh air, feel the sun, breed or groom naturally, roost in trees, or establish social orders within a flock—capacities their ancestors in Southeast Asian jungles enjoyed exercising.

I knew that similarly horrifying things could be said of the cows, pigs, chickens, and turkeys raised in confinement farms.[11] But I just didn't feel anything for these nameless, faceless billions. Like word of a tornado warning four counties over, the knowledge of these things was vaguely concerning but not viscerally moving. My emotional disengagement allowed the concrete terrors of individual animals' daily suffering—mutilated bodies, brutal confinement, the denial of every instinctual creaturely delight, and the total effacement of any life at all beyond "market weight"—to vanish into the dark, hovering abstraction of "factory farming."

It was the copious amounts of carrot-laden feces in my own backyard that ultimately showed me the light. I dread few things more than mass poop collection. A first-order dread comes from my distaste for picking up shit, which sucks. Far more formidable a foe is the second-order dread that the first-order dread will trigger a gagging episode. Not a quick dry heave or two—relentless uncontrollable retching that doubles me over from the muscular trauma of my pharynx and larynx repeatedly pummeling my throat so hard it seizes my pelvic floor.

One fateful day on the soggy edge of a Michigan spring, our Gus-sitter called in sick and I had to rush home between classes to let Gus out. Lumbering from his crate almost two hours behind schedule, he seemed bored and resentful to start but looked crestfallen upon surveying the winter-neglected yard. Fence-to-fence carrot mush and not a feces-free patch of tundra on which to relieve himself. Our eyes met and I felt an absurd mélange of sympathy for Gus, anger that dogs defecate, shame over my fretful gag reflex, and utter disgust at the state of things: a yard so fouled by waste that a lonely dog can't even do his business.

I secured two plastic grocery bags from the kitchen, wielded them respectively as scooper-glove and waste bin, and returned, determined, to the yard. I had dispatched the remains of maybe three bunches of carrots when my eyes started watering and the gagging started. I call what happened next an epiphany because there's no sufficient word in English for the experience of feeling the universal flood into the particular with such force that life itself becomes a perfectly heartrending poem, leaving one leavened but burdened with intuitively complete yet inarticulable understanding.

In the twinkling of a watering eye, rendered receptive to the will of the cosmos by unwilled muscular repulsion, I felt it all: Gus, standing bewildered at my mercy, was every abject creature raised and slaughtered for food. My yard, desecrated by waste, was the blasted Earth struggling to support life under the crushing weight of self-defeating, comfort- and convenience-seeking neglect. I, incapacitated by the fallout of my indifference, was humankind writ pitifully small, reaping the self-inflicted just deserts of failing properly to care for my own.

The most powerful truths are not the ones we're taught but the ones that dawn on us. In that mystical moment of illumination, the sort of radiant certainty that sometimes only pain can deliver, it was as if my desperate gagging broke something loose, allowing a torrent of apocalyptic articles and abject video clips that had dammed up in my uncurious mind finally to overwhelm my ever-loving heart. The abstract "facts of the matter" about the fallout of industrial agriculture for the daily lives of animals and the Earth had irrevocably become affronts to Gus's being and thus to my own.

And what more fitting vehicle for this awakening than an experience of visceral disgust over the execrable management of excrement? Shit happens when a system extracts value from life-giving inputs and then excretes the toxic remains. Extracting and excreting without taking good care both of what is extracted and the place where the leftover toxins land is disgusting in large part because it is potentially deadly. We don't shit where we sleep because our old brains know that proximity to poop can make us sick or kill us—a primordial awareness we share with pigs who wouldn't dream of fouling their living quarters if we didn't force them, for love of their carcinogenic corpses, to wallow by the billions in their own excrement.

Ironic, then, that in feeding on our animal-based food system, we collectively shit the bed in ways that have toxified our environment from the soil to the stratosphere. If there's a more compelling example of wanton extraction resulting in toxic excretion, literally or figuratively, I can't think of it. We extract mind-boggling amounts of mono-cropped corn and soy from once rich farmland and excrete infertile dust, threatening our potential to grow nutrient-dense food into the twenty-second century.[12] Why? So we can extract an average of one calorie of animal protein from every nine calories of plant protein we invest, annually excreting billions of tons of river- and ocean-defiling manure and climate-killing gases along with increased risk of deadly pandemics. Why? So that while the Global South starves and burns, affluent Westerners can extract hundreds of pounds of meat per person per year, excreting epidemic levels of heart disease, cancer, stroke, and diabetes.

But there I go again lapsing back into what we already "know" as the most repellant horror of all recedes behind the "facts": all this excrement results from a system that consigns hundreds of billions of creatures as clever and feeling and beautiful as Gus to the grossly inefficient, world-destroying, and cruel fate of metabolizing scarce resources that sicken and fatten them unto a violent, premature death. Amidst the overwhelming sounds and smells of their fellow creatures' terror, they die at the hands of disenfranchised people who have little choice but to bear the devastating physical and psychological trauma of repeatedly ignoring cries for mercy.

This system is repulsive.

Gus's death was one of the most beautiful and heartrending experiences of my life. Just before his twelfth birthday, we found out he had cancer. We tried chemo but it destroyed his immune system. He stopped eating, drinking, and walking. He couldn't sleep through the night. When we shared news of our decision to end his suffering painlessly, our devoted community of Gus-loving friends and family responded with photos and tributes to mark the life of a dog who loved a spirited tug-of-war, emitted copious flatulence as musky as a truffle, inspired multiple books (including *Philosophy Comes to Dinner* and the one you're reading now!), and passed almost 3,500 pounds of carrots.[13] When his time came to die, he was enveloped in the adoring presence of his family—four human beings and an ornery Lhasa apso called Charlie. The vet who put the needle in his arm had saved his life twice already (from the poison of paint and the obstruction of a hockey puck) and here she was to deliver him with love for the third and final time. We put our hands on him and felt him leaving and then gone. We wept over his body, burying our faces between his burly shoulders at the brown ticking that reminded us of chocolatey fingerprints.

So compelling a companion was Gus that Charlie followed in a matter of months, giving up the ghost in the very same manner, room, and company. In the moments after Charlie's death the grief of releasing two irreplaceable family members to the mystery in such short order had rendered three of the remaining four of us speechless. But our three-year-old daughter had an epiphany. "Gus and Charlie are dead! We have no more dogs! Time to get a chicken! Bawk! Bawk!" Finally someone who gets it. Unless we change and become like children, we will never enter the kingdom of heaven.

Wasteful, despoiling, toxic, exploitative, cruel, and farcically self-defeating, our animal-based food system is manifestly disgusting. When confronted with the gory details in safe and emotionally honest company, most of us intuitively and immediately recoil from it, recognizing at a visceral level that this system can't be good for us.

But even as our disgust opens the possibility for an honest reckoning of the catastrophic environmental and moral fallout of our food system, the momentum of this disgust-fueled repulsion from the system is rarely enough, by itself, to break us free from the orbit of the status quo. And this fact raises a puzzling question.

Why is it so difficult to turn away from a system that is so manifestly disgusting and counter to our best interests? Why does the practical and moral urgency of going vegan come as such terrible news to most people?

To make headway on this question, we need to get curious about a feature of human experience that often goes unnoticed: most of us, in most of our everyday activities, are not primarily the sophisticated reason-guided creatures we fancy ourselves to be. Most of the time, we're under the influence of cultural and social shaping forces from which we have inherited the lion's share of our beliefs and practices, often without noticing how we're being shaped or even that we're being influenced at all.[14]

What we do notice, usually by way of emotional discomfort, is when the inherited matrix of beliefs, preferences, and practices that anchors our unique identity is called into question or threatened in some way. As James Baldwin writes in *The Devil Finds Work*, "An identity is questioned only when it is menaced, as when the mighty begin to fall, or when the wretched begin to rise, or when the stranger enters the gates, never, thereafter, to be a stranger: the stranger's presence making *you* the stranger, less to the stranger than to yourself."[15]

There is nothing more alienating or more likely to summon the defenses of deflection and denial than the realization that we are not who we believed ourselves to be—not at peace with this new stranger within. What we're most hungry for, most of the time, is the security, approval, and control we achieve through belonging with our people. The food we eat is often the gateway to satisfying that hunger.

So while disgust is a visceral emotional educator that can leverage important critical distance from the self-defeating aspects of our foodways—the cultural, social, and economic practices that govern our approaches to producing and consuming food—there is another primordial force of the old brain at work in our eating habits that makes changing them for the better seem an insurmountable challenge to many of us: our fear of estrangement from the communities of belonging that make us who we are.

CHAPTER 2

ANYTHING BUT VEGAN

A WORLD IN DENIAL

IT'S THE EARLY NINETIES. A MAN IN OVERALLS IS STANDING in a church parking lot on a makeshift stage of plywood and milk crates singing, "Sent my brown jug downtown." I am peeling blistering skin off a pig on a spit, watching a bunch of Mennonites square dance. I eat the skin and a spray of fat leaves a key-shaped stain on my concert tee that will moisten my eyes some twenty years later when I clean out my childhood bedroom. Friends summon me across the lot. The dessert table has materialized. We scramble to stockpile brownies and blondies and millionaire bars, cut small to feed the many but destined to land like toppled Jenga stacks on the plates of just a few shameless teens. This is my happy place. It's the harvest pig roast at Lombard Mennonite Church.

It's also the ideal setting, though pride makes me reluctant to say so, for clarifying how eating animal products serves as a unifying medium of expression for many of the most fundamental shaping forces of our identities—forces that make it exceedingly difficult to imagine going vegan and harder still to commit to living out this aspiration. Realizing that our foodways are usually the products of socially and emotionally encultured customs and habits (rather than evidence-based reflection) can be an embarrassing and even traumatic experience, confronting us with unwelcome truths that sit ill with our rosy self-perceptions.

So much the better, dear reader, to experience this embarrassment and trauma vicariously through examples drawn from my ample treasury of food misadventures. The work of this chapter is to show how the necessity of a new vegan normal activates all our panic buttons at once, threatening our deepest needs for security, comfort, and approval and making the challenge of going vegan seem insurmountable to our culture at large.

To the pig roast, then. At this shining moment in time, I'm a muscle-bound, no-neck seventeen-year-old who eats five thousand calories a day and rises at five a.m. to get ninety minutes in the weight room before school starts at seven thirty. I couldn't be prouder to be the starting left guard for the Wheaton North Falcons. Football is still the god of the mainstream Midwestern social imaginary, and Journey songs are still the backdrop of the romantic montages I daydream in chemistry class. But Nirvana's *Nevermind* is feeding on the corpse of '80s optimism, the cool kids are increasingly ironic, and unisex chin-length bobs will soon outnumber the buzz cuts and bangs on the homecoming court. Whether you're rocking preppy pastels, heavy metal denims, grungy flannels, or hip-hoppy tracksuits, lunch finds you at the Smoke House eating gyros.

I'm growing out my hair, thanks to an emo streak sparked by a passion for "college music" and fanned to flame by my first real girlfriend—an artist and costume designer whose irresistible aura of dark academia somehow compels a gridiron lunkhead who loathes musicals (me) to try out for *West Side Story* just to get near her. She's a vegetarian and we both love The Smiths, but when Morrissey croons "Meat Is Murder," I laugh and make like I'm eating a monster turkey leg and she frowns and looks down at her black Mary Janes. She politely declines to attend the pig roast where I am now, and though I won't realize it for years, it's the beginning of the end of both our relationship and my unconflicted meat-eating.

We live in the western suburbs of Chicago in a town that supposedly once boasted the highest number of churches per capita in the United States. I'm ambivalent about organized religion, especially of the evangelical Christian variety, but I've been heavily shaped by the vision of the world that modern Christianity bequeathed to the twentieth century—one in which human beings are the apex of creation and everything else on Earth is here to serve our pleasure and use. Whether or not one believes in God, one knows God made animals for food.

I celebrate my apex predator status on the regular with my best friend from church, a jacked wrestler from a rival high school. We sit together in the back of the sanctuary, wait for our parents to see that we are there, and then slip out during the first hymn to the tip-top of the food chain—Old Country Buffet. We harass the carver in the paper toque until he cuts us each a pair of inch-thick slabs of roast beef and then we put popcorn shrimp between them and eat it like a sandwich. Tonight, we won't even need to hit Taco Bell before it closes at one a.m. We're four pork sandwiches and eleven brownies in.

Despite my skepticism of evangelical Christianity, I still strongly identify with my Mennonite Christian heritage, even at my teenage surliest. I love that Mennonites don't talk much about religion but try to serve others and make the world a more peaceful and just place. For most of my forbears, this service took the form of lives devoted to feeding people. Great-Grandpop butchered hogs. Grandpop farmed eggs. There were distant cousins at family reunions whose much nicer shoes testified to their parents' ownership of prosperous local dairies and packing plants. As a small child, I overheard a man I'd never met beaming to someone twice removed that my Poppop's patents in herbicide chemistry were saving hungry people across the globe by making animal feed cheaper. I felt a surge of importance so abundant and indelible that it sufficed, years later, to swamp the panic and humiliation I felt as a ten-year-old on my first trip to a slaughter plant (even though I still cried). No tears, though, for the pig whose skin I'm peeling at this very moment.

Notwithstanding predictable teen angst and family of origin drama, I greatly admire my parents for the authentic way they live out their values. My dad was a conscientious objector in the Vietnam era, and here in the early '90s he models that moral resolve as an economics professor offering critiques of capitalism and militarism at an elite Christian college where markets and country are golden calves. My mom is a spiritual director and a fair-trade activist who understands that genuine openness to the mystery requires concrete acts of neighbor love. *More-with-Less*, a famed Mennonite cookbook that proclaims eating as an act of justice, is the most dog-eared book in the house.[1] But my sister and I live for Tuesday nights when we order two large pizzas brimming with bacon, sausage, and ham. There are never leftovers.

As proud as I am of my Mennonite farming heritage and family commitments to social justice, I'm also a painfully self-critical high school senior surrounded by more affluent peers. I'm thus acutely aware that my people aren't fancy. They don't have trust funds or second homes or storied family histories. They haven't gone to prestige schools. They don't ski or play squash. They put hamburger in the chili and chicken in the curry, but steak and lobster aren't on the menu and nobody's even heard of foie gras. For celebrations? Tonight's pig roast is about as posh as it'll get. We're square dancing, for heaven's sake.

And so I'm a little ashamed, a little jealous, and a lot smitten when I hang out with folks who casually eat luxury foods. A neighbor went to Harvard, gave me a summer job (jacket required), and took me to a club luncheon where I met Defense Secretary Dick Cheney over lamb chops with mint jelly. Close family friends with a country home and impeccably seasoned cast iron had a kitchen that smelled of cardamom and afforded me my first tastes of stilton and fennel-rubbed pork loin. A significant other's father practiced radiology, collected antiquities, and cooked beef as marbled as handmade Italian paper in a mayonnaise of avocado oil, egg, fresh lemon, and black salt. As my teeth and fingers folksily strip flesh from the pig skin, a force so deep that I can't even feel it hates how much I love this and longs ineffably for something like effortless facility with an oyster fork.

The miraculous thing about time and being is that these moments are not past, but woven into an ever-simultaneous present, exerting silent pressure, heightening pleasure but also simmering shame and building anxiety, creating an oscillating torsion between delight and humiliation that, despite all the expended energy, holds me right where I am. I lick pork fat from my lips and attempt to coax the stain from my shirt with the moistened corner of a fall-themed napkin, thinking (without a hint of irony), "If my girlfriend only knew what she is missing..."

In reflecting on this narrative of my life in food at the tender age of seventeen, one can discern a wide variety of shaping forces in play, regulating and negotiating my identity between and among them. Being able-bodied and athletic predisposes me to certain conceptions of physical health and fitness and the routines and rituals necessary to maintain them. My gender and sexuality predispose me to certain leanings, behaviors, and roles, and my specific friendships and relationships mold these into dispositions and habits. My religious tradition assumes a certain vision of the order of things and how it all hangs together. My racial identity and ethnic heritage root me in the folkways of a specific group of people who see and do some things better than others. My family of origin transmits those inheritances along with the special inflections, expectations, and blind spots of parents and siblings. My social class imposes capacities and limits as well as allegiances and yearnings that are in complex tension.

Now notice how deeply entrenched the practice of eating animal products is in each of these shaping forces. If eating animals were just one shaping force of our identity among others, matters might be easier—perhaps we could just find a way to target that specific issue (as we might by seeing a doctor for a health issue, a therapist for family drama, or a spiritual director for a crisis of faith). But our meaty foodways are notoriously difficult to divide and conquer, because for most of us they are distributed pervasively across the most powerful shaping forces of our identities. For teenage me, it's not too dramatic to say that each defining aspect of my identity is constituted in significant part by the act of eating animal products in precisely the way that aspect of my identity predisposes me to eat them.

I crack raw eggs into protein shakes like an athlete, eager to unleash explosive power in a body I hope to sculpt into a fine-tuned sporting machine. To give up animal protein is to compromise performance and sacrifice my health.

I eat steak like a straight white man, visibly, voraciously, and in amounts that proclaim to various target audiences, "I take what's mine!", "You know you want me!", and "Mess with the best and die like the rest!" To refuse steak is to reject an opportunity to assert dominance and raise unwelcome questions about my status, virility, and orientation.

I eat Easter ham like a Christian, grateful for the divinely granted privilege of my spiritual superiority to the creatures given me for food and bolstered in my existential confidence by the power exercised through this privilege. To refuse ham is both to reject a gift of God and to risk disrupting the proper order of creation.

I eat Ghanaian chicken groundnut stew like a Mennonite, at a church potluck table with family and friends after a sermon on neighbor love and the impact of industrial agriculture on food production in West Africa. To refuse the stew is a missed opportunity for cross-cultural learning, a churlish rejection of hospitality, and a barrier to fellowship with members of my community.

I eat meat-lover's pizza like a Halteman, anticipating, savoring, and finding comfort and joy in this weekly family indulgence, loving it even more when my sister becomes a vegetarian and I can needle her with bacon jokes. To sabotage pizza night is to meddle with the fundamental forces of attraction and repulsion that keep our nuclear family together.

I eat lamb chops with mint jelly like a middle-class white kid dying to impress, petrified that I'll make a mistake but resolute that I'm not throwing away my shot. To balk at the lamb chops is to raise suspicion about my pedigree and risk outing myself as an inexperienced rube unworthy of the city club set.

Mind you, as I'm consuming these egg shakes, steaks, hams, chicken stews, meat-lover's pizzas, and lamb chops, I'm not reflectively engaged in any of this consumption. I'm just an ordinary high school kid doing what my people (and the people I hope to impress) are doing and it's completely automatic. But if I lack explicit reasons for choosing these foods that I could articulate under criticism, my unstated emotional commitment to consuming them is total. I'm meeting my deepest emotional needs for security, approval, and control through these acts of consumption, proving through my relish of them that I belong, naturally and obviously, to the various communities that make me who I am: an athletic, middle-class, straight, white Mennonite Christian seventeen-year-old man-child named Matt Halteman. Eating animal products authenticates my entitlement to each of these aspects of who I am.

And because I experience these forms of belonging as morally and spiritually grounded (I am in solidarity with these communities and called to serve their missions!), it's easy to forget that

I'm physiologically dependent on these shared foodways, too. I'm conditioned—even driven—to continue craving and eating animal products by a chemical dance of performance and reward that I've been rehearsing since before I could speak.

At nine months of age, I precociously say "Poppop!" and my ecstatic grandfather envelops me, serves me a victory spoonful of chocolate milkshake, and floods my tiny brain with happy juice. I don't know what oxytocin, dopamine, and endorphins are, but they're just what I'm getting, respectively, when Mom hugs me as I eat spritz cookies on Christmas Eve, when my neighbor reassures an incredulous block-partier that I need my protein as I tuck into a quadruple-decker cheeseburger, and when my team-mates and I get high on a midnight workout fueled by Italian subs the circumference of my biceps. That's a lot of mortadella.

Because eating animal products is woven into most of my best memories of feeling happy, proud, and fit, it makes perfect sense that I turn to these foods, too, for comfort and assurance in moments of sadness, shame, and ill health. My heart has learned with some help from the pharmacy in my brain that these foods give succor to my soul. When I am lonely, a ham and egg sandwich on sourdough feels like smoking away the wee hours with a diner-full of friends. When I fail, a pulled pork sandwich envelops me in the unconditional embrace of Mennonites square dancing. When I am too sick and exhausted to get out of bed, a soup of chicken and rice mothers me into good enough shape to smile for a hair-tousling.

In declining my invitation to the pig roast, my vegetarian girlfriend was kind enough not to make it about me. There was no confrontation, no arguments exchanged, and no judgment implied in her declining to attend. It just "wasn't her thing" and we left it at that. But even though I didn't realize it at the time, it's not surprising that her skipping the pig roast left a mark. There's a profound sense in which this event was very much about me, and about all the shaping forces at work in me, invisibly projecting the parameters of my taste and judgment, steering my decisions, and shoring up my comfort and consolation. Had my girlfriend chosen to pick a fight over the pig roast, perhaps by reminding me of pigs' intelligence or showing me videos of animal cruelty or citing statistics about environmental impact or worker injustice, my response would have been entirely predictable. But protein! But powerlifting! But God's will! But hospitality! But family! But social ambition!

Any one of these rebuttals might feel sufficient at any given moment to parry the incoming threat, but it's worth recognizing that they are all intimately intertwined and mutually supporting, such that when one of the shaping forces is challenged, the others rush to its defense like a woven fabric cinching around a snagged thread. A health-based defense of eating animal products, for instance, is usually already tinged (and often fully dyed) in family-, gender-, and hospitality-based defenses, and our conceptions of family, gender, and hospitality are always socialized and almost always spiritualized.

If this description seems too abstract, you can make it more concrete simply by imagining your particular version of the master defense that firmly, if unconsciously, held my dietary commitments in place well into adulthood: "My family raised me to believe that God gave us animals to nourish and clothe our bodies so that we, in turn, can feed the hungry, clothe the naked, and have the strength to search out the unique ways that our talents and gifts can bring us joy and serve the world; as an athlete and an intellectual called to be a team leader and a teacher, I need my protein and lots of it!"

Depending on my mood and the identity of the conversation partners challenging me, I might offer varying versions of this defense calmly and confidently, in anger, or maybe even silently to myself as I nod in feigned concern to minimize conflict. Whatever style of delivery I choose, I make the same unstated admission in each case: I experience eating animal products as essential to who I am, and I cannot imagine being me—having the security, approval, and control on which my happiness depends—without eating them.

Your story is unique and likely very different from mine. Perhaps cooking wild game and fresh-caught fish over an open fire rather than chugging whey shakes in a room full of dumbbells is how you stay strong. Maybe it's Shabbat brisket or Eid mutton korma or pastor's pork and beans instead of Easter ham that radiates holy favor and belonging across your celebration table. Or maybe fellowship around your uncle's Swiss steak is the way mystery moves in your family of skeptics. You may not give a hoot about spritz cookies, but some days you might consider trading a fortune in gold for just one bite of your abuelita's pupusas or your memaw's bacon greens or your zayde's knishes. We all have our precious foodways and they are mighty different from one another.

But the shaping forces behind our foodways are likely similar, even across the markedly different ways they influence our sense of who we are and what we can imagine for ourselves. Whether we realize it or not and whether we like it or not, for most of us, consuming animal products is a practice so deeply entrenched in the ways we embody and express identity that eating these foods is like breathing air or speaking our native language—doing it is so effortless, unreflective, and essential for social and emotional well-being that not doing it is simply unimaginable.

So when a social media post, magazine article, talk show segment, or (heaven forbid!) a real-live vegan provides an occasion to confront the unimaginable, we tend not to love this experience but find it easy enough to dismiss. When the arguments for going vegan get trotted out in impersonal contexts like these, most of us find ourselves as naturally immune to them as we are to a tract from a bizarre religious cult. We simply can't imagine how the pitch could pertain to us, given the way it seems to cut against the grain of everything we hold dear.

For many of us, this natural immunity to the possibility of going vegan remains ironclad until someone from our circle of trust unexpectedly defects to Team Veg. The best friend stops doing Shotz-n-Wingz night at Baloneez and starts blathering on about Impossible burgers. The sibling goes on a plant-based health kick and wonders aloud if your life insurance is paid up as you gorge on Chicago-style pizza. The favorite professor takes every opportunity to spotlight the horrors of industrial agriculture in class. The adult education coordinator at your place of worship hosts a workshop on food justice, inviting participants to go veg for a week. The kid whose diaper you changed for years is suddenly an endless font of vegan wisdom at every meal. The veg girlfriend gives you the old "It's not you, it's me!" and skips the pig roast (hypothetically).

Whichever defector is responsible for nudging us from indifference to attentiveness over the case for going vegan, it doesn't take long for anxiety to spread past the sphere of the initial contagion into every corner of our identity. We feel all the shaping forces of who we are cinch up into a knot in our stomach, closing ranks around our cherished sense of self. If we can imagine living in this strange new vegan world at all, the commitments that await us there can appear only as a series of negations of the things we love:

> I can't be healthy and strong without animal protein.
>
> I can't use meat-eating to prove my vitality, success, or devotion to my crew.
>
> I can't give thanks to God for the gift of these delicious foods provided for me.
>
> I can't take pride in my agricultural heritage, which I now worry is cause for shame.
>
> I can't eat in the campus dining hall unless I want to settle for plain pasta or white rice.
>
> I can't go to my favorite restaurants without asking nitpicky menu questions.
>
> I can't let my grandparents treat me to my annual birthday steak.
>
> I can't enjoy family holidays eating all my favorite celebratory foods.
>
> I can't afford the ingredients required to eat a delicious, nutritious vegan diet.
>
> I can't spare the time to cook every meal for myself and to relearn all my favorite recipes.

I can't feed my family this rabbit food, so meal prep is a nightmare.

I can't express my gifts as a brilliant home cook treating friends to comforting favorites.

I can't be hospitable to my hosts at social events when animal foods are served.

I can't go to zoos and aquariums or let my kids go on field trips to those places.

I can't wear my favorite leather boots or cashmere sweaters.

Any one of these maddening no-can-do's is a serious put-off for many people. The lot of them together is a full-on deal-breaker for all but the most earnest do-gooders and aggressive social shapeshifters. Faced with this onslaught of potential deprivations of the security, approval, and control we usually enjoy as engaged members of our cherished communities, most of us will simply fall back on what Yale Law professor and cultural cognition expert Dan Kahan calls "identity protective cognition": "As a way of avoiding dissonance and estrangement from valued groups, individuals subconsciously resist factual information that threatens their defining values." In drawing out the social implications of Kahan's research, journalist Ezra Klein notes that our resort to this welcome shelter of denial makes perfect sense, given that "the most important psychological imperative most of us have in a given day is protecting our idea of who we are and our relationships with the people we trust and love."[2] Trying to imagine our way into a brave new vegan world is threatening and our brains are wired to give us an easy out.

But let's suppose you fall into the elite crowd of rare individuals who can somehow imagine themselves secure, accepted, and powerful enough even in the face of these stringent deprivations to try going vegan. For you, dear hero, a herculean act of will awaits on the flipside of every can't, as you become beholden to a corresponding slate of brand-new musts:

I must meet my nutritional needs in a healthful way with unfamiliar foods.

I must find other ways to project confidence and belonging.

I must justify my practices to my religious community, which is skeptical of my decision.

I must overcome the grief associated with estrangement from my agricultural past.

I must make alternative arrangements to feed myself at school and at work.

I must advocate for alternatives at my favorite restaurants and try a bunch of new ones.

I must explain myself to family and friends without alienating or disappointing them.

I must experiment with new holiday traditions without seeming exclusive or threatening.

I must tighten my budget to afford vegan foods that are satisfying and healthful.

I must plan my leisure time to allow for additional cooking and recipe development.

I must prepare multiple meals per mealtime for family members who eat differently.

I must rethink my approach to entertaining to avoid disappointing my friends.

I must prepare for awkwardness or drama when I refuse
certain foods at social events.

I must find alternative foods and entertainment attrac-
tions for my kids' birthday parties.

I must purchase a new wardrobe or prepare to be judged
for wearing non-vegan clothing.

The two stages of this can't/must double whammy constitute
what I call the challenges of imagination and motivation.[3] At
stage one, a denial-induced lack of imagination prevents us from
envisioning going vegan as compatible with continuing to be
happy, healthy, engaged members of our communities. And even
if we rise to the challenge of imagining a vegan life worth living
among all the "can'ts," the looming prospect of a demoralizing
failure of motivation amidst all the new "musts" threatens to sabotage even the most earnest fledgling aspirations to go vegan.

Accepting the practical and moral urgency of establishing a
new vegan normal is excruciating, then, both because we often
can't imagine that going vegan is compatible with being who
we are, and because—even if we do succeed in imagining that
possibility as worthwhile—it seems impossible to will ourselves
to follow through as the pressures of everyday life assail us. And
because vegans themselves are living, breathing reminders that
these common challenges of imagination and motivation can in
fact be overcome, we find them excruciating too!

Vegans don't even need to misbehave to incur our wrath: like
the ultra-fit colleague who effortlessly runs marathons while our

gym memberships lapse, or the brilliant classmate who breezes calculus while we struggle to pass, the mere existence of vegans is a reminder of our limitations at best and more often feels like an indictment of our very being. Better to kill the messenger (or at least ignore or demean them) than to face the drudgery of stringent prohibitions and burdensome new obligations required to take the message on board.

The upshot is that our culture's default practice of framing vegan commitments in terms of what vegans can't do (and must therefore do instead) limits our vision and breaks our will by making it seem as though going vegan is incompatible with full participation in our most cherished activities, communities, and institutions. As long as going vegan is perceived as a threat to our traditional personal and cultural identities, our collective denial of the need for a new vegan normal will persist and hostility will abound for those attempting to be the change they want to see in the world.

What to do? According to Wharton School organizational psychologist Adam Grant, "Research shows that when people are resistant to change, it helps to reinforce what will stay the same. Visions for change are more compelling when they include visions of continuity. Although our strategy might evolve, our identity will endure."[4] As far-fetched as it may at first sound, the vision for change we need to bring about a new vegan normal is in fact deeply grounded in a vision of continuity.

Surprisingly, most of us are much better off than we typically believe ourselves to be when it comes to our potential alignment with a vegan vision of the world. For though the challenges of imagination and motivation can project the illusion that our values are wildly out of sync with whatever magical thinking we suspect vegans of indulging, the reality is that most of us already know, believe, and feel everything we need, not only to harbor hope for a vegan world but to discover with delight that making our own unique contribution to its realization is deeply desirable.

CHAPTER 3

THE VEGAN IMAGINATION

YOUR STANDARD MORAL OUTLOOK, EXPANDED!

WE SPENT THE DAY ON A SECLUDED GREEN-SAND beach several miles' hike from where the southernmost edge of Hawaii's Big Island plunges into the Pacific. Back from the beach, I am dining al fresco at an oceanside Kona eatery. I should be basking in the glow of the day's pure glory, chatting with wife and friends about tomorrow's New Year's Eve festivities. Instead, I'm consumed by the thought that the segment of swordfish resisting my fork recently belonged to a free-living creature, probably in the very waters at which I'm staring. I'm hungry, but the realization that the ocean and its former denizen are reduced in this moment to mere objects of my pleasure makes the situation impossible to enjoy. I am acutely aware that this may be my last bite of swordfish and the feeling is uncanny. Never to be the same again is both terrifying and exhilarating.

As usual for me when it comes to life-changing experiences, my current opportunity is other people's doing. My wife, my friend, my bulldog, and my students—all decidedly more resolute in the "Try something new!" department than I—have collectively persuaded me to teach a course on the ethics of how we treat animals. For three weeks in January, my students and I will devote an intensive seminar of three hours per day to investigating what other animals are like, what cultural attitudes and forms of commercial exploitation govern their existence, and what philosophy, advocacy, and food system reform might do to ameliorate their miserable lot.

Susan has prevailed upon me to go vegan for the duration of the course to set a good example for students and err on the side of caution as my own engagement with this new material evolves.

"Wouldn't you rather be a little too conservative now than a lot more regretful later if it turns out changes are requisite? Plus, I love a good cooking challenge! It'll be fun!"

I don't think it will be fun. "The class doesn't start until after Hawaii," I plead.

"Good enough. We'll start then."

But here we are over four thousand miles from my looming professorial duty, and it's already started in my mind and heart if not yet on my fork. As I beg the beauty of the Pacific Ocean to distract me from the posthumous judgment of a former swordfish, I harbor both a deep sense of foreboding and an equal and opposite hope about the coming teaching experience.

My fear is that going vegan will demand my transformation into someone radically new. I fretfully imagine that this experiment will usher me onto some higher plane of enlightenment that, however uplifting, wrenches me away from everything I know and love on the ground.

My corresponding hope is that going all the way to vegan will turn out to be unnecessary. My days of unconstrained meat-eating are probably over, but maybe I'll discover that eating kinder, gentler animal products is not only possible, but a crucial step toward realizing the best possible world: the one in which human beings get to keep eating their favorite foods while cows, pigs, chickens, and turkeys get to be their fullest creaturely selves. Like on Old MacDonald's farm or in Michael Pollan's fantasies, at least until the fabled circle of life turns in our favor, and animals "sacrifice themselves" for our culinary pleasure. Is it a coincidence that the most charismatic guest speaker on my syllabus in the pivotal final week is a Wendell Berry–loving grass-fed dairy farmer? You decide.

Genuine learning has a way of dispelling fears and reorienting hopes. What I couldn't yet imagine, dreading the coming vegan experiment from distant Pacific shores, was that this decision could result in my becoming a more joyful, confident, and consistent version of my oldest self. Yes, of the six-year-old child who rooted so hard for Wilbur in *Charlotte's Web* that I wrote a fan-fic endowing him with a longhorn rack to gore the butcher. But of my aspiring adult self, too, steeped since I was knee-high to a grasshopper in the hope for a world where good living cultivates the long-cherished values of curiosity, humility, fairness, honesty, courage, respect, kindness, cooperation, authenticity, the promotion of happiness, and the prevention of suffering. I've come to think of this collection of timeworn values as kindergarten ethics. Not because it's childish or oversimplified, but because it's the ground level for doing well as soon as we're able to conduct ourselves in public no matter who we are.[1]

The biggest surprise of teaching that fateful course was discovering that going vegan is just a matter of aspiring to live out kindergarten ethics. What my students and I realized, much to our shock and initially to our dismay, was that most of us were already vegans-in-waiting: people whose deeply encultured orientation within kindergarten ethics (or something very much like it) had already infused us with all the beliefs, feelings, and values we needed to resonate with and even desire to enact a vegan vision of the world.[2] The standard moral imagination that we had all brought into the course was already a *vegan* imagination—the trick was to get enough experience in this arena to see it. Far from triggering a radical change in identity, going vegan held out the possibility of living more continuously and mindfully toward who we already aspired to be, ushering us into deeper resonance with and more consistent application of commitments we already cherished but often unwittingly betrayed.

I'm not suggesting this was an easy transition for all (or even any) of us. It certainly wasn't for me. Like a panicked search for missing keys that ends with their discovery in one's hand, it was humbling and disorienting to realize I was a vegan-in-waiting. And like ending a relationship with someone you really like but reluctantly realize you just can't love, it was sad and grief-inducing even if eventually liberating. I had to let go of some things that brought me comfort and that I genuinely thought I wanted but ultimately couldn't keep because they were blocking my access to even deeper desires, thwarting my aspirations to change for the better. Chief among these obstacles was my hope that it was possible to be honest, courageous, and authentic to myself and curious, humble, fair, respectful, and kind to other animals while continuing to support their gratuitous exploitation and slaughter for my pleasure.

The work of this chapter is to help you discover your inner vegan-in-waiting, remove some of the obstacles that threaten to block you from aspiring to change, and inspire you to see that the adventure unfolding in this seemingly new direction is in fact a journey of incremental progress that you started long ago. If we commit to changing our lives in going vegan, we do so to stay the same—to become more fully who we thought we already were and thus to become more fully who we deeply desire to be.

To clarify the initially surprising idea that many if not most of us are already vegans-in-waiting, let's go back to kindergarten. What I have in mind by "kindergarten ethics" is the aspirational, formative set of values, feelings, and behaviors that we learn as young children to empower us to enter social situations and eventually thrive in them.

In describing kindergarten ethics as "aspirational," I mean that it emphasizes striving over arriving—the goal is not stringently to achieve shared ideals so much as to persist in trying for incremental progress toward them within the limits of our individual circumstances. When the hope is to corral a ragtag band of impulsive, self-centered six-year-olds into a functional learning community, aspiring to make progress by learning from inevitable failures and always trying again is a more sustainable and empowering approach than expecting total compliance. Kindergarten is no place for moral perfectionism.

In calling kindergarten ethics "formative," I mean that it aims to shape students over time through repetitive practice into a particular sort of person—not into a slavish, tattling opportunist who follows a set of inflexible rules to gain reward, avoid punishment, or relish seeing it inflicted on others, but rather into a discerning, empathic student of life who aspires to practice and eventually habituate attitudes and actions that are good for them, good for their classmates, and crucial for ongoing social success as they grow into adults.

It's not important that kindergarten be the place (or the only place) that one learns to aspire to these values and begin working toward them. One might just as well learn such things (or have them reinforced with various tweaks and additions) at one's home, summer camp, sports club, or place of worship. The point is that these values are widely acknowledged across the wisdom literatures of many cultures and by contemporary social science to be ground-level tools for social coping that it's best to inculcate early and practice often if we wish to improve our chances of living well together.

For our purposes here, I'll think of kindergarten ethics as including, but certainly not limited to, curiosity, humility, fairness, honesty, courage, respect, kindness, cooperation, and authenticity. These are mainstream, baseline values that many of us have been taught, from an early age and within a variety of traditions, to see as indispensable for promoting happiness, preventing suffering, and creating the conditions for general flourishing in community.

In kindergarten, curiosity emerges in the thrill of discovering that the world outside your small experience is teeming with exciting people, animals, places, and processes that inspire deep wonder and burning desire to understand what is happening and to imagine what might happen next. That you need a night-light while bats can see in the dark, that your sandcastles last mere hours while rivers carve canyons over millions of years—these are bedazzling discoveries that hold you delightfully in thrall and help you to zero in on what you really love.

Your curiosity is a natural gateway to humility, which dawns as an awareness that the world doesn't revolve around you even though your limited perspective and abilities sometimes tempt you to act like it does. Humility surfaces in realizing that Roger G. is much better at drawing dinosaurs than you, in finding story time easy when the topic is sports but difficult when it's the alphabet, in struggling to share favorite toys while generosity comes naturally to your friend Chi L., and in learning that Regina the class guinea pig can hear things that no human being will ever hear. You are but one among many, your skills and opportunities are limited, and your classmates are in the same boat. It's good to know your limits and to recognize and rely on the strengths of others to help you on your way.

With curiosity powering your delight in the world's wonders and your discovery of special talents, and humility spotlighting your vulnerability and your needs for social cooperation and support, your teacher's insistence on fairness becomes increasingly intuitive. When you realize you're not the center of the universe, and that you share it with other wonderful, needy creatures like you, it makes sense not to take more than your share or act in ways that fail to give wonderful, needy others their due. You might still hoard the coveted glitter markers to complete your masterpiece when you know full well it's the green table's turn. But you also know it isn't fair and you'd be justifiably angry if they did it to you.

When you're striving for fairness, it's crucial to be honest. You can't give others their due if you haven't been truthful about the circumstances in question. And telling the truth in kindergarten often requires courage. Sometimes you must admit to hoarding glitter markers and suffer the consequences. Other times you must report that your best friend Marquis W. did in fact call Stacey G. "toilet-facey" even though you'll pay for it after school.

Practicing curiosity and fairness paves the way for respect. The combination of delighting in experiences of difference and recognizing that others are owed their due enables you to acknowledge the unique personal integrity of every other and honor their existence as worthy and dignified apart from your personal feelings about them. When Mrs. S. says it's time to put the LEGOs away you're disappointed. But she's the teacher and you follow instructions. Maryam Z. wears different clothes and celebrates different holidays. Dennis B. uses leg braces to walk. Maria S. is really into math. In moments of frustration with them, you might defy, tease, taunt, or name-call. But when you land in the principal's office, you're neither surprised nor proud.

At the horizon of respect lies kindness. For as you practice honoring the inherent worth and dignity of others, you find both that your heart goes out to them when they're sad and that responding to their suffering with compassion makes you feel happy and fulfilled. You also notice when others are kind. You're more excited to play gaga ball with them, and they sit atop the list of preferred recipients of your llama-themed birthday cupcakes (even if your own efforts to be fair and kind ultimately result, with a little nudge from your parents, in everyone getting a treat).

The self-confidence and affinity with others created by practicing these values makes cooperation possible—discerning together what you and your classmates love, what your unique talents and struggles are, and how you can help and challenge each other to activate your potential as individuals and as a class. With enough practice, you can make headway toward authenticity—being who you aspire to be in your community even when the going gets tough.

Granted, trying to act in accordance with these values can feel unnatural or begrudging at first. When Remi F. skins their knee, you pretend to care, rush to help, and reluctantly admit your role in the accident but are secretly glad. They deserved it for hogging the twisty slide. As you gain experience acting toward these values, you begin to anticipate the benefits of their repeated use and the drawbacks of acting in ways that run afoul of their leavening wisdom. Things just go better for you and everyone else when you're the sort of person whom your teacher and classmates can trust to show up and consistently elevate the group in these ways.

This account is idealized. Holly B. is still going to spray an entire juice box in Tasha K.'s face, Mike A. is going to pee in Alex R.'s Moon Boots, and Matt H. will interrupt the pledge of allegiance with underarm fart noises. But on good days, when everybody's trying, kindergarten ethics can be remarkably effective at promoting happiness, reducing suffering, and creating a space where flourishing happens—growing in knowledge and experience, learning from and correcting mistakes, building self-esteem and community, and delighting in the rewards of cooperative work and play in a safe, nurturing environment.

To say the least, kindergarten ethics doesn't fully take in kindergarten. Most of us find ourselves struggling with the challenge of living out these values well into adulthood and often fail to model them to the extent we'd like, especially in times of fear or stress. Still, most of us adopt some version of the moral imagination that animates these values. That is, when we imagine what an ideal world would look like and what attitudes and values people would generally live by in that world, we're not surprised to find curiosity, humility, fairness, honesty, courage, respect, kindness, cooperation, and authenticity on that list, because we've experienced their value firsthand for promoting happiness, preventing suffering, and creating conditions conducive to personal and communal flourishing.

It doesn't take a huge leap of moral imagination to see that consistent application of kindergarten ethics in the arena of our eating habits would ideally result in a considerably different food system than the one we have.

As flattering as it is to believe that our failure to face the necessity of changing these habits is a matter of our "just not getting it," the hard truth is exactly the opposite. It's precisely because we *do* get it, intuitively, immediately, and harrowingly, that we find it so difficult to look ourselves in the proverbial eye when called to account for it. The disconnect between our values and our actions is so glaringly, indefensibly extreme that bewildering shame is the natural response upon becoming emotionally engaged with it. And because shame is a destabilizing emotion, everything in us wants to change the subject, defend the status quo, kill the messenger—anything to escape the vertigo of suddenly becoming moral strangers to ourselves in our most routine and pleasurable daily activity.

I advise against killing the messenger. But the impulse is not entirely mysterious to me, given that vegan advocates often proceed by spotlighting this yawning chasm between our professed values and our eating habits, leveraging our shame and attempting to blame us into a chastened effort to "stop doing bad things" or "live up to our values." Such strategies wave our commitments in our faces, backing us into the corner of some corresponding "should" or "ought" that threatens to muscle us into submission on pain of being a moral monster.

If you're reading this book, you've probably already been on the receiving end (maybe even the giving end, too?) of any number of these charming rhetorical cudgels:

If you gave a hoot about curiosity and rigorous research, you'd commit to learning more about what the animals you eat are capable of thinking, feeling, and doing, and to confronting how awful it is to consign them to lives of abject misery on factory farms. I dare you to expend even one tenth of the effort you put into sleuthing out the environmental impact of plastics or cryptocurrency into understanding the true cost of your food. But nooooooo! You'd rather sit here eating hot wings in ignorance than investigate those questions!

You talk a big game about humility—"God put us here to be stewards of creation, not lords of it!," "Humans are just one small part of a much grander divine dance!," and yada, yada—but you eat like your trivial interest in steak trumps the most basic interests of cows, the workers forced to kill them in deplorable conditions, and the creation you're so humbly committed to "stewarding." If this is what humility looks like, I'd hate to see your take on arrogance.

When it comes to your political advocacy, it's always "Every vote counts!," "Time to start knocking on doors!," "If we come together and cooperate, we can do anything!," "All hands on deck!" But every time the food question arises, you're like, "What can one person really do?," "The system's just too big to change," "It's not like ordering the salad is going to resurrect any pigs." I guess collective action and doing your part only matter to you when they're not coming for your bacon double cheeseburger.

A cheese omelet? Does authenticity mean anything to you? Here you are, touting vegetarianism as the moral response to violence against meat animals, only to turn your back on the even worse suffering of dairy cows and laying hens who must endure the additional cruelty of having their reproductive systems highjacked for months or years before they are killed for low-grade meat. And that's not even to mention the forgotten collateral damage of your "breakfast"—the male calves sold into veal crates because they can't give milk and the male chicks ground up alive because they'll never lay eggs. It's hard to take your "love of animals" seriously when you're a living contradiction.

So you "respect" farmed animals enough to propose that we dismantle the entire industrial farming system and replace it with less cruel, much more labor-intensive farms that provide an idyllic existence for these creatures. But you don't respect farmed animals enough to believe that their interest in continuing the idyllic life you imagine for them on pasture might outweigh your interest in eating bougie pasture-raised pork loin for $15 a pound?[3] Let me guess: humane slaughter, right? That compassionate practice by which one violently and prematurely kills a thriving animal who doesn't want to die nor benefits from the death so that the killer can eat or profit from the animal's dead body? Sounds like respect to me!

It's not that these kinds of rebukes don't ring true in some register, or even that they are incapable of shaming some of us into action, at least temporarily. The problem is that, for most of us, they're recipes for identity-protective cognition to kick in and defend the status quo.

In these moments, we are seriously vulnerable. Here we are, on the unnerving threshold of meeting our inner vegan-in-waiting, disoriented by the encroaching shame and grief of realizing we are not who we thought we were when it comes to our eating habits. Then, at precisely the moment we most need calm to counteract shame and create space for curiosity playfully to open the way to progress, the vegan brigade charges in to catch us red-handed in unspeakable acts of hypocrisy and cruelty.

Naturally, forceful reminders that we're failing to do something we're allegedly supposed to do (but habitually predisposed not to do) puts us in a defensive posture. Such unattended obligations spotlight our deficiencies, calling attention to something we're missing, guilty for overlooking, ashamed for ignoring. And the more compelling the argument—the more we worry that it might be right—the harder we'll work to vindicate the behaviors we don't want to change. Failing that, we'll turn to the loving arms of denial or compartmentalization. It can't really be that bad. One shouldn't be expected to mend all the world's ills, for heaven's sake!

Upon reflection, it's not surprising that blasting a floodlight onto shame-inducing unattended obligations is a clumsy way (and at times, ironically, a cruel one) to try to engage our reluctant inner vegans-in-waiting. What we should be offering these emotionally attuned but often intellectually timid parts of ourselves is an inviting space to welcome new information that can expand the imaginative reach and motivational power of our oldest, most cherished commitments.

So let's turn the page on accusing others and ourselves of flunking kindergarten ethics. Let's imagine what it might be like if our inner vegans-in-waiting could return to kindergarten for a fresh look at our eating habits, now animated by a spirit of enthusiasm instilled by a patient, kind, enthusiastic teacher who lives to help us bring out our best. What exciting opportunities for coaxing out our best selves might appear in the absence of shame-inducing pressure to conform to looming obligations that threaten to block our inner vegans-in-waiting from coming into their own?

Remember the stakes. The goal is not to rigidly follow the rules, but to work at becoming an empathic person who knows from experience what's good for you and others and strives to pursue those goods as your special talents and challenges allow. When your teacher encourages you to be curious, humble, fair, honest, courageous, respectful, kind, cooperative, and authentic, it's not because she expects perfection or wants you to achieve some distinction or award, but because she knows you and your classmates will learn more, have more fun together, and be much happier if you practice thinking and acting in these ways whenever possible.

In curiosity, your inner vegan-in-waiting discovers myriad intriguing paths to explore: the wonders of other animals' intellectual, emotional, and social capacities; the astonishingly far-reaching ripple effects of our food choices across human, animal, and environmental boundaries increasingly revealed to be artificially drawn; the sumptuous plant-based offerings of international cuisines never before encountered; the health advantages of experimenting with these delicious new foods.

In humility, your inner vegan-in-waiting is awed by your relative insignificance in the face of all these underexplored territories and yet invigorated and empowered to have a small but important role to play in your unique community of influence as the potential cause of wide-ranging effects that can have a profound collective impact. With the weight of the world off your shoulders, and the freedom to do what you can at a sustainable pace, the feeling of overwhelm subsides and your confidence to face the challenges ahead grows.

With curiosity's newfound delight in your connectedness to other animals and the Earth, and humility's freedom to focus on your own small part, your need to be at the center diminishes, igniting your desire to understand the complex needs of those affected by your choices and do right by them. In the light of fairness, your inner vegan-in-waiting sees clearly that we all deserve much better than our current food system allows: our shared earthly home, animals, people who raise and slaughter them, people who eat them, and people who are hungry or destitute because of the resource intensity and climate consequences of farming them.

In honesty, you feel the weight of ugly truths to bear, but also the galvanizing resolve that comes from departing a fool's paradise for reality's embrace. The truth sets you free from self-serving illusions and forced participation in their ultimately self-defeating consequences, emboldening your courage to be the change you want to see in our food system.

With your eyes opened to the realities of the current system, and your courage primed to do what you can to change it, your respect for and kindness toward the many animals and human beings harmed by this system are greatly enlarged. Instead of shrinking from the knowledge of their unique capacities and their burdens that demand our deference, you can affirm and advocate for their right to our moral attention. And instead of retreating into a hardened heart that would refuse them compassion, your fellow-feeling for them makes you ever more painfully aware, daring you—to revisit the words of Pope Francis—"to turn what is happening in the world into your own personal suffering and thus to discover what each of us can do about it."

Empowered by the freedom and confidence earned from practicing curiosity, humility, fairness, honesty, courage, respect, and kindness, your inner vegan-in-waiting feels invigorated to join the grand act of cooperation that transforming our food system requires precisely through cultivating your own authentic contribution, leading by example in the communities you serve as only you can.

This account is idealized. You'll probably still eat burgers in airports sometimes.[4] You'll continue to pilfer Milky Ways from your unsuspecting kid's Halloween haul. In certain company, you might hide your vegan aspirations under a bushel or at least fail to be as loud and proud as you'd like to be. Maybe you'll save a pepperoni pizza from the trash at a work party, eat a birthday dinner you'd refuse on an average Thursday, or worry less about what goes down the hatch when your old friends are in town, or grill-master Granny's on the smoker, or you're on vacation. You might even occasionally forget to key in your frequent buyer number at the checkout so that the stroopwafels that accidentally fell into your cart don't generate any incriminating coupons in the next mailing (hypothetically).

But overall, when you're at your best, the aspiration to go vegan makes perfect sense and feels good too, now that you appreciate the difference between living toward the ideal of a vegan world and trying to be the ideal vegan person. Far from requiring adherence to an esoteric "-ism" full of burdensome obligations, going vegan is a natural extension of the standard moral imagination into a host of invigorating opportunities to benefit ourselves, other animals, and the earthly home we share.

You might be thinking: "Fine, fine. We need to transform our food system and it might even be inspiring to try. But do we really have to go all the way to vegan here? How about we just settle for coaxing out our inner agrarians-in-waiting so we can keep fennel-rubbed, pasture-raised pork loin and fresh-caught local Pacific swordfish on the menu?"

That's what I was thinking as I stewed over an untouched swordfish steak in Kona, hoping against hope that a charismatic grass-fed dairy farmer would come through in the clutch in that final week of my looming seminar, opening a path for me to have my transformed food system and eat my pork loin too.

But it simply wasn't to be.

Curiosity led me to marvel at the intellectual, emotional, and social capabilities of cows, pigs, chickens, turkeys, sheep, and fish.

It felt entirely fitting to respect them as unique individuals worthy of our moral consideration and our deep empathy and kindness, living, suffering, and dying as they do with alert minds and fragile bodies biologically like our own.

Humility helped me see the lack of fairness in supposing that my trivial interest in the pleasure of eating their bodies could outweigh their most basic interests in living and enjoying their lives.

Honesty compelled me to acknowledge that "humane slaughter" is an oxymoron. One cannot compassionately give gratuitous death to a thriving, unwilling creature.

Courage helped me to see that prioritizing animal welfare only to snatch it away before flourishing animals even reach adolescence is a profound failure of resolve. If animals are the sorts of creatures whose lives demand our respect and kindness at all, then they are the sorts of creatures whose lives should not be cut woefully short for our pleasure and profit.

As comforting as the agrarian ideal of producing high-welfare animal products initially seemed, I couldn't find inspiration there.[5] The vision simply didn't afford opportunities for continued growth in living out my dearest commitments. Beyond that, it just wasn't beautiful. "Humanely raised" animals suffer and die in the same blood-soaked abattoirs at the hands of the same exploited workforce as their confined cousins. Their deaths are no less gratuitous and perhaps even more cruel, given that they have tasted the good life and experienced a semblance of trust with those who ultimately betray them.[6]

My hope for authenticity—that deep-seated desire to be true to my commitments in the company of others even when the going gets tough—turned out to be animated by a vegan imagination. My inner vegan-in-waiting had come out into the open. The question now was whether I would remain blocked by the obstacles of habit, convenience, comfort, and laziness, or aspire to move forward toward the opportunities held out to me.

It's one thing, after all, to know what is true and thus to see what is good for you and quite another thing to desire to do it fervently enough to overcome the inertia of the status quo. Whether your inner vegan-in-waiting ultimately becomes an aspiring vegan or what Carol J. Adams describes as a "blocked vegan" depends a great deal on how you adapt to the expansion of your moral imagination and whether you commit to cultivating the desire to live into it.[7]

Most of our inner vegans-in-waiting initially emerge as a combination of blocked and aspiring—the general resonance with the ideal of a vegan world is there and we have all the commitments we need to pursue it, but on some fronts the way is blocked and on others we feel positive energy gathering to push us forward.

In my experience, the best way to unblock your capacity to accept difficult truths and cultivate fervent aspirations to live accordingly is to catch wind of the irresistibly beautiful possibilities for renewal, fulfillment, and joy that await those who strive to live truthful lives. As artist and filmmaker Alejandro

	Blocked		**Aspiring**
	(defensive, backward-looking, obligation-focused)		(curious, forward-looking, opportunity-focused)
Curiosity	"Don't tell me! I don't want to know!"	vs.	"What exciting culinary journey awaits?"
Humility	"But human beings are more important!"	vs.	"How else have I under-estimated these amazing creatures?"
Fairness	"But I love the taste of steak!"	vs.	"Is my pleasure really as important as their lives?"
Honesty	"Surely not all farms are that bad!"	vs.	"When profit is the motive, isn't exploitation inevitable?"
Courage	"I could never give up cheese!"	vs.	"Might it be worth the effort to find new culinary loves?"
Respect	"They're just animals!"	vs.	"How can I show respect for these unique individuals?"
Kindness	"Stop manipulating my emotions!"	vs.	"What is my empathy for animals trying to teach me?"
Cooperation	"I can't do it all and it's not my thing!"	vs.	"Even if I can't do much, what can I contribute right now?"

Jodorowsky thrillingly puts it, "The beautiful is the sparkling of the true."[8]

With this illumination of the difficult truths of our food system behind us, let us turn to a more robust exploration of the vegan imagination, envisioning the dazzling abundance of a world transformed by redemptive responses to these truths.

PART II

IMAGINATION

THE JOYFUL ABUNDANCE OF
A NEW VEGAN NORMAL

CHAPTER 4

HUMAN BEINGS

TOWARD FLOURISHING SELVES AND JUST COMMUNITIES

THIN RIBBONS OF DARK GREEN FALL CRISPLY FROM A chef's knife onto a walnut cutting board. Wafts of minced garlic and orange oil escape the well-worked surface of the board with each cut, foretelling the imminent transfiguration of these humble leafy greens into Citrus Collards with Raisins, the opening recipe of Bryant Terry's celebrated new cookbook, *Vegan Soul Kitchen*.[1] Rare funk and soul tracks homegrown in Michigan infuse the room with an elevating chemistry.

Dee Edwards's "(I Can) Deal with That" drops into the mix, inviting the capacity crowd to "get ourselves together." That's just what we're doing, because the promise of a live cooking demonstration and book signing with rising culinary star and bestselling author Bryant Terry has our beloved Brick Road Pizza Co.

packed shoulder to shoulder. That the pizza will yield center stage on their all-you-can-eat brunch buffet to a smorgasbord of sumptuous dishes from *Vegan Soul Kitchen* is just the icing on the cake. Or rather the Molasses-Vanilla Ice Cream with Candied Walnuts on the Maple Yam-Ginger Pie, as luck would have it.

It's almost showtime.

Bryant's demo is the most anticipated event of this year's Wake Up Weekend, a fledgling vegan festival I cofounded in hopes of infusing some extracurricular joy into teaching an intensive animal ethics seminar in the bleak midwinter. Facing the hard truths of our food system is a tall order in the best of times, but in the frigid dark of a brutal Michigan January? My students and I can barely imagine an evening without the comfort of a meat-lovers pizza, much less the prospect of a livable vegan world. We get that it's all just kindergarten ethics. But our inner vegans-in-waiting are famished for inspiration.

So Wake Up Weekend devotes two action-packed days of talks, workshops, demos, art exhibitions, film screenings, concerts, food, food, and still more food to envisioning a vegan world and celebrating the immense beauty of striving to realize it. The exhilarating inner harmony of our physical, social, emotional, intellectual, and moral selves! The concentration of our power to liberate food systems from the ignorance, indifference, impotence, and injustice of the status quo! The hope of an invigorated Mother Earth renewed by foodways that preserve scarce resources and nourish biodiversity! The balancing fusion of compassion and courage that catalyzes our kinship and solidarity with other hungry beautiful animals! And most importantly, the chance for your top-secret signature recipe to prove ascendant in West Michigan's most prestigious (and only) vegan chili cook-off!

With Bryant Terry anchoring our panel of celebrity judges this year, an astonishing thirty-four contenders are vying for plant-based chili supremacy. We're encouraging people to ditch plates and bring muffin tins so they can sample a dozen chilis per sitting. We scheduled the cooking demo early and the chili cook-off late because crowds this big eating food this good will want to take their precious time. How could life in a vegan world be anything but gorgeous with a delectable new chili for every day of the month (and three extra days besides)?

The work of this chapter is to imagine this new vegan normal in rich detail with Bryant's invitational approach to advocacy as our inspiration and my adventures in Wake-Up-Weekending as our guide. The goal is to envision the many ways that the beauty of a vegan world can woo us into striving with joy toward flourishing selves and just communities, harmonizing our deepest inner desires with the greatest needs and most hopeful prospects of the world outside.

With fifteen minutes until Bryant's cooking demo goes live, the line to get into Brick Road Pizza is out the door and around the block. Volunteers scramble to get overflow seating and a video feed installed in an adjacent dining area. I negotiate the expectant crowd to deliver a box of coconut water to Bryant as he concludes his demo prep. From his cooking station at the front of the restaurant, the beauty of this strange and wonderful gathering suddenly grips and dazzles me.

My path through this packed-out pizzeria has traversed in unlikely succession the pleasures of high-fiving a food justice activist from a neighborhood nonprofit, meeting Rosa Parks's personal assistant, directing a group of health-conscious seniors to accessible seating, greeting members of an evangelical Christian youth group with a passion for creation care, shaking hands with an Ivy League philosopher, bear-hugging the drummer of a local hardcore band, and returning a fallen sippy cup to a wandering toddler in a "GO VEG!" romper.

Everyone is here, together amidst our differences in age, race, socioeconomic status, spirituality, and vocation, coaxed into improbable fellowship by our shared hunger and hope for something elevating and sustaining: sumptuous soul food born from ideas and set to sounds that invite us to imagine liberation on a cosmic scale that only a vegan world could offer.

My first glimpse of the capaciousness of the vegan imagination came from my friendship and work with Bryant Terry. In the philosophical debates around "veganism" that had initially piqued my interest, the discussion was usually abstract, nearly always focused on discerning obligations, and often humorously bereft of practical appeal. "Is it permissible to consume this pepperoni pizza I found in a dumpster? Yes, because the act of consuming it bears no causal relationship to the bad act that produced it, just like eating roadkill." Not really the stuff of imagination-building, however clarifying of the thorny questions hiding in the weeds.

For Bryant, the vision was much more expansive: foodways are *life*ways and life unfurls profusely and abundantly in many directions simultaneously, encompassing our physical health, spiritual creativity, and social history, our partnerships, friendships, parenting, careers, and civic engagement. So Bryant integrated art, music, books, and political history into his advocacy, paid close attention to how children understand and enjoy food, and most importantly, was not uptight about what specific acts qualified or disqualified a person as an aspiring vegan. His focus was on the beauty of a vegan world and the pleasures of being a part of it, not on the list of obligations demanded of the perfect vegan person. One came away from his interventions believing it was possible to go vegan while remaining in deep spiritual communication with the foodways one grew up in even as one takes them into daring, fascinating new places.

Bryant's joyful charisma emanates from this invitational holism. Preparing a recipe from any of his books will treat you to a personal feast for the body, mind, and heart, but also an invocation of collective spirit to grow food, community, and society in our work together. Prepare to encounter the olfactory pleasures of fresh ground spices that can require a satisfying resourcefulness to procure. The extravagant loveliness of meticulously curated textures, colors, and tastes mingling on the palate. The suggested pairings of recipes with soundtracks and books that seduce one into moving to and being moved by the cultural and political rhythms of ingredients and foodways that built the bodies and powered the wisdom of ancestors.

What Bryant understands is that eating good food is the animating force of both personal autonomy and global flourishing. Good food liberates us to raise bodies that can strive, suffer, recover, abide, and delight in growing and disseminating our unique gifts and passions. And building a better food system to power our collective striving is essential to our survival, especially as our hunger as a species increasingly threatens the beauty and balance of animal life on the planet.

But Bryant knows equally well—and this is where the irresistible appeal of his work lies for me—that eating good food is just too personal, too pleasurable, and too communal an experience to be reduced to a philosophical argument or an activist's tool. We're not typically looking for a regime of health warnings, moral prohibitions, and political agendas when we sit down to eat. What we want from our food is to be comforted, pleasured, dazzled, delivered from life's hardships, brought together around tables of acceptance, love, and solidarity. We want to taste and feel the deep beauty and delight of freely expressed belonging.

That's not to say that good food lacks the power to enlighten us and sing to our better angels. It's just that food must delight us first, capture our imaginations, coax us into deeper relationships in communities that nourish our collective spirit, emanating soul: that elevating chemistry that allows inspired individuals cooperatively to create a whole grander than the sum of its parts. As Bryant always says, "Start with the visceral, move to the cerebral, and end at the political."

This experience is precisely what Wake Up Weekend aims to offer: an inviting space simply to enjoy ourselves, to eat delicious food together, to experience communal joy around a common cause, only to discover—through this pleasurable immersion—that our deepest desires and our grandest hopes for the world are drawn compellingly together in going vegan.

Like a heaping plate of Bryant's Citrus Collards with Raisins, this communal act of envisioning a vegan world and feeling drawn to seek its beauty is enticing all by itself, but also brimming with nourishment and radiating goodness—from healing phytochemicals to the wisdom of ancient foodways, dignifying labor for the people who grow our food, an Earth-healing harvest, and justice for animals.

Far from the threats of stringent restriction and grudging abstinence, the promise of a vegan world is *beauty*—the gathering together of inner longing and outer abundance, just as the poet David Whyte describes it:

> Beauty is the harvest of presence, the evanescent moment of seeing
> or hearing on the outside what already lives far inside us; the eyes,
> the ears, or the imagination suddenly becoming a bridge between
> the here and the there, . . . eras[ing] our separation, our distance, our
> fear of the other.[2]

This beautiful experience of erasing our fear can initially feel daunting, especially when the others to whom we must draw near include such strange and wonderful creatures as other animals, the green planet itself, and—perhaps most fearsome of all—our own inner vegans-in-waiting. For most of us, "what already lives far inside us" is a decidedly complicated affair. Bryant's advice to "start with the visceral, move to the cerebral, and end at the political" honors this timeless wisdom that each human being is always already a family of many members—parts that need each other but are often at cross-purposes, especially when we fail mindfully to acknowledge and honor their different roles and complex interrelations.[3]

In *How to Relax*, famed Zen master and political reformer Thich Nhat Hanh frames the challenge of being human as akin to that of a monarch charged with ruling peacefully over a territory of provinces (body, heart, and mind) among which disharmony and conflict often reign.[4] To establish benevolent regency over this complex inner ecology means coaxing power from a system that has been ruling us since before we were born.

We all share the humble origin of flesh, emerging in a physical system of bodily reception and excretion that takes in nourishment, regulates growth, and dispels toxins. Surviving the rigors of fleshly finitude requires sustained socialization into deeply formative human relationships even as we gestate. We are seven months beyond the womb before our oldest emotions, fear and anger, dawn in primordial response to our desperate need of others' caring. Our intellectual capacities crackle forth, as powers to detect and recollect our caregivers' presence or absence give rise to the meaning and use of words within a year. By toddlerhood, the joys of shared treats and heartfelt hugs and the sorrows of hoarded toys and hurtful names begin to sort themselves as rights and wrongs, morally charged acts of justice or injustice.

We live and grow thereafter as an evolving whole of intermeshed parts, negotiating well-being with others and the world to the extent we succeed in harmonizing the physical, social, emotional, intellectual, and moral aspects of our being. Meeting this challenge can be as easy as thwarting hangry parenting by vigilantly eating oatmeal before the kids wake up for the morning routine. Or parrying writer's block with a furious elliptical run to Journey's "Don't Stop Believin.'" Or bracing for a work-day that might otherwise elicit one-finger salutes to all comers by lingering in a hug from a loved one. Ah, the calming effects of oxytocin!

Managing our inner ecologies can be mighty difficult too. Like when your heart blissfully ignores both your gut and your head as a toxic relationship sends you careening toward implosion. Or when a month of poorly managed work travel transports you predictably from Lonely Valley through Booze Gulch onto the floor of the dingiest room at the Motel Dicey Choices. Or when your gut wants a burger, your heart wants to nuzzle a cow, and your head bobbles about between defending old habits and exploring new ones as your friends look on befuddled.

To fully express our capabilities for well-being—to "flourish," as Aristotle would say—we need relative harmony across the provinces of our territory.[5] When we are unwell, chances are that two or more of the provinces are at war. If we want to bring peace among them, it pays to know each of them intimately—their points of strength, their weaknesses, their insecurities, which ones naturally collaborate well and which ones are temperamentally at odds. Perhaps most importantly, we must know who to approach first to start building the requisite alliances.

Here's where the genius of Bryant's advice to "start with the visceral" really comes home. It's hard to imagine the beauty of a vegan world while your stomach churns at the thought of endless turnip porridge and your heart sinks into dread of the social death sentence sure to follow. Disgust and anxiety are imagination killers. If you want to open a window from our inner ecology into the beauty of a vegan world, go first and with gusto for the gut, preferably with a superabundance of delicious food and comforting company.

I'm not saying you need to roll out thirty-four plant-based chilis sparkling with the sacred foodways of five continents to a crowd so diverse that everyone could both find their people *and* break (corn)bread with a bunch of wildly different new friends. But whether you're serving chili to hundreds or tacos to two, the first and most formidable challenge is to remove all doubt that the visceral pleasures of food and fellowship can be abundantly enjoyed in going vegan, and enjoyed, too, in a wide variety of circumstances.

It's not enough to have a surprisingly good meal in a trendy restaurant. We need to know in our bones that there's a perfect foldable slice of pizza to power us through a breakup. A superlative Friday night takeout to rinse off the week and a Saturday brunch worth showering for. A dynamite date night. Portable power foods for cookouts and camping. Quick eats for the busy times and cheap eats for the lean times and stuff that won't provoke a hunger strike from picky kids. A Super Bowl spread we'll live to regret. If we can't imagine both feeding our children and overenjoying a vegan party, we can't imagine flourishing in a vegan world.

And so Wake Up Weekend made hospitality job one, inviting participants to envision a new vegan normal as delicious, comforting, and fun. Neighborhood restaurants ran specials offering an embarrassment of riches around the clock. A breakfast of vegan chicken and waffles. A lunch of mouth-busting deli sandwiches for the parentals, crustless PB&Js for the littles, and for everyone, cupcakes the size of a beaming toddler's face.

A platter of Ethiopian stews for dinner. Hot wings and beers at nine. Loaded baked-potato pizzas at midnight. Student activists led cooking demos to show how a simple homemade salsa could transform inexpensive staples like beans, corn, rice, and greens into a week's worth of glorious burritos. Sponsoring food companies sent cold cuts for your lunch box, trail mix for your fanny pack, and candy bars for your plastic jack-o-lantern.

And yes, West Michigan's proudest home cooks made chilis by the dozen, each inflecting their own culture and history, bringing a world of foodways from Accra to Mexico City to Shenzhen to Zagreb to a muffin tin near you. If there's any other comfort in the world like being stuffed to the brink of delirium with twelve standing O performances of the planet's most soul-warming food (knowing all the while you've got nearly two dozen chilis left to try!), I have yet to experience it. In the loving embrace of thirty-four chilis, fears of dying alone on a diet of raw celery disappear faster than fellow partygoers from philosophers querying the ethics of eating roadkill.

If the faintest doubts remain, the presence of Bryant Terry and other visiting chefs and bloggers provided proof positive that there is no occasion under heaven—no picnic or party, no wedding or funeral, no dinner in a dive or swanky tasting menu—that vegan cuisine can't elevate, all the while serving up ample sides of additional benefits we didn't even know we craved.

Coming to see the beauty of these additional benefits is a matter of "moving to the cerebral." With our tummies and hearts full of assurances that gustatory pleasure and communal belonging needn't be sacrificed, our heads start to clear of the intellectual defenses mounted to protect vulnerable viscera. The beauty of a satisfied gut is that the head can talk openly to the heart, directing our attentions and nourishing our loves from a space of curious imagination rather than stultifying skepticism.[6]

Our guiding assumption at Wake Up Weekend was that if the feast we prepared for the head was as extravagant as that offered to the gut and heart, we could woo every member of our inner ecology, sparking mutually supporting collaborations among our provinces and awakening consciousness of the beauty of a vegan world across our entire territory.

A jubilant gut could free the head to be more curious and the heart to be more compassionate. An imaginative head could teach new tricks to a naïve heart, expanding its empathy into wider worlds of experience. An open heart could whisper to a stubborn head or an anxious gut that the world is infinitely less threatening and more resplendent in love's embrace. And with the gut, heart, and head killin' like the Ramsey Lewis Trio (iykyk), our social instincts and moral judgment can pulse with possibilities that simply aren't in our bandwidth without the provocations of this inner improvisation.

But our inner ecologies are all unique. It's difficult to predict, too, what intellectual dishes will be most appetizing on a given day to a given person when it's time to move to the cerebral. So our aspiration was to serve an interdisciplinary smorgasbord—to create a microcosm of a vegan world by inviting activists and professors, artists and scientists, documentary filmmakers and public health experts, pastors and economists to illuminate how their particular patches of ground would be beautified by a new vegan normal.

The vision was to flood every lovely corner of a vegan world with light, allowing us to glimpse the whole—a world transformed!—that inspires our desire to keep working enthusiastically at each of our small but critically important parts. The hope was that exposure to this vision could help us to more vividly imagine ourselves flourishing as aspiring vegans across all the life-shaping places and practices that make the world what it is and thus enfold us into belonging there, from the family room to the classroom to the breakroom to the protest line, at the gym, on a hike, or in places of worship.

If I'm honest, this was an intellectual feast that I needed more than anyone. As a professional philosopher whose strategic playbook was heavy on abstract theoretical reflection and light on killing it at parties, I had intellectual insecurities aplenty about how going vegan and advocating for others to join me might complicate my relationships with fellow human beings.

For one thing, my students, friends, and family were less captivated by the philosophical arguments for going vegan than I was. They seemed effortlessly to intuit a worry that had been gnawing at me for years: as helpful as philosophical reasoning can be for spotting flaws in our timeworn traditions and getting clearer about where we stand, it can also tempt us to overvalue the intellect's power of abstraction and undervalue other facets of our intellectual lives (not to mention other parts of our inner ecologies) that are crucial for sustaining complex commitments in unique circumstances.

We've all experienced the inner challenge of having to break an intellectual tie between equally compelling ideas by consulting our emotional awareness, listening to our bodies, or taking the social temperature of the room. And beyond the self, abstract arguments can incline us to oversimplify complex communal realities, leading us to gloss over or completely miss key differences in the situations of people for whom the challenges of going vegan can weigh heavier or feel particularly foreign. If we're not careful, such arguments can push us toward a one-size-fits-all "veganism" that both individually and collectively fails us.[7]

Folks in my orbit were most worried about two such perceived failures in particular: a lack of attention to how going vegan sits with the system of food apartheid that consigns many communities of color in the United States to receiving few benefits from our industrial food system even as they endure greater risk of harm by its costs;[8] and a lack of respect for religious communities in spite of the fact that religion figures centrally in the social, emotional, intellectual, and moral lives of a significant majority of human beings.[9]

Among that significant majority are many of my students, friends, and family. Oh, and me too. Hello, intellectual alienation! I'm out here offering secular arguments for animal liberation, but that's not where most of my people live. And the books I'm recommending in hopes of persuading my community to share my concern? They're written by people who think religion's mostly to blame for the very problems we're trying to solve. On a narrow if culturally dominant reading of the history (if hopefully not the future!) of religious engagement on the animal question, they've got a point. I'm effectively saying to my majority religious community, "Hey guys! Check out Peter Singer's 'Man's Dominion: A Short History of Speciesism' where the plight of animals is laid at the doorstep of Judeo-Christianity's human exceptionalism! Are you excited? Let's go vegan! Wooooooo!"[10] I might as well have been running a workshop on how to trigger counter-productive identity-protective cognition!

I felt insecure that people in my family, social, and professional circles were clearly intuiting both the limits of my intellectual tools and my inner ambivalence about their value. It was clear when they yawned at the philosophical arguments I found impressive. It was clearer still when they found the arguments intellectually compelling but ultimately inadequate for catalyzing their social, emotional, and moral transformation. I hoped they were wrong but worried they were right when they objected that going vegan is for white elitists, and no place from which to cultivate genuine solidarity with communities under oppression. My heart sank when they countered my argumentative challenges just as our nonreligious critics predicted ("Human beings have dominion!"; "God gave us animals for food!"), and I had no exciting counternarrative with which to challenge or inspire either side.[11]

The feast for the mind we hosted at Wake Up Weekend changed all that—a joy I owe to my colleagues and closest collaborators on the festival, Adam Wolpa and the Reverend Dr. Michelle Loyd-Paige.

Wolpa showed me how to get beyond the abstract arguments into experiential curiosity. A sculptor, printmaker, and professor of studio art, he curated a major exhibition for Wake Up Weekend each year with a closing artist's reception at our university's urban art gallery that coincided (not coincidentally) with the chili cook-off. The "free chili," "gallery hopping," and "vegan advocacy" demographics didn't overlap much, but that was precisely the point.

Wolpa's genius, both as a collage artist and community organizer, is his ability to spark creativity and openness to provocative ideas through unlikely but hospitable and often humorous aesthetic juxtapositions. Whether you encountered this genius in his hand-printed programs, the art on display, or his roving megaphone commentary, Wolpa channeled the power of the visual and performance arts to captivate attention and coax transformational curiosity from inquiring minds that often respond defensively to more teachy-preachy forms of intellectual engagement.[12]

My favorite example of his myriad successes doubles humorously as a critique of my own pedagogy. Wolpa invited Detroit artist and urban farmer Kate Daughdrill to offer a workshop on churning fresh ice cream. Drawn in by a quaint little table set with a stand of waffle cones and all the sundae fixings, visitors were invited to join Kate in a lace tent to make the ice cream by hand in an old-fashioned wooden churn.

Fewer people ate the ice cream than churned it, however, because it was made from donated human breast milk that they'd have to sign a waiver to try. It was a humbling yet exhilarating moment when a student from my seminar emerged from the tent with an eye-opening reframe, waving a box of Tofurky cold cuts from his cook-off spoils to flag me down: "Not gonna lie. When you were going on about the ethics of drinking cow's milk in class, I was like whatever. But duuuuude."

If Wolpa showed me a world where provocative experiences could take thinking to places that arguments alone couldn't go, Michelle showed me a world beyond my racial and religious experience that helped me to envision going vegan in a much more holistic and personally inflected way.

What you must know about Michelle is that her signature commitment to "eating like a vegan" is fully legendary across a dizzying array of contexts with her family, church, university, and all the communities she serves as a professor of sociology, a pastor, a worship dancer, a diversity consultant, an entrepreneur, a podcaster, and a personal health coach. For heaven's sake, I once discovered Michelle at a holiday vegan trade show presiding over a vendor's booth of the most stylish vegan handbags I've ever seen, because—you know—going vegan doesn't have to mean losing that flash and sparkle and she's got the purses to prove it. I just kept eating my vegan donut in sheer awe.

We had been colleagues for years, but it was our mutual love of vegan chili and Bryant Terry's recipes that made us coconspirators. In teaming up to align departmental budgets to fulfill our shared dream of bringing Bryant to campus, we got talking about my animal ethics class. My usual hemming and hawing ensued about the vanilla demographics of my syllabus, and Michelle volunteered to share a draft of a piece she had written for a forthcoming book and to visit my class to discuss it.

That book turned out to be Dr. A. Breeze Harper's genre-defining classic, *Sistah Vegan: Black Women Speak on Food, Identity, Health, and Society*—a volume that invited the world to envision going vegan not as an exclusive and legalistic niche diet, but as a holistic and hospitable way of life that each of us must live according to our own awakening, generating benefits that radiate far beyond ourselves to our communities, our fellow creatures, and the planet.[13] In addition to revolutionizing my understanding of how going vegan can serve the intermeshed causes of civil rights, women's liberation, combating environmental racism, and ending food apartheid, *Sistah Vegan* catalyzed my conviction that the transformational healing power of vegan living simply can't be captured in a one-size-fits-all vegan fundamentalism. "The beauty of this edited volume," Harper concludes in the introduction, is that "even though we do identify as Black and female, we are not a monolithic group."[14]

Michelle's chapter in *Sistah Vegan*—"Thinking and Eating at the Same Time"—crystalized this insight in a way that couldn't have spoken more directly to my insecurities about arguments, race, and religion. "Thinking," in Michelle's usage, is not a matter of mastering abstract arguments that apply universally to all comers, but of becoming better attuned to what we can learn from those mystical moments of experience when hidden connections between who we are and the way the world is suddenly and indelibly become manifest.

For Michelle, the awakening came while waiting in line to pick up a six-piece chicken wing snack for her husband, as her mind wandered to the question of what happened to the rest of the three birds who were killed to facilitate her casual purchase. You should receive the good word about how this small act of curiosity led to a world-transforming epiphany straight from the pastor's pulpit:

> My thinking and eating habits changed as a result of what I call a *Kairos* moment. Kairos is an ancient Greek word meaning the "right or opportune moment." In my faith tradition it also means "the appointed time in the purpose of God." At this appointed time, four previously unassociated thoughts—the content of a lecture I had just presented on the global inequities in food distribution;

a vague recollection of a statement from PETA about the cruelties associated with chicken production; the remembrance of how surprisingly good I felt physically while on a forty-day spiritually motivated fast from meat and dairy; and my own desire to live an authentic life—yanked me into an uncomfortable realization that, when it came to food consumption, I was not living according to my beliefs.[15]

This permission to understand going vegan as a highly personal, experientially catalyzed call from the cosmos to live more authentically toward a holistic vision of justice was precisely what the (reverend) doctor ordered to calm my insecurities and set my mind ablaze for communicating the promise of vegan living to my community.

Moving to the cerebral may look very different for you. Perhaps your "*Kairos* moment" occurs while you're churning ice cream from human milk and you realize in rapid fire that cow's milk is for calves, consuming a fluid made to pack five hundred pounds onto a bovine baby maybe isn't so healthful for an adult human being, and believing that cow's milk is delicious while skunk milk, sloth milk, whale milk, and human milk are disgusting is kind of weird. Maybe the idea of a nudge from the universe feels too grandiose for you, but becoming mindful of the synergies among physical health, moral awakening, and social justice nonetheless feels intellectually energizing.

As Oprah likes to say, riffing on the wise words of Billie Jean King, "If you can see it, and believe it, it's a lot easier to achieve it." Together, the good folks at Wake Up Weekend demonstrated in living color how vegan life, work, and advocacy can instill the empowering spirit of resolve that accompanies belonging to a visionary community committed to provoking cultural awakening and social transformation at a time of unprecedented moral and spiritual crisis. Together, these good folks gave us not only a window into a beautiful vegan world, but a model for how to synchronize our inner ecologies for optimal participation in the blessings of striving to realize that world, whoever we may be, whatever unique perspectives, passions, and gifts we can contribute.

They showed that it is not only possible, but pleasurable to be an aspiring vegan athlete, or parent, or friend, or scientist, or artist, or religious adherent, or scholar, or activist, or—perhaps most beautifully—all of them at once. The beauty of going vegan is epitomized by the way that envisioning and striving toward a vegan world engenders inner ecological transformation— nourishing all that we are, liberating and empowering our physical, emotional, social, intellectual, and moral aspects to cooperate without the friction and frustration that often characterize our lives before our inner vegans-in-waiting are fully awake.

For most of us, these unsettling, sometimes even shame-inducing, existential dissonances are all too familiar. The stomach-churning fear of the truth and those who tell it that makes us lie to ourselves. The unenviable conditions of "knowing" but not caring ("It's bad, but they're just animals"), "caring" but not knowing ("Worker justice now! Pass the meatloaf!"), knowing and caring but not doing ("I shouldn't eat this, but . . ."). The defensive social postures of fight, flight, and freeze that these inner conflicts bully us into taking even and especially when we acutely feel the embarrassment and well understand the injustice of our selective forgetting of kindergarten ethics.

But in going vegan, a resolute gut, a compassionate heart, and a curious head can engage in full and open collaboration, enabling social awareness and moral discernment unencumbered by squeamishness, indifference, and defensiveness. The heart is free appropriately to feel moved by circumstances that are moving, whether they are beautiful or terrible, without the head rationalizing away legitimate concerns. The head is free to follow science and scholarship away from mawkish attachment to attitudes, traditions, industries, and practices that no longer make sense. Going vegan thus aligns our respect for the findings of science with our personal ethics and the daily attitudes and actions we take at home, at work, and as consumers, symbolically and practically extending the caring, respect, and empathy we delight in showing to beloved family, friends, and animal companions to all creatures deserving of that delight.

Lest you feel I'm blowing sunshine up your knickers, let me state unequivocally that our efforts to keep beauty front and center should not be confused with ducking or denying the realities of our current ways of life. No honest engagement with the complexities of our food system and the personal and collective challenges of striving to transform it can breathe in only sweetness and light.

But the spotlight at Wake Up Weekend was always trained on what we gain from responding with courage and joy to this honest assessment of our lot, emphasizing first and foremost not what "veganism" is *against* but what going vegan is *for*: the pursuit of cosmic liberation for flourishing selves and just communities that the beautiful vision of a vegan world holds out to us. If kindergarten ethics calls us to a new way of eating, it's not to shame and blame us into lives of abstinence, rigidity, and scarcity, but to pull back the curtain on the world of liberation, opportunity, and abundance for all that we stand to enjoy by working together to transform the status quo.

The potential abundance of a vegan world is breathtaking. In over two decades of teaching and scholarship devoted to discerning what a true, beautiful, and good world might look like and how a life enjoyed in pursuit of this vision might take shape, I've never come across a more lavish abundance aggregator than the practice of going vegan, conserving and concentrating inner and outer powers as it so effusively does for their reallocation toward transformative service to self and world.

In going vegan, we stand inwardly to save ourselves physical inflammation, cognitive dissonance, emotional incoherence, and moral hypocrisy, and outwardly to save ourselves the unconscionable amounts of land, water, grain, pharmaceuticals, pandemic risk, worker injustice, and animal suffering we currently exploit to feed ourselves, freeing up vast energies with which to pursue more abundant ways of being for all. Establishing a new vegan normal is a slam dunk for human flourishing from the perspective of both egoistic analyses of what we stand to gain as individuals and altruistic accounts of the benefits we stand to gain as a collective.

When I say "we" here, please have no illusions of a homogeneous solidarity or a perfectly united front. In my early years of teaching animal ethics, the four authors whose work provoked the most intriguing class discussions were a Presbyterian ecofeminist whose advocacy work began with women's reproductive rights and whose latest book critiques effective altruism (Carol

J. Adams),[16] an atheist moral philosopher known for defending the right to euthanasia and founding effective altruism (Peter Singer),[17] a pro-life Republican strategist who published blistering critiques of industrial animal farming while serving as senior speechwriter for President George W. Bush (Matthew Scully),[18] and a sociologist, pastor, and diversity consultant with whose work we're already familiar (Rev. Dr. Michelle Loyd-Paige).[19]

They agreed that the state of things would be vastly better if we set our sights on a vegan world and began living toward that ideal in whatever ways we could manage. But their perspectives, experiences, and styles of approach were and are radically different.

Wake Up Weekend's events happened under a similarly big tent. When the tent is large, there will be disagreement. Even controversy. But beauty can be so much bigger and bolder than a bowl of cherries—a fact that is urgently important to remember at a time when social movements are so susceptible to the divisive forces of culture wars and digital fracture. Activist and author Adrienne Maree Brown puts as lovely a touch on this wisdom as I have seen:

> There are way too many people in critique mode who belong to no formation, who spend their lives writing volunteer think pieces in 140-character bursts of Internet. It makes me feel defensive of the messy chaotic beauty of transformation. Uprisings and resistance and mass movement require a tolerance for messiness, a tolerance of many, many paths being walked on at once.[20]

Between the ugliness of the status quo and the beauty of a world transformed lies the "messy chaotic beauty of transformation"—the divergences, wrong turns, collisions, and convergences of many, many paths traveled simultaneously in hopes of achieving the progress we all desire.[21]

And here is where the last step of Bryant's advice—"to end at the political"—finally gets traction. Once the gut and the head are well-fed, packed, and ready for the journey, it's time to start mapping the unique paths to flourishing selves and just communities that each of us is best suited to travel given our unique inner ecologies and the different shapes of our influence out there in the world.

In my experience, it's much easier to discern one's place in the *polis*—that sweet spot where a citizen's gifts and passions serve the flourishing of the whole city—when one's inner politics are peaceful and productive. If one can take wise leadership of one's own inner ecology, as going vegan helps us to do, the prospects are much better for promoting peace and justice outside in the places where one is uniquely gifted to contribute.

Grace Lee Boggs said it with authority: "Transform yourself to transform the world." Adrienne Maree Brown sets this sparkling gem just right: "This doesn't mean to get lost in the self, but rather to see our own lives and work and relationships as a front line, a first place we can practice justice, liberation, and alignment with each other and the planet."[22]

Admittedly, our efforts to "end with the political" at Wake Up Weekend were modest and aspirational. Whether we're talking about the "inner citadel" of the self (as Marcus Aurelius described it) or the wider world beyond, Rome wasn't built in two days. As we'll see in Part III, blazing the trail from an inspired vegan imagination to engaged daily striving toward the vegan world we envision is typically a slow burn that requires selective attention and strategic patience to tend.

Even so, we sought to inspire audiences to imagine how their own unique paths from the personal to the political might unfold by giving them concrete examples of how those already on the journey were striving to live out their inner transformations in the communities they served.

The final workshop of our inaugural event, for instance, gave students an opportunity to engage a panel of animal advocates from national and local nonprofits on how best to start an advocacy group on campus. Within weeks, Students for Compassionate Living (SCL) had a charter. Within years, the group's leadership had built a network of relationships among faculty, students, and other campus organizations that leveraged changes in dining services, provided regular fellowship and support for veg and veg-curious students, and furnished a crack team of committed volunteers for annual Wake Up Weekend events.

One intrepid SCL cochair even volunteered to administrate a service project for all first-year students with the express intent to leverage her influence to adopt catering services that better reflected the university's stated commitments to justice and sustainability. One thousand veg lunches later, it's fair to say that she was being the change she wished to see in her city.

In those early years, the most political thing I could imagine doing to push past my intellectual insecurities and move toward being the change I wished to see was to take animal advocacy to church. It took a few years to get up the gumption, but we did it, inviting the late Marilyn McCord Adams, a renowned philosopher and Episcopal priest, to collaborate with other visiting scholars and local parishioners on a full slate of Sunday activities focused on the flourishing of all creatures. Adams created an original liturgy and led a worship service that centered animals and celebrated their creaturely kinship with humankind. In the adult education hour after the service, I led a panel on eating as an act of justice and then we all sat down to a vegan potluck to give it a try.

In this buzzing church basement, now five years and counting from the day Bryant Terry made Citrus Collards with Raisins for a packed house at a local pizza joint, I find myself gripped and dazzled again by that beautiful feeling of belonging so overwhelming that, for a moment, the warm blurry hum of everything's embrace both erases and energizes me. The potluck table is admittedly thirty-three chilis shy of my ideal, but my joy is complete. I am eating vegan chili at a plant-based church potluck after a Sunday school class on how going vegan can harmonize our inner ecologies even as it concentrates our power to show the world and everyone in it something closer to love.

That I am still very much the boy for whom happiness in church once felt like lips glistening with pork fat makes the chili before me that much more sumptuous. This infinite embrace is not the province of words, but upon my return the travelogue reads: *I can live differently toward a rejuvenated same, the forces that shaped me can be reshaped, the world can change, and I can be a servant of its transformation, if only one church basement, one philosophy class, one vegan festival at a time.*

What I felt at Bryant's cooking demo amidst wafts of orange oil and garlic and the electrifying energy of belonging in difference, what I felt radiating into my hands and through my body from the bottom of a bowl of chili after vegan Sunday school, is what I feel as I share these transformational experiences with you now. Gratitude. Because the poet succeeds where the philosopher fails, here's David Whyte again:

> Gratitude arises from paying attention, from being awake in the presence of everything that lives within and without us. . . . Gratitude is the understanding that many millions of things come together and live together and mesh together and breathe together in order for us to take even one more breath of air, that the underlying gift of life and incarnation as a living, participating human being is a privilege, that we are miraculously part of something, rather than nothing.[23]

Going vegan, for me, has been an experience of following beauty into gratitude, a journey of desire finding fulfillment in mutual dependence on others—*inter*dependence with different parts of ourselves, other human beings, and members of other species. Cultivating gratitude knits together our inner and outer lives, inviting us to discover our unique if beautifully small parts in the transformation of everything.

But as a more gracious inner ecology increases our power to strive for flourishing selves and just communities, it simultaneously diminishes our hubris. As our inner vegans-in-waiting become more confident and resolved, the conceit that we human beings are the only ones for whom individual and communal flourishing are possible begins to feel unlikely. We become increasingly open to delighting in the flourishing of other creatures for their own sake and increasingly committed to promoting their flourishing, regardless of what we might stand to gain.

Released from the delusion that our best interests are served by the unnecessary suffering and death of other creatures and the exploitation of human beings made to inflict these atrocities on our behalf, we are free to see members of other species for who they are—fellow hungry beautiful animals, subjects of their own lives who experience the dependent desires of their being according to pleasures, pains, and purposes uniquely theirs, however foreign or unknown they remain to us. In a vegan world, our gratitude would serve their flourishing.

CHAPTER 5

ANIMALS

___

TOWARD EXPANDED CONSCIOUSNESS OF CREATURELY FLOURISHING

E VERY SUMMER OUR THREE EXTENDED FAMILIES CON-verge at a gorgeous destination in the Salish Sea off the coast of Vancouver to eat like crazy, celebrate our decades of friendship, and knit our clans together across the distance that separates us most of the year. We're not related but we might as well be. It's one of those situations where we'd call each other's parents "Uncle" and "Auntie" if we were inclined to that sort of thing.

Most years, seventy to eighty of us make the trek. In a good year, there might be four generations in the mix across the three families. Thanks to our prosperous elders, we live free from want for the summer and basically just take over the place. The local businesses expect us and are always very happy to see us. Don't hate me, but in 2010 we kept the party going for almost four months.

Like distant cousins that somehow manage to stay close, our disparate familial dialects, tastes, quirks, and high-maintenance relatives occasionally make for minor drama when we're together. It can take some doing to find food that everyone is happy to eat. We stay vigilant of the folks who have something to prove or are inclined to have a little too much fun.

Our moms run the show. They pick the place, communicate the details, wrangle the reluctant, temper the overzealous, and most of all, they decide who gets to do what with whom when the gathering is on. Every summer, a couple of the kids who were playmates in previous years are suddenly interested in becoming more than friends. Suffice it to say that no one gets any quality time alone until the matchmaker mamas weigh in. There is no need to smash the patriarchy in this crew. It's settled. There is none.

When it comes to travel and leisure, we're a wild bunch and we're all outdoorsy types. No vehicles, off-road only, and we move as a unit, drawing and building on one another's energy. Everyone communicates incessantly even from a distance while racing along at full speed, some of us chatting, some singing, some scanning for meals with sonic flashlights. As we cleave the deep, our faces effortlessly gather meaning from words reverberating through our skin—signs of inner life and shared purpose that you hear as mere clicks and whistles, bereft of our world as you are.

❧ ❧

On the day that a crestfallen bulldog and a carrot-desecrated yard conspired with the universe to convince me of the moral equivalence of dogs and pigs, I would still have been deeply skeptical of the idea that orcas enjoy personal experiences in complex family cultures within a shared dolphin world.[1]

As impressive as dolphins are, I might have argued back then, their accomplishments are still modest compared to skyscrapers and symphony orchestras. And when you're out there trying to be taken seriously as a vegan, you're not going to lead with animal biographies, especially those of apex predators allegedly so brutal in their ascendance that they deserve the epithet "killer." The only quicker way to achieve Annoying Vegan status is to mount a campaign for termite liberation at a pest control trade show. A better strategy, or so it seemed to me in the early years of going vegan, was to keep the focus tight on shame-inducing comparisons between the two classes of animals that most depend on our mercy: the companions whose bodies we hug, and the "food animals" whose bodies we eat.

As my inner ecology has become more unified and my vegan practice has gained confidence, it's slowly dawned on me that the stories of free-living creatures striving to flourish in a wider world that provokes their desires and challenges their efforts can powerfully unveil the beauty of a new vegan normal in ways that appealing to the suffering of domesticated animals often cannot.

This is certainly not to say that free-living animals are more beautiful or morally important than their domesticated fellow creatures. To render any such comparative judgment absurd, simply feast your eyes on the beauty and dignity radiating from every page of Isa Leshko's magnificent *Allowed to Grow Old: Portraits of Elderly Animals from Farm Sanctuaries*.[2] The point is to interrupt our regularly scheduled program of seeing animals primarily in contrast to assumed human ascendence as dependent, oppressed, and suffering, so that exposure to their flourishing might invite us to imagine who they are beyond the human/animal binary that renders them lesser-than before we even know the first thing about them.

By retraining our consciousness of the lives of animals on narratives of free-living creatures doing well, we can transform our default vision of them as underlings, even and especially the domesticated animals we thought we already knew. By these lights, astonishing capabilities for living well on their own terms come brilliantly into focus that must hide in plain sight when we experience animals primarily within the overwhelmingly negative valences of our most common inherited conceptions of them. Instead of seeing animals merely as docile pets, expendable tools, brutal predators, cringing prey, or destructive pests—beings who, in all cases, are either servile underlings we feel entitled to dominate or encroaching aggressors we feel entitled to destroy—we can envision them as potentially flourishing creatures free to pursue ends uniquely their own.

Drawing on two life-changing experiences from my own journey into deeper animal consciousness, the work of this chapter is to achieve heightened awareness of the complex worlds and awe-inspiring capabilities that dignify other creatures and explode our comparative, inaccurate, and ultimately oppressive conceptions of them as subhuman. Because of our collective history of oppressing animals—and indeed, weaponizing the very idea of "the animal" to facilitate the oppression of fellow human beings—it is unsurprising and even fitting that our aspirations to go vegan often begin in lament over the cruel treatment of victims of this oppression. But going vegan can progressively lift us into heightened consciousness of members of other species as creatures whose lives are their own to cherish, beautiful in themselves and alive to possibilities we can never experience even as they provoke our deepest awe and respect.

"Animal consciousness" may sound a little spooky, but I think most of us have ample experience with what I have in mind. Just think of it as the felt human awareness that other animals have personal lives—that they are creatures who, like us, must make their own way in a world that pushes back.[3] To have animal consciousness is to understand at some level, even if only occasionally in inklings, that other animals have lives that matter to them, lives that could be better or could be worse from their own perspective. Such creatures have experiences, desires, abilities to seek things they want and avoid things they dislike, and their desires are often personally inflected. Some dogs eat six pounds of carrots a week while others never touch the stuff. But all dogs are cognitively, emotionally, socially, and physically invested in doing well for themselves, as their gorgeously shameless trash-rummaging, pre-vacation pouting, backyard showboating, and massage-begging ways attest.

Animal consciousness comes in degrees and waxes and wanes situationally in keeping with how presently threatening or invigorating one finds the prospect that human beings are not the only creatures on the planet who cherish doing well. As children, many of us enjoy such high levels of animal consciousness that our fierce caring for the feathered and furry extends even to our stuffed animals (as any unlucky parent who accidentally smothers a plush sloth at bedtime is abruptly reminded). As we age, sustaining such high levels of animal consciousness becomes increasingly inconvenient, as our perceived interests in doing well come increasingly into conflict with those of other animals.

To the extent that our well-being seems to depend on steaks, chops, milk, and eggs, our animal consciousness contracts to the point of seeing animals, if we see them at all, as instinct-driven ambulatory objects ready to serve as tools for human use. But when a squirrel darts in front of the car or a tufted titmouse careens into the house, our consciousness intuitively if temporarily expands to receive these creatures as having interests in striving and surviving that soccer balls and paper planes clearly lack. And every now and then, when a mother mallard emerges from the brush with ducklings in tow, or a family of raccoons crests the garage roof on a moonlit quest for ripening grapes, our animal consciousness can instantaneously dilate into capacious curiosity, wonder, or even awe at their strivings. Most of us have it in us to be dazzled by other animals, at least when their flourishing demands nothing of us. In thrall to this bedazzlement, we can't help but wish our fellow creatures well.

One needn't have especially or consistently high levels of animal consciousness to go vegan. As we observed in Chapter 4, human beings stand so much to gain in doing so that one could readily adopt vegan aspirations for human-centered reasons alone. What's more intriguing in this context is that many of us who do go vegan thanks to waxing animal consciousness owe our initial awakenings not to awe-inspiring positive experiences of animals flourishing, but rather to shame-inducing negative experiences of animals languishing under oppression.

The uptick in animal consciousness we experience in situations like these is often reluctant and even grudging, trained more on human exploitation of the dependent creatures reduced to objects under our rule than on any concrete hope for their independent flourishing, whatever that might mean. We feel intuitively that industrial animal farming is a moral travesty and we're right! But we're hard put, in most cases, to say much of substance about what the good life might look like (or even if there is such a thing) for the pigs, cows, chickens, and turkeys whose suffering we oppose. For many (maybe most?), going vegan begins with protesting against animal suffering rather than standing for animal flourishing—the promotion of life, liberty, and the pursuit of species-appropriate happiness for other-than-human creatures.

My own conversion was just such an experience. Witnessing Gus's languishing from my overbusy schedule and underutilized pooper scooper allowed me finally to experience the languishing of animals used for farming as intolerable. But in the immediate aftermath of that epiphany and for quite some time moving forward, my inner ecology remained a chaotic mess that seriously hamstrung my initial efforts both to live a fulfilled vegan life myself and to make the riches of going vegan accessible to others in a winsome way.

There was the emotional overwhelm of realizing that hundreds of billions of creatures just like Gus live abject lives of unremitting suffering, a realization that swamped my inner ecology with guilt and shame. There was the social and moral confusion about how to communicate these horrors without overwhelming or alienating others whose consciences were shockingly less burdened by it. There was the physical challenge, both of adapting to new foods and staving off cravings for old favorites.

Worst of all, for a professional philosopher, at least, was the unique intellectual confusion raised by the animal question. I've already confessed the intellectual insecurities I suffered repping vegan commitments early on even just for human-centered reasons. But advancing the outrageous proposition that animals have dignified lives they value living on their own terms really escalates the tension. To make the scandal vivid, just imagine the difference in your least sympathetic uncle's reaction to learning that someone is "allergic to dairy" or even "vegan for health reasons" versus discovering they're "vegan for animal rights reasons." Allergies? No further questions. Animal rights? Permission to consider hostile!

In the wake of my conversion, it was suddenly clear to me that what animals experienced in our food system was textbook oppression and obviously morally wrong, at least from the standpoint of your average kindergartener. But the most readily available conceptual machinery for identifying industrial animal agriculture as oppressive and communicating to more sophisticated audiences exactly why the offending system should be dismantled and transformed had been built for diagnosing and dismantling *human* oppression.

To mobilize this conceptual machinery for the cause of animals meant trying to defend comparisons between human beings and animals that most adults were simply unwilling to entertain, conditioned as we are by a lifetime of human supremacy messaging at home, in school, and in our religious communities. Few people (including me) knew anything whatsoever about the lives of pigs, cows, chickens, and turkeys, and that was expectable given the uninterrogated confidence of the culture at large that they were "just animals," and thus subhuman and unworthy of serious concern outside the imaginations of kindergarteners and unduly sentimental adults. Unsurprisingly, efforts to frame the suffering of animals in industrial farms as evidence of "speciesism" akin to the sexism of patriarchal culture or the racism of white supremacist culture, and to speak, thus, of "animal liberation" in the same breath as the causes of women's liberation or the civil rights movement seemed to most people deeply counterintuitive at best if not outright offensive.

A related intellectual challenge that arose from starting with the suffering of domesticated animals in my efforts to get folks to pay attention was that doing so unwittingly reinforced the cultural assumption of a human-animal hierarchy by simultaneously exaggerating animal dependence on human purposes and obscuring natural behaviors that could otherwise give us a window into animals' remarkable capabilities for independent living. In watching videos of sows languishing in filthy gestation crates, row upon imprisoned row, their collective abjection silently imploring our empathy, could my students imagine anything at all of the clean, curious, clever nest-building matriarchs whose cacophonous wrath at our incursion might put us up a tree or end us entirely should our paths cross in the woods? It is indeed a cruel irony that the creatures who most often turn our hearts and minds to the unpopular truth that animals have value in themselves independent of human purposes are precisely the ones whose well-being hinges so unequivocally on our mercy and their compliant dependence on it.

When we survey the lives of domesticated creatures—the dogs we hug and the pigs we eat—there is a certain comfort in it even when we must confront their suffering. We see our own world and its values reflected back to us in their station and behavior and we judge their aptitude and worth by the degree to which they succeed or fail in making our priorities their priorities. The "good dog" obeys her master and stays at heel. The "bad dog" follows the urine maps that delight her brain from spot to seemingly random spot (random, at least, to those of us who lack the hardware to reveal and regulate our social worlds by the scent of others' urine). The "good pig" returns to her gestation crate without prodding. The "bad pig" resists returning to a place that frustrates her capacities to move, feed, groom, socialize, or even defecate as she would prefer. And obviously there's no such thing as a "good" sewer rat or cockroach.

The truth is that we don't have a ready conception of the good for most nonhuman creatures, much less an understanding of the breathtaking abilities at their disposal to pursue it. We deem them capable or incapable, worthy or unworthy, relative to the extent their existence seemingly helps or hinders our own perceived good. It usually goes without saying that even our most trivial interests are more important than their most basic ones (not that we usually know what those are).

This state of intellectual confusion over how to think about the lives of other animals and communicate my fledgling but urgent sense of our collective duty to improve their lot led to expectable ripples across the other aspects of my inner ecology. Because I didn't have intellectual permission to accord animals the moral worth that seemed fitting given how I felt about them emotionally, I worried that I had been duped by guilt or bullied by shame into irrational sentimentality. Socially, this intellectual

Animals

insecurity manifested in unbecoming if predictable ways. I over-
sold my confidence to family, friends, and students. I undersold
it to the brink of moral cowardice among professional peers. I
overperformed masculinity to remove all doubt that "real men"
could go vegan. I loudly extolled the virtues of human mercy and
good stewardship to drown out skeptical inner whispers over the
scandal of animal liberation.

Perhaps the most intriguing bit of inner ecological fallout was
the way my intellectual hesitancy incited and sustained emotional conflict in the face of my newfound moral conviction.
When residual desire for favorite foods flared up, my skeptical
mind seized the opportunity to rationalize this desire ("What
difference are you really making?"), and the empathy for animals
that usually powered my resolve would suddenly deflate, leaving me a prisoner of unwanted obligation, both salivating and
self-flagellating over intrusive thoughts of a Philly cheesesteak.
Aesthetically, few things seemed more alluring. Morally, few
things seemed more repugnant. This persistent unrest among my
intellectual, emotional, and moral selves made for much inner
adventure in my first couple years of going vegan.

And then things changed forever in a single moment one fateful afternoon. I was in the custom, at this stage, of mourning the
loss of my favorite foods by going out of my way to see them, smell
them, and imagine tasting them. One of my more absurd rituals
during this era was to drive at a crawl with the windows down past
my former favorite restaurant where ribs were always smoking in
the parking lot. I'd allow the car to fill with smoke, quickly close
the windows, and then hit recirculate on the air conditioning to
marinate in the aroma of slow-cooked ribs all the way home.

The day things changed, I was listening on the radio to an interview with Nobel laureate and Holocaust survivor Elie Wiesel, famed for—among many things—the memoir *Night*, which recounts his experiences as a prisoner at Auschwitz and Buchenwald. I was listening inactively as one does while driving, attention drifting and diffused across the tasks of getting home, deferring an oil change in defiance of the warning light, fixing dinner, piloting a dangerous projectile through traffic. With me in the car were Wiesel's voice, years of inner ferment around going vegan, self-congratulatory disgust for the Germans who knew, a burgeoning haze of meat smoke, and an attending lament that I would soon be making carrot soup.

Up go the windows. Recirculate. I draw the deepest possible breath through my nose—the one you luxuriate in among the gardenias or amidst the sillage of an all too familiar perfume, where your chin drifts upward and your eyes begin to close. I hear the word "crematorium."

Bile rises and vision blurs and everyone in me runs for cover from the blast. I find us regathering in a parking lot, dry heaving and ugly crying and pummeling a steering wheel that repeatedly sounds the horn in protest. This is the day that my moral and emotional universes converge in full aesthetic revolt—the day that not eating meat enters the company of not ingesting feces, not smelling vomit, and not handling medical waste on the list of "things in my best interest that require no effort of me." The sweet, comforting smell of my church harvest festival—the perfume of my people celebrating plenty—had irrevocably revealed itself as the stench of a burning body taken by violence from a potentially flourishing creature who did not and would never choose this end.

But if my moral and emotional provinces made peace that day and longing for meat became a thing of the past, my intellect still felt estranged from both. One of the most uncanny features of being human is living in the temporal gap between experience and understanding, ever enduring a vivid present whose meaning must be retrospectively coaxed from shifting and suggestible memory with conceptual tools that are rarely of recent vintage and often dulled by years of misuse or neglect. If our current conceptual machinery is inadequate to the challenge of grasping the complex effects of an experience on our inner relationships, our ecologies can remain in turmoil, plagued by cognitive dissonance, moral confusion, and emotional unrest.

At that point in my journey, the most available conceptual machinery for interpreting my experience was the human/animal binary and its accompanying comparative logic. When I looked within myself through that lens, it initially seemed to me that my transformation must have been provoked by an intensely felt similarity between the suffering and death of Jewish people in the Holocaust and the suffering and death of pigs in our food system, and that—through this problematic comparison—I had intuited parallels between the repugnance of antisemitism and speciesism.[4] As a result, I inferred, I could no longer take pleasure in the smell of meat (or in the act of imagining eating it) any more than I could take pleasure in the smell of Nazi crematoria.

This hypothesis left me intellectually unsatisfied, morally conflicted, and emotionally unsettled about whether and how to communicate my experience. Whatever parallels I imagined myself to have intuited, it seemed to me that the subjective experiences of human beings and pigs are undeniably different in a wide variety of specifiable and unspecifiable ways that make them difficult to compare with any precision and morally dubious to try to compare at all. And while it felt liberating that my circles of moral and emotional concern had widened and converged in this experience and I wanted to share that with others, it felt ghoulish to try to leverage gains for pigs by instrumentalizing moral atrocities suffered by human beings. The reasons are both obvious and perfectly distilled by Cynthia Ozick: "The Jews are not a metaphor for anyone else. They're their own people."[5]

Given that I am neither Jewish nor any sort of scholar of Jewish history, it seemed crystal clear that this comparison was not mine to make. For nearly a decade, I rarely mentioned this transformational experience and at times felt ashamed of it. When I did share it, I'd choose the audience wisely and recount the tale apologetically, even as it continued to function as a watershed in my inner life and a fountainhead of my passion to advocate for animals as subjects of their own lives rather than patients of our mercy.

It wasn't until I got my hands on a copy of Aph Ko and Syl Ko's *Aphro-ism: Essays on Pop Culture, Feminism, and Black Veganism from Two Sisters* that I found the conceptual machinery I needed to piece together what I now believe began happening in me on the day things changed.[6] Hailed by *Laika* magazine's Julie Gueraseva as a "paradigm-shifting perspective on the entanglements of race, species, and gender," *Aphro-ism* spotlights how the social construction of the human/animal binary in Eurocentric culture functions as a sort of master concept in the logic of white patriarchal supremacy. Though it is tempting to frame racism, sexism, and speciesism as separate forms of oppression that sometimes link up at various "intersections" of historical or demographic overlap, Ko and Ko argue that we'll have better luck dismantling these social ills if we understand them holistically as different dimensions of the same white patriarchal edifice and organize our movement to strike at this common foundation.[7]

The human/animal binary, they maintain, functions as the "ideological bedrock" of this edifice, weaponizing "the negative notion of 'the animal'" as "a category that we shove certain bodies into when we want to justify violence against them"—the bodies, more specifically, of anyone who doesn't conform to the assumed ideal state of being human, that of the white European man.[8] By "animalizing" these groups of people as falling outside the realm of the ideal "human"—"they are irrational, they hold 'barbaric' values, they have 'inferior' systems of beliefs, they behave 'like animals,' and so on"—"we legitimize acting against these groups in ways that would otherwise be considered grossly inappropriate and criminal," Syl Ko explains.[9]

That the human/animal binary functions primarily in our inherited conceptual landscape as an exploitative social and political partition rather than as an informative biological one is clear both from our white patriarchal history of animalizing biologically human people of color to justify their domination, and from the vapidity of "the animal" as a biological classification (i.e., every other "animal" but *homo sapiens*, the human animal).[10] Anti-racist movements have understandably sought to "humanize" vulnerable groups in protest of this injustice and seek protections on the basis of their humanity. But Ko and Ko worry that such efforts uphold and strengthen the very human/animal binary on which white supremacy was built, allowing that edifice to continue to dictate the terms on which liberation is sought and obscuring the intimate connection between racialization and animalization that must be destroyed to bring the edifice down.

A better strategy, the Ko sisters propose, is to dismantle the binary—a task that will involve "a deep commitment to animals, the direct bearers of the unfortunate consequences of the negative status-marker "the animal."[11] Going vegan, they conclude, can be a powerful material practice for contesting the conceptual ascendance of the human/animal binary, forging "connections between the oppressions we face with the oppressions other groups face, whether human or not, in order to see the big picture."[12]

Of the many things I love about reading philosophy, my favorite is receiving the gift of new language for clarifying inchoate inklings, overcoming insecurities, expanding imagination, and inspiring bolder practice. What the Ko sisters helped me to see is that the inner workings provoked by the coincidence of meat smoke and crematoria that fateful day in the car need not be interpreted, as I first feared, as an abstract, disinterested, and ultimately callous comparison of the unlike subjective experiences of human beings and animals.

I could understand the experience instead as a fledgling intuition of a horrifying consistency in the way that oppressors exploit (and attempt to justify exploiting) their victims regardless of species. The subjective experiences of human beings and other creatures who suffer under oppression are experientially and morally incomparable, but the methods of their oppressors are consistent: frame the person or creature as bereft of autonomy (and thus of owed independence and inherent value), revalue them as a tool for achieving the oppressor's gain, and then use them for whatever purpose the oppressor sees fit. Animalize. Instrumentalize. Consume.[13]

The inner liberation I experienced in receiving this reframe of oppression outside the human/animal binary spanned my entire ecology.

I finally had the conceptual language for articulating my discomfort with the problematic comparisons of racism and sexism to speciesism and for understanding my confusion over why the term "animal" seemed at once so socially and politically powerful and yet so biologically flaccid. I could see with clarity for the first time the disorienting but compelling truth that members of the wild profusion of radically different sentient species who call this planet home are conceivable collectively as "animals" only insofar as we have pre-reflectively animalized them—relegating them conceptually to a sphere of being where their unique material subjectivities and idiosyncratic forms of agency are effaced in advance and only their extractable utility can appear, whenever and wherever perceived human needs, wants, or even whims demand it. I felt emotionally emancipated to turn from comparing to caring about other oppressed creatures without worrying that I was somehow disrespecting fellow human beings under oppression. I felt socially empowered to share how going vegan (even for other animals' sake) could support and strengthen my advocacy for human justice.

But if a carful of meat smoke was sufficient to force open a window into the world outside the human/animal binary, it took another life-changing experience to break down the walls and bring me face-to-face with the awe-inspiring mystery of a world fully teeming with independent other-than-human flourishing. For this story to land, I need you to know two random facts about me that fate decided to use as the backdrop for one of the most transformative experiences of my life.

Fact number one is that I grew up deathly afraid of geese. The provenance of this fear is straightforward, originating in an exuberant but catastrophically failed attempt to offer bread to a protective gander on a grade school nature walk just steps away from his life-mate's clutch of eggs. If my pride has finally recovered from treating my peers to the spectacle of repeatedly scream-ing "Goose attack!" while tumbling backward across a patch of soggy, feces-laden grass, the sound of infuriated hissing coupled with the sensation of a wet bum even through the impenetrable denim of my Toughskins remains for me the epitome of shame.

Fact number two is that nothing throws me into a blind rage faster than the discovery of bird shit on a freshly washed automo-bile. I grew up in a family that both prized clean cars and made a weekly event of washing, waxing, and detailing them. The car wash kit I received for my sweet sixteen was not just a red bucket with Turtle Wax and an Armor All wash pad nestled into a chamois flourished at the rim of the bucket like superabsorbent gift-bag tissue. It was a shining symbol of wisely stewarded adult freedom and an invitation to practice it with honor. So when some incontinent feathered foe had the audacity to let fly on my jet-black, pristinely bathed 1981 Chevy Impala coupe, it was hours of scrubbing and buffing lost, yes, but also a wanton attack on my life project. The sort of thing that tempted me, helpless in the clutches of a high school athlete's fragile masculinity, to fantasize about mowing over a gaggle of the offending species in a parking lot (and even idly boasting to teammates that I had).

Fast-forward maybe two decades. I'm about three years into going vegan and perhaps a year or so into the inner ferment provoked by the meat smoke. Ribs no longer tempt me, but my aerial defecation rage-reflex remains intact. It's presently on a hair trigger given that we've just taken possession of a gorgeous jet-black 1997 Volvo 960—an aging hand-me-down from family but still far and away the finest automobile I'd owned.

After a painful and costly bout of dentistry, I emerged into the car park to find my spirits lifted by the sight of the Volvo, just washed and shining like polished onyx in the far corner of the lot at a safe distance from nearby construction dust. Adjacent to the edge of the lot was a retention pond teeming with geese—a fact of which I would have remained blissfully unaware were it not for the divine intervention of a nearby forklift dropping its payload as I drove out the lot, causing a panicked exodus of geese, several of whom narrowly missed hitting my side window as they crested the banks of the pond and one or more of whom violently and voluminously evacuated themselves across my windshield. The shock of mad flapping on the periphery, the terror of expected collision, and the obstructed view through my obliterated windshield brought me to the proverbial screeching halt. As the panic subsided and I realized what had happened, I braced for the rage.

Instead, I laughed. Deliriously, uproariously, desperately, as if this shit were manna from heaven as I lay starving in the desert. The thought that cracked me up is so juvenile that I'm convinced my goose-traumatized grade-school self must have resurfaced to think it and so to experience redemption: "These jokers don't give a shit about my freshly washed car." So to speak.

And then my mind and my eyes simultaneously flooded as the sublime ramifications of this realization dawned on me all at once. Geese get scared shitless. They care about their lives and each other. They mate for life. They take emergency measures to protect themselves and their kin, such as flying into the fucking sky under power of feathered flapping wings, effortlessly extracting enough oxygen with the aid of hollow bones to sustain flight at altitudes that would find us drowning in our own fluids. Cars and pretty much everything else we make are nothing to them but noise pollution, occasional obstacles, and accidental fecal repositories. They want for nothing from me, except maybe to step back and make room for them to be more fully who they are—agents, communities, beings striving and surviving together to endure and enjoy their fierce but fragile lives in ways I'll never fathom.[14]

That my childhood nemeses, the geese, ushered me into this beautiful new world is a turn that I cherish, not least because an avalanche of elephant dung might have killed me, but also because taking this lesson from creatures I despised made the transformation feel that much more momentous and authentic. If the loathsome goose could raise in me this torrent of awe, this involuntary enthusiasm, this overwhelming feeling of wonderous solidarity even in radical difference—and by defecating on me, no less!— surely the myriad other denizens of this untamed world were equally magisterial in their own ways, large and small, terrestrial, aerial, and aquatic.[15] Suddenly nothing seemed more hilarious than the conceit that this gorgeous profusion of beings, millions upon millions of species as different from one another as ostriches, octopuses, orb weavers, and orcas, could be straight-facedly lumped together into a single category: "animal."

For those seeking awe-inspiring confirmation of this experience without the risk of fecal contamination, it's a joy to report that we live in a golden age of scientifically grounded, empathy-informed research on the pleasures and travails of independent flourishing in the lives of other creatures (or at least the breathtaking inklings we've gathered so far from our own limited perspective). Jennifer Ackerman invites us to behold *The Genius of Birds*.[16] Jonathan Balcombe pulls back the curtain on *What a Fish Knows*.[17] Michael Tye considers how consciousness animates the lives of *Tense Bees and Shell-Shocked Crabs*.[18] Carl Safina shows how *Becoming Wild* for sperm whales, macaws, and chimpanzees is a matter of culture-making that encompasses raising families, creating beauty, and achieving peace.[19] Ed Yong unveils scintillating places within *An Immense World* that only those who see by echolocation, move in concert with magnetic fields, or smell through forked tongues will ever experience.[20]

These beautiful books and the wonderful and complex lives of their subjects decisively give the lie to the old saw that "nature is red in tooth and claw," by which we've always really meant that (some) members of our species can dominate every other because it's all just a meaningless bloodbath without our civilizing presence. But as much as I've gleaned from books, the truth is that—since the geese, anyway—it's much less about accruing additional facts than about learning to experience what has been hiding in plain sight all along just outside the frame of the human/animal binary. In the dazzling world of other-than-human flourishing, a simple walk through the neighborhood can be mind-blowing. Every squirrel is a park-our master. Every bee is a hive-minded oracle. Birdsong once charming or irksome depending on my intention to relax or to work is now a language at which I marvel, sent forth from inner lives I can't imagine to summon, tease, entice, repel, or collude with others outside who share their world.

Domesticated animals appear differently, too. After the geese, Gus's walks got much more olfactorily interesting for him and much more chaotic for me as he followed his nose and I trundled along for the ride. Pigs, cows, chickens, and turkeys on farms seem so much more grievously entitled to my caring and advocacy (and these responses come so much more easily) now that I see them in light of the dignity and resourcefulness of their free-living counterparts in forests, plains, mountains, and jungles. With the unimaginable scale of animal suffering and death in industrial farming, it can be difficult even to see individuals at all through the collective abjection if you don't know what flourishing looks like.

This is perhaps the most life-changing lesson I've learned from two decades of teaching: if you want to free yourself fervently to love justice, train your imagination on the beauty and joy of flourishing lives so you can see with clarity what oppression steals away. For a domesticated animal like me, primed for docile service to the self-defeating falsehoods and joy-thieving comparisons of the human/animal binary, liberation from this tool of oppression has expanded my consciousness of other forms of flourishing and vastly improved my capacities to pursue and realize my own.

I don't know what it says about me that other species' feces are so often harbingers of my transformation, but the path I traveled between a yard full of Gus shit and a windshield full of goose shit taught me that going vegan is a journey of evolving consciousness—anything but the instantaneous toggle from ignorance to enlightenment that I hoped for in abstaining from my first cheeseburger. What began with a guilt-ridden and grudging acknowledgement of a duty to prevent suffering unfolded into an increasingly emboldened desire to promote flourishing. In my experience, the most beautiful thing about this evolution of animal consciousness from the initial dilation that generates guilt to the level of expansion that generates awe is the movement it catalyzes away from self-focused and reluctant obligation *to* others toward self-effacing and joyful solidarity *with* others.

With the Gus shit, my inner vegan was ready to face the sadness and shame of how badly people like me treat farm animals. But it was still ultimately about me. What was sad and shameful was that I—we, human beings like us—failed in our obligations and did nasty things to these poor, abject, lesser animals for whom we have a duty to care. That was where I had to start. And it's not wrong to begin in lament over dependents suffering—indeed, as we saw in Chapter 1, becoming painfully aware of the horrors and injustice of the system is an essential ingredient of the process of change. But when the human/animal binary went up in meat smoke and I was suddenly free to begin seeing other creatures for who they are outside that frame, my inner vegan began to grow in confidence and my focus began to shift away from lamenting human frailty and animal suffering toward seeking a more holistic understanding of creaturely flourishing.

With the goose shit, I got my first experience of independent free-living creatures commanding sheer awe, a force powerful enough to convert enmity into fellow feeling and to deliver the big reveal: it's not ultimately about me, or us, or our ethics at all—it's about them and their mandate for being, their embodied desires to enjoy being and striving to be. Our ethics can put stops on our selfishness and guide us on the way to this epiphany, but the light only really goes on when we experience them for who they are: magisterial creatures, destined to be in ways unfathomable to us, free to live and strive and thrive for as long as the gift of an embodied life is tenable. They are worthy of this gift of a dignified life well-lived—the gift of an opportunity to flourish.

When you've stood in awe of other creatures, dazzled by the wonders of their worlds, the idea that an externally imposed mechanism like obligation should be necessary to motivate respect and caring for them can seem bizarre. Yes, we have these duties. And yes, we must build a world where those who lack respect and caring for others have external incentives not to do their worst. But in awe and wonder, we can discover ourselves already respectful and fervently caring without even cognizing (much less feeling encumbered by) these obligations. When we feel solidarity with someone—when we truly care about their well-being and appreciate the extent to which our own well-being is always already bound up with theirs—our desire for them is not just the prevention of their suffering, but the promotion and enabling of their fullest possible flourishing, even and especially when it costs us.

For me, living into this expanded consciousness was a gateway from scarcity into abundance. My rigid commitment to a *veganism* driven by shame over my superior species' abandonment of our duty to minimize inferior species' suffering was evolving into a free and joyful practice of *going vegan* to promote and celebrate creaturely flourishing in all its myriad forms. My imagination had been captured by the vision of a world beyond the human/animal binary whose awe-inspiring beauty seemed capable of powering our desire to seek the flourishing of all creatures on a shared planet no longer imperiled by the ever-expanding and rapidly destabilizing domination of one species over all the others.

Even so, in sober moments unaided by the intoxicant of mystical goose shit, I harbored lingering skepticism about a vision that could seem just a little too rainbowy and unicorny to be a candidate for wide adoption. What would such a vegan world look like, exactly? What attitudes and actions toward other creatures would a more abundance-loving, less scarcity-fearing humankind ideally exhibit in a new vegan normal? How might our shared planet be changed, assuming that a utopia of vegan pie in the sky is too much to expect?

Glimmers of answers to these huge cosmic questions would soon sparkle forth from fellowship with some of the smallest creatures in my own backyard.

CHAPTER 6

EARTHLINGS

TOWARD FLOURISHING TOGETHER IN OUR COMMON HOME

I'M ABOUT AS EARTHY AS A PALETTE OF ANTISEPTIC wipes locked in an underground containment bunker at the Centers for Disease Control. I went to sleepaway camp exactly once. Legend has it I wrote a letter home bemoaning the unendurable grit in my nether regions from the only night of wilderness camping I'll ever attempt. I have repressed this experience. I do recall arriving home with my dirty clothes folded neatly in my pristine backpack, which never once touched the cabin floor. I occasionally still have stress dreams about the water pressure in the bunkhouse showers that reeked of nickels and urine.

The fact that failing summer camp in fifth grade is the most recent example I can muster of appreciable time spent "in nature" tells you everything you need to know about how much I suck at the great outdoors. It's hardly surprising that the trailhead of my vegan journey was not environmental concerns over the devastating impact of animal agriculture on everything from ice caps to rainforests, air pollution to ocean dead zones, biodiversity to climate stability. To the extent that I was thinking about these earthier matters at all before going vegan, it was in the high-altitude manner that thirty years of proudly preferring "culture" to "nature" had primed me for.[1] "What a pity the planet is warming!" gasped the City Mouse from his planetarium IMAX recliner as he beheld ice sheets vanishing across time-lapsed footage from outer space.

It was the evolution of my consciousness beyond the human/ animal binary that eventually brought me down to earth. Not into the rarefied realm of "nature," mind you, over whose wilds and resources civilized human beings must more efficiently preside. But rather into the common ground of "home," where all creatures must find places of belonging together in our shared desire to flourish, even though, admittedly, our modes of flourishing are vastly different and there's a special urgency for human beings to take better care given the outsized impact of our attitudes and actions on all earthlings.

The vehicle for this homecoming was the conversion of our tiny little suburban backyard from a pesticide-laden dead zone into a lively sanctuary for native plants and other creatures who call West Michigan home. I'll draw on this experience in this chapter to clarify in microcosm how the heightened consciousness of other creatures' flourishing that attends to going vegan can broaden our vision of justice and generate a liberating interspecies solidarity alluring enough to power the transformation of our shared world.

If a new vegan normal can't deliver utopia, a global transition away from animal agriculture toward a plant-based food system nonetheless remains our best hope for pursuing environmental justice for all by cooling the climate, restoring key ecosystems and biodiversity, and refreshing the air, land, and water that make the green planet a beautiful, fertile, habitable home for all who strive to flourish here.

My membership in the cult of the great American lawn came standard with growing up in the west suburbs of Chicago. The ideal backyard in my childhood imagination was a bright green, freshly mowed, and meticulously edged but otherwise untrammeled quarter to half acre expanse of chemically preserved Kentucky bluegrass. Maybe with some piney shrubs and vivid annuals at the margins. My idyllic perception of these monocultural monoliths shifted somewhat across the transition from playing in them as a kid to profiting from mowing them as a teen, but by early adulthood, I knew the drill: a beautiful yard is the product of uniformity imposed through relentless control, resource investment, and—when necessary—merciless extermination of interlopers. Rain shortage? Drench that luxury lawn all night without a stray thought about efficiency or runoff! Got crab grass, clover, or dandelions? Spray 'em! Got bugs, grubs, or—God forbid!—groundhogs? Poison 'em! Better life through chemicals, baby!

My deprogramming began when I married a forest-loving New Englander. But it took going vegan to achieve liberation from the lawn and order paradigm and begin reimagining my station as an earthling, starting with my relationships to fellow creatures in our own backyard. Straightaway, our vegan journey gave us several compelling reasons to lose the lawny monoculture and return our small patch of earth to a more biodiverse state befitting of our place in West Michigan.

First, we fancied a less toxic, more interesting place for Gus to nose around and do his business. Preferably a place more resilient than a twenty-five-by-twenty-five-foot square of struggling grass, better at hiding and recycling his daily deposits, kinder to my gag reflex, and less needful of costly treatments and thirsty watering cycles. Second, we aspired to grow our own food. Nothing more ambitious than a symbolic bed of greens raised in protest of the industry whose products we sought to replace, but a bed that would nevertheless require more fecundity to thrive than that afforded by the dust beneath the turf toupee that came with the house. Third, as the human/animal binary fell away and I became more attentive to the other-than-human lives around me, the culture/nature boundary started wobbling too. I began to suspect that human beings' incessant drive to secure social approval by "civilizing" our yards beyond their "natural" stations was yet another symptom of the same oppressive hubris that had blinded me to the beauty and dignity of other creatures.

Powered by Susan's resolve and a burgeoning reading list of ecofeminist and environmentalist literature (and aided, if I'm honest, by my own ineptitude and sloth at gardening), I began to see the backyard anew.[2] The maintenance of exotic flora that required extra watering and repeated interventions, the application of pesticides and fertilizers, and the constant mowing, raking, and blowing to reassert seasonal order revealed themselves as unnecessary obstacles to everyone's flourishing from the ground up.

These soil-stripping, water-gobbling, habitat-polluting, time-consuming, and expensive practices were disadvantaging, displacing, or killing many others with whom I could choose to live in more symbiotic community. And though I had read about it in books, my existential initiation into environmental consciousness was this awakening to the possibility that treading more lightly in my immediate material environment could help me realize my hope of living more hospitably toward other creatures without delay.

So it came to pass that an organic soil amendment, some fieldstone hardscaping, and graded beds of native plants, trees, and grasses replaced all but a small crescent of lawn in our backyard. Though we couldn't afford so thorough a transformation of the front yard, we abandoned chemical treatments, expanded garden beds piecemeal with lower maintenance plants, and made peace with the clover, violets, and dandelions that appeared throughout what remained of our once traditional suburban lawn. It's a testament to how little lawn was left that we even ditched the gas lawn mower and got one of those rinky-dink push mowers with the revolving blades that I still haven't managed to sharpen even once.

And then, slowly but surely, just as the guidebooks said, our grounds were newly alive with worms, beetles, spiders, bees, butterflies, birds, chipmunks, squirrels, rabbits, and opossums, visitors who grasped even before we did that a movement from scarcity to abundance was afoot in this place, an evolution from fearful control to hopeful hospitality. I worry that it's a bit too on the nose to dwell on the parallels between the recalibration of outer ecology that rejuvenated my backyard and finding peace across the provinces of my inner ecology and wonder at the worlds beyond their borders. And yet, these things are true and their coincidence felt beautiful. The backyard and its denizens had a great deal to teach me about what I could reasonably hope for from a new vegan normal and what I could not, at once tempering my expectations and heightening their allure.

To clarify these developments, I need to say more about how the shift away from seeing suffering prevention as the beating heart of my vegan desire was changing my understanding and practice of my commitments. As my journey from scarcity into abundance progressed, I found that the most common disciplines associated with going vegan—eating a plant-based diet, educating others about the shortcomings of our food system, becoming a more mindful guardian of companion animals, and giving to sanctuaries and shelters—began to feel more like ripples downstream of my vegan imagination than the wellspring itself.[3]

Don't get me wrong. I fervently adopted these disciplines from the outset and reaped significant rewards from practicing them. Assiduous abstention from animal products led to a rapid uptake of exciting new cooking skills and culinary adventures. Educating all comers about the costs of industrial animal farming and the benefits of plant-based eating rejuvenated my teaching and scholarship. Striving to love Gus better completely remade me. Visiting and giving to sanctuaries enabled us to put our money where our mouths, minds, and hearts were and to build community with other vegans and other creatures lucky enough to get a second chance at flourishing. I continue to practice and recommend these disciplines as among the most empowering expressions of the vegan imagination I know, albeit not quite as fearfully or judgmentally as I once did. Without the inner ecological ferment these disciplines catalyzed, the lesson from my geese teachers would surely have been rage-inducing rather than enlightening.

But the illumination that accompanied their gift from above left me with a deep desire to be more intimately involved in supporting and promoting the kind of independent creaturely flourishing the geese had dared me to imagine—not just as a more conscientious consumer, guardian, or charitable giver leveraging my buying power to stand against captive suffering (as essential as that is), but as an active collaborator with the free-living creatures in my immediate environment striving to flourish on their own terms. I wanted to go beyond just the prevention of their suffering to the creation and maintenance of real opportunities for their creaturely flourishing.

Philosopher Martha Nussbaum captures the beauty of such opportunities in describing the richness and range of other creatures' agency beyond their capacity to feel:

> Sentience mark[s] a very important boundary. But although pain is very important, and ending gratuitous pain is an urgent goal, animals are agents, and their lives have other relevant aspects: dignity, social capacity, curiosity, play, planning, and free movement, among others. Their flourishing is best conceived in terms of opportunities for choice of activities, not just states of satisfaction.[4]

If other creatures have dignity, if their desires are not fleeting instinctual impulses in the vacuum of a meaningless "now" but are in fact curiously, playfully, socially braided into being from experiences, memories, relationships, and plans, born from attitudes and freely taken actions that can go better or worse for them from their own point of view, and that can be helped or hindered by those who bear witness to their striving—well, then the beings we've referred to collectively as "animals" are ends in themselves, unique individuals by whom we can do right or wrong, and in view of whose existence we must ask ourselves: How can we seek justice for these creatures? How can we create, as Nussbaum elegantly puts it, "spaces for them to seek flourishing, each in their own way"?[5]

In my own backyard, this query began in wonder-driven attention to the lives of those who visited or even chose to make their homes here. Eastern cottontail rabbit mothers nesting their kits in April and May and feasting on clover throughout the summer. Robin families in June and July, building nests from last year's grasses that would soon host daylong alternating feedings from both parents for the first two weeks of their fragile fledglings' lives. Bees from the first blooms of April to the brink of winter hibernation, visiting trees and flowers to draw out their nectar and—one glorious summer day—swarming by the tens of thousands around a limb of our once-weeping cherry (the hybrid tree was actually in the process of abandoning weeping cherry grafts onto its traditional cherry trunk, but I fancy it just stopped crying for the joy of being chosen by bees).

The beauty of showing fidelity to wonder is the way it opens you to seeing a purposeful whole of meaningful mutualities where once you had seen only isolated parts. Before my yard became a more hospitable place to free-living creatures, my experience of virtually all animals other than our companions and a gaggle of incontinent geese had been fleeting, objectifying, and instrumentalizing: a creature would enter my purview, announce itself as a particular type of thing relative to my interests, and elicit a practical response that turned the encounter to my credit or at least allowed me to escape unscathed.

There were the majestic spectacles: "A red-tailed hawk! Give me the binoculars!"

The captive entertainers: "Let's hit the primate house! Gorillas are hilarious!"

The hunted trophies: "A forty-inch striper, at least! We'll need a bigger grill!"

The surprise adversaries: "There's a skunk in the garbage! I'm out of here!"

And, of special relevance for this discussion, the ecologically necessary nuisances: "A bee! Flee, but don't kill it! Without pollinators, our food system will collapse!"

Animals were things in my world.

But the wonderful creatures who made their homes in my yard took me out of my world and into theirs. Mother cottontails aren't absentee parents; their infrequent visits are a form of vigilance to keep predators from trailing them back to their helpless kits. Mother robins don't have poor hygiene; their breasts are muddy from shaping and cementing the bowls of their nests. Swarming worker bees aren't angry; they're in the process of moving an old queen to a new hive, and—fat with honey for transport, free from the duty of hive defense, and distracted by the elaborate dances of scouts plumping prospective new digs—they pose little threat of aggression.[6]

These creatures pursued flourishing in very different ways, but they collectively taught me something that's true of every earthling who must strive to thrive as a unique individual: if there's no material place that supports the delicately calibrated matrix of soil, air, water, flora, fauna, food, and social opportunity that lights your peculiar spark, you'll never get the home fires burning. To make a home here, we must each have a world of possible material involvements that sustains our bodies, stokes our desires, elicits our unique forms of ingenuity and craft, and rewards cooperation and competition with others. Our free-living independence is fundamentally Earth dependent.

I may be a desk jockey who couldn't start a proper campfire with a flamethrower, but this realization that the ground level of pursuing justice for individual creatures of any species is securing *environmental* justice for them finally brought the wobbling culture/nature distinction tumbling down. For all my technology, sophistication, and loathing of sandy shorts, I was no less dependent on my earthly home than any other hungry beautiful animal who leaves tracks in the snow or scat in the grass (at least once, anyway, before I retired from wilderness camping at age eleven). In fact, I was much more heavily dependent on the Earth than members of virtually all other species, given both the vastly disproportionate resource intensity of my way of life relative to theirs and my complete lack of ability to fend for myself without the resulting comforts.

That's what impressed me most about our backyard denizens: how remarkably little they required of me to do their thing and, by all indications, resiliently to enjoy doing their thing. I was so used to humankind being the hero of the story that I naturally assumed the dawning of my environmental consciousness would result in a complex regime of ecological interventions through which I'd shepherd these creatures into their own. I had come to terms with our mutual dependence on this shared patch of Earth and I understood the importance of my agency for safeguarding their flourishing. What I didn't yet grasp was the importance of their agency—their unique earthly life projects—for giving place to my own.

If geese opened me to the wonders of other creatures independently flourishing, it was the bees who brought home the wisdom that all creaturely independence is ultimately Earth-bound interdependence. The significant uptick in bee visits to our yard was a special point of pride for me, both because they vindicated my always laissez-faire but suddenly virtuous approach to dandelion management and because I felt I owed them one for taking a deflationist tack in debates over their honey. The question of whether to eat or not to eat honey is one that newly vegan philosophy professors can expect to be asked a lot, given that it's a favorite topic both for omnivores and vegetarians seeking to portray vegans as extreme and for vegans seeking ever higher planes of enlightenment.

It's almost always a setup for a gotcha moment. My preferred evasion strategy was to counter the question with enough additional questions to escape into the weeds of specific bee experiences: Honey from what sort of hive? Are local populations stressed? Are the beekeepers profiteers or conservationists? Are they culling queens? How much of the honey is harvested relative to the needs of the colony? How disruptive to its members and their hive or nest are the harvesting methods?

In the process of figuring out how to forestall accusations of extremism or exploitation (depending on the audience), I learned many astonishing things about the life and work of bees, including that their pollinating activity is responsible for roughly one in every three bites of the food we eat. More personally, I realized that my abiding love of almonds, apples, blueberries, broccoli, cashews, cherries, cranberries, melons, pumpkins, and squash might have gone undiscovered without bees and could one day go unrequited if we human beings don't take wiser approaches to managing soil and growing food.[7]

This information landed much differently now that I was actively inviting bees to the yard, enjoying their burgeoning presence among our flowers and trees, admiring the feats of spatial memory achieved in their search flights as I might a neighbor's pianistic virtuosity gifted through the window. The old me, operating from scarcity, might stop killing bees or even start paying for habitat preservation to keep the cantaloupes coming. But transactional concern has its motive in anxiety. Once the melon supply is secure, "the pollinators" and "the environment" can safely recede from "things that matter" back into the abyss of indifference. The new me, operating from something closer to abundance, was free to care first for my neighbors, the bees. And because caring flows from mutuality, the cantaloupe is not the crux of the relationship even if it remains a potential fruit of the delightful reciprocity of friendship.

By cultivating soil that is hospitable to native plants and flowers, I help to make a home for bees and to make it possible for them to eat. And by pollinating the plants and flowers that come up from that soil, they help to make a home for me and to make it possible for me to eat. We're in this together. We share common ground and so naturally our flourishing is interlaced. And I'm happy and proud to see my neighbors making good, with or without a slice of melon on my plate (thank you, bees!), or richer soil (much obliged, ants!), or grounds drenched in color, song, and mystery blooms I didn't plant (cheers, birds!). These relationships felt redolent of friendship, both in terms of my delight in their well-being for their own sake and my joy in the gratuitous reciprocity among us.[8]

At the same time, the households of bees, rabbits, robins, and ants operate very differently from my own. And to respect those differences, what careful attention and good hospitality clearly required of me was to step back, stop intervening, and simply let them be. After the initial soil amendment and native repopulation, it turned out that making our yard as friendly as possible to the needs and wants of other creatures was largely a matter of *not* doing things I might otherwise have done.

Not using fertilizers, pesticides, or regular watering discouraged heavy lawn growth, making space for clover, seed-bearing grasses, dandelions, and wildflowers, and making a happy place, in turn, for insects, bees, and butterflies. Not raking, power mowing, weeding, or clearing seasonal brush as often created lush, undisturbed groundcover for insects, and food and nesting materials for rabbits and birds. Not spraying our Concord grapes made a place for robins' nests, and not harvesting all of them at peak ripeness brought memorable night visits from raccoons and possums. Not letting the dogs out without a few good raps on the windowpane gave the free-living peeps out back time to get to safety. Not filling the tiny tunnels under the fence gave rabbits, chipmunks, and squirrels a fighting chance against aerial predators and prowling neighborhood cats.

The mention of killer cats furnishes the perfect occasion to state an obvious truth that is nonetheless tempting to cheat on while indulging fleeting vegan fantasies of a return to Eden: the pursuit of (and even the realization of) a new vegan normal will not result in a pain-free, deathless utopia for all or even any earthlings. When we aspire to the ideal of a vegan world, we're not envisioning a pie-in-the-sky paradise in which bodily limitations, suffering, predation, and existential conflicts of interest among human beings and other species somehow magically disappear, even if we do hope to significantly reduce and prevent *unnecessary* suffering and death.

The beauty of a new vegan normal lies not in transcending our creaturely limitations, but in aspiring to attitudes and actions that empower us to live much lovelier lives within them, turning away from self-defeating practices and institutions that degrade and destroy our capabilities (and those of many others) and toward liberating practices and institutions that open much more fertile spaces for all to seek flourishing, each in their own way. Suffering and death, for human beings and everyone else, are here to stay. In fact, they're indispensable features of the bodily equipment necessary for earthly striving and thriving (if you doubt it, consider how long you'd last without the aversive benefits of feeling pain or how happy you'd be to remain conscious past the expiration of your most basic physical capabilities).

And while going vegan is a beautiful path into *human* flourishing that can also give generous place to the flourishing of other creatures and the Earth, it is clearly not a viable path to flourishing for members of many other species. The ladybugs on our cherry tree must keep eating the aphids, and the ants must fight the ladybugs to keep the aphids feeding so they can harvest the residual sugars. Out there in the world (even the most fully realized vegan world that human beings could ever hope to achieve), owls gonna owl, orcas gonna orca, and cats gonna cat. The big cats must keep felling antelopes and the little ones must leave dismembered cottontail kits on my back porch (even if their guardians should probably make indoor living more exciting for them, all things considered).

Reckoning respectfully with the agency of other creatures sometimes requires lamenting the kit without blaming the cat. And it always demands of us the delicate balancing act of taking responsibility for the centrality of human agency in determining the possibilities of earthly flourishing at large without negating or taking ownership of other creatures' agency in the process. Syl Ko and Lindgren Johnson articulate this tension skillfully enough to justify a long quotation:

> What attributes to human beings a moral heaviness is not some distinct property, capacity, feature or trait but rather it is the human [being] that is the proper object of the human moral inquiry and whose subsequent behavior sets out the conditions under which other animals (and other humans) must live. This is the same reason we do not foist our moral expectations upon, say, Bruno the family cat; it is not right to say that Bruno is intellectually or cognitively

disabled to a severe degree, or—on the other hand—lacks empathy and harbors antisocial tendencies, and so he cannot be reasonably asked to participate in the results of our moral deliberations, such as we might say for some humans. Instead, Bruno belongs to an entirely different form of life, which is specific to his species, subjectively closed to us and which we cannot (and ought not attempt to) take intellectual possession of or subsume under our intellectual rubrics.[9]

This framing of the unique station of humankind as a matter of heightened moral responsibility rather than superior existential value has been a literal lifesaver in my yard when conflicts of interest make it burdensome or impossible simply to let beings be. When carpenter ants would make their homes too close for comfort or paper wasps would show up on the porch, the old me would see trespassers and reach for the poison or call the exterminator. But we're in solidarity now. I see them as fellow earthlings striving and surviving, looking to secure the material conditions for thriving in this common ground, just as they should be (and often even in ways that richly benefit me and mine, if I have the eyes to see it). And I recognize in myself a disproportionate power to shape their lives for better or worse, and an ever-burgeoning desire to bless them.

With help from wonder and the Internet, I have found that harmlessly encouraging their departure for more hospitable shores is usually just a matter of figuring out who they are, what they're looking for, and how my own negligent housekeeping has unwittingly encouraged their arrival. What appears to me as encroachment is to them the reception of an invitation. I didn't caulk properly, keep up the masonry, clean up the picnic, or install the insulation correctly, and so I made them an offer they couldn't refuse. Good fences make good neighbors, and in failing to set proper boundaries, I communicated an openness I did not intend and could not sustain.

Not all conflicts can be resolved with a little redirection, some water, and the strategic placement of caulk, duct tape, cinnamon, paprika, or peppermint oil. But it's amazing how many can be defused or prevented entirely through simple, inexpensive means that are intriguing to research and gratifying to implement when the desire is there to preserve dignity and achieve mutual benefit. It's difficult to describe the leavening that attends to approaching conflicts free from the impulses to vilify, target, and exterminate, enamored instead of opportunities to understand, bless, and leave room. But the feeling is exquisite. And the loveliness of receiving with gratitude an admonishment to better housekeeping from paper wasps is something to relish, especially if you've had occasion to marvel at their gorgeous homes.

I am acutely aware that I am not everyone. My backyard is not the world. A soil amendment on a single tiny plot in suburban West Michigan does not a global environmental transformation make. But that's precisely why we must take this beautiful journey together, each on our own path to going vegan, each through our own process of soil amendment, both for the ecologies within us and for the patches of ground where we live and work and hold sway over who is welcome and what goes on.

I love the metaphor of soil amendment for framing both the enrichment of our inner lives that going vegan can foment and the process of working toward a new vegan normal wherever we find ourselves in the world at large. We are billions, each of us contain multitudes, and how we envision, pursue, and make room for flourishing in the places we call home profoundly shapes the lives and livelihoods of all earthlings. Whether we're feeding our inner soil or the ground beneath our feet, going vegan is about propagating desire and potential to thrive, introducing an elevating chemistry that boosts fertility and opportunity in the places that make earthly flourishing possible for each of us in our own way.

In envisioning the abundance of a new vegan normal, our hope is not to bring about utopia, but to stoke our desire to cultivate attitudes and actions that can increasingly channel our unique, world-shaping power as a species into letting beings be—opening and maintaining places for hungry beautiful animals of all species to live their best interdependent lives without exploitative human interference. In cases where conflicts of interest make leaving room for others temporarily or permanently impossible, progress toward a new vegan normal will find us creating infrastructure, sanctuaries, and preserves to save the lives of displaced creatures and give them safe harbor. And where existing industries and institutions profit from degrading or destroying the flourishing of sentient creatures in conditions where their languishing is a foregone conclusion, progress toward a new vegan normal will find us abolishing these practices as a baseline. Letting be is the ideal. Saving is second best. And sparing is the bare minimum.

Admittedly, we are still at the inception of the complex process of social and political reimagination it would take to institute a new vegan normal. Within a scarcity mindset, there's plenty of room for fear, doubt, and a foreboding sense of futility. But from a more abundant perspective, our position is exhilarating and the possibilities breathtaking. We have an opportunity to be the vanguard of a movement with a fighting chance to vastly improve the lives of quintillions of earthlings, not least ourselves, and to supplant some of the most degrading and destructive forms of exploitation we've ever devised with much more beautiful and generous alternatives.

Some of the ways our world changes for the better will be astonishing in their simplicity. As our understanding and respect for other creatures' unique subjectivities and forms of agency grow, we'll be able to construct roads, buildings, and energy infrastructure that make it easier for other creatures to live among us and work around us. Wildlife overpasses and underpasses in our highway systems and bird-friendly glass and wind turbines are some of my favorite windows into a vegan world—a world where we think in advance from the perspective of all-species kinship about how our diverse modes of being, seeing, and moving engage the same built environment in radically different ways that can be perfectly compatible if we design with that diversity in mind.[10]

Other innovations will be mind-bogglingly complex. The race to replace animal protein with environmentally sustainable foods that cost less, taste the same or better, and provide superior nutrition—now known as the "alt-protein" movement—is negotiating fascinating challenges on scientific, technological, commercial, political, and psychological fronts. Remarkable progress is already underway in the arenas of using plant proteins to mimic muscle, developing cell cultures to make real meat and dairy products without animals, and harnessing the power of mycoproteins (which means, but sounds decidedly better than, "fungal protein"). But the feats of scaling production, convincing industry and policymakers to fast-track the R&D and regulatory approval, and enticing the general public to get on board are yet to be accomplished, and emblematic of our need for cooperative, holistic, cross-disciplinary problem-solving to secure our food future.[11] Environmental activist and bestselling author George Monbiot believes these challenges are well worth rising to meet: "This transition could be our best hope of stopping the sixth great extinction. . . . We could rewild most of the land now used for farming, while protecting the remaining wild places."[12]

Reclaiming this land from industrial animal agriculture is potentially the most transformative soil amendment in human history and would set off a cascade of Earth-healing developments from which all earthlings would benefit. Vastly reduced greenhouse emissions and vastly increased carbon sequestration. Reforestation of grazing lands. Rebounding biodiversity in areas where animal agriculture has crowded out free-living wildlife. Cleaner water, fresher air, and safer living environments in rural areas that have been degraded by decades of industrial animal farming.

At the ground level, this collective, world-transforming work of establishing a new vegan normal is based in the daily commitments of aspiring individuals. It's up to each one of us to follow our desire for flourishing lives to the nearest corners of the Earth where our unique aspirations, gifts, and talents can introduce elevating chemistry to the places we live and work and, thus, to the common ground we share with others of all species.

The truth is that moving toward a new vegan normal is in our individual and collective best interest. And the beauty of this vision is compelling for the flourishing of earthlings of all kinds. The trick now is to turn it to our good—to channel the beauty of pursuing this truth into powering us through the daily challenge of living within our limits as we strive to bring the world of the vegan imagination down to Earth in our everyday attitudes and actions.

PART III

MOTIVATION

LIVING WELL TOWARD A NEW VEGAN NORMAL

CHAPTER 7

ASPIRATION

GOALS FOR OUR OWN VEGAN GOOD

MONDAY EVENINGS IN 1984 WERE DEVOTED TO HAR-vesting promising rubbish from my suburban neighbors' curbside trash. Waste collection took place on Tuesdays, and my chums from down the block and I commonly spent garbage day's eve loading our wagons with discarded treasures to repurpose for use in Creators' Combat—the decidedly non-utopian kids-only civilization we had illicitly erected from trash in a wooded lot behind an unsuspecting neighbor's house.

Where most people saw splintered broom handles, molder-ing mattresses, soggy pressboard, and spent appliances, we envi-sioned potential nunchaku, possible stunt equipment, future fortress walls, and would-be automated pulley systems—essential ingredients to the vision of freedom and adventure that transfig-ured ordinary trash into integral parts of an extraordinary world.

Through the work of imagination, mere garbage gave way to sublime liberation from suburban boredom. At least until our makeshift elevator collapsed and one of our buddies fell two stories and broke his back.

He survived and thrived, thank goodness.

But our misadventures in world-building taught me an important lesson at a tender age. Working to bring beautiful visions of a world transformed down to earth in the real world can set us up for deep disappointment—even catastrophic failure—if we don't think carefully in advance about our very particular strengths and limitations and set individual and collective expectations accordingly.

With luck, the vision of a vegan world we developed in Part II has more going for it than that of a glorified garbage fort masterminded by '80s tweens. But the cautionary tale is well taken. On the other side of every Wake Up Weekend is Monday through Friday. The occasional mountaintop experiences of the perfect vegan chili and the odd deluge of mystical goose shit are not going to see most of us through the average day, with its stubborn family members, smirking coworkers, and servers disappearing to remove the cheese from our iceberg lettuce. Not to mention the self-doubting, self-defeating, self-medicating parts of ourselves just waiting to sabotage us the minute the going gets tough. If our vision of a new vegan normal is beautiful and there are many reasons to deeply desire and fervently pursue its realization, our success depends on setting expectations appropriate to our varied circumstances and preparing for the challenges that will inevitably confront our own special brands of going vegan as unique individuals facing different opportunities and obstacles.

As creatures with limited understanding and experience who are also prone to error, we must recognize at the outset that working toward personal and social transformation is always a balancing act. We must be bold enough to push beyond obstacles to social change that are tractable with the help of resolve, creativity, and innovation. But we must be wise enough to accept necessary limits on what we can expect to achieve in even the brightest future given the finitude and fragility of embodied experience. Setting our expectations accordingly can be the difference between happiness and disillusionment. Like all hungry beautiful animals, our best chance to realize our good—to activate our capabilities for flourishing—is to live with our desires and limitations in proper balance.

Discerning this balance presents a unique challenge to every person and requires an ongoing commitment to courageous experimentation. To set realistic goals, we need self-understanding that is confident enough to discern and prioritize our desires but humble enough to forecast pitfalls and remain open to changing course. To make progress toward these goals, we need self-discipline that is challenging enough to bring out our best but forgiving enough to accommodate our worst. And to take the measure of our progress, we need self-love that is effusive enough to praise our smallest victories but resilient enough to laugh at our biggest failures.

The aim of Part III of this book is to bolster your self-understanding, self-discipline, and self-love as an aspiring vegan to nurture and sustain your motivation from the earliest stages of inner soil amendment to the growth that comes with persistent discipline to the harvest that blesses your longer-term labors.

With a strategy for discerning the goals, tasks, and practical effects of pursuing a desire-driven, delight-savoring approach to going vegan, living well toward a new vegan normal can be both approachable and invigorating.

As we embark on this last leg of the journey, it's worth noting that we'll be traveling at a lower altitude. After the catharsis of coaxing our inner vegan-in-waiting from the felt tragedy of our food system in Part I and the exhilaration of imagining a world transformed in Part II, preparing to tackle the workaday challenges of going vegan in Part III might feel a bit planned and predictable by comparison. There is admittedly less drama. Not a single shit-induced epiphany to speak of, alas. Like writing a book or plucking your eyebrows, it's more fun having done it than doing it. But we can't have nice things if we skip this step. This is how we get what we want.

The work of this chapter is to learn how to leverage self-understanding to set realistic goals for our own vegan good, custom fitting our personal aspirations for going vegan to the concrete details of our specific embodied circumstances. In the opening pages of this book, I made you a promise:

The destination of this journey is an inviting, empowering, and inclusive understanding of everyday vegan living that abandons the demoralizing goal of arriving once and for all at a perfected individual identity in favor of inspired but practical striving toward a global aspiration—to do what one enthusiastically can, within one's limits and always imperfectly, to live toward a truer, more beautiful, better vegan world. Instead of framing our individual efforts to go vegan unrealistically in terms of the achievement of a one-size-fits-all state of being (a "cruelty-free" identity), we'll envision going vegan as a liberating journey of becoming that unfolds uniquely for every person based on what their individual and communal situations inspire and enable them to contribute.

We're much better positioned now to articulate what is at stake in this global aspiration to live toward a vegan world: our collective allowance of abundant space for creaturely flourishing that we all deeply desire. We're also better equipped to explain why each of us should enjoy the freedom to go vegan on our own path: to allow abundant space for cultivating the most fertile collaboration possible between our inner ecologies and outer involvements as we negotiate the new vegan normal that is appropriate to our unique circumstances.

Because customization is key to discerning how going vegan can introduce an elevating chemistry to your peculiar patch of ground, this chapter is primarily about *how* to set goals rather than *which* goals to set. I hope a philosopher's input on the advantage of self-understanding for human flourishing in general and for setting your personal goals in particular makes your discernment process easier. But you don't need me to tell you what your new vegan normal should look like any more than you need me to assemble your workout playlist, even if you should know that a one-hour elliptical run through four consecutive viewings of T-Swift's short film *All Too Well* burns mad calories. Anyway. Our respective "new normals" might have a song or two in common, but they'll be remarkably different, too. That's lucky for everyone. Especially those whose lives depend on as many of us as possible turning our desire to live more beautifully into redemptive action on the ground.

Coming to this realization took me a minute. Once I had discerned my desire to go vegan, the initial temptation was to think that my primary goal should be to achieve what I then believed to be the vegan apotheosis—never to eat or use animal products ever again, ever! My secondary goal? To strong-arm everyone else into doing the same, naturally. Purity plus proselytization plus policing equals perfection, right?

It was only after I came into a more expansive appreciation of the vision of creaturely flourishing motivating my new dietary commitments that I realized the perfect is often the enemy of the good, and that a sustainable commitment to going vegan is like every other human aspiration: relative not only to different people's situations but also to different times in history and even to different stages in the same person's life. There is a long and winding road between the worlds of tofu and rice milk in 1970s Berkeley and Impossible burgers and Just Egg omelets in 2020s San Francisco even though they're just across the bay. Fifty years is plenty of time for an anarchist activist to evolve into a techno-capitalist entrepreneur. Or for a timid veterinary technician to become a pioneering professor of animal law. Or for a techno-capitalist entrepreneur to evolve into an anarchist activist. Or for all of us to find and lose and find ourselves again as we strive to sift joy from the slings and arrows of outrageous fortune.

We human beings understand ourselves, experience our needs and wants, and set our goals for satisfying these desires in the shelter and shadow of very particular places and times. Places inside, like the inner ecologies across which our loves, liabilities, and limits are shaped and reshaped over decades. And places outside, like the homes, neighborhoods, workplaces, commercial and leisure environments, civil institutions, and places of worship where our communal strivings apply both liberating and constraining pressure to the horizons of our imaginations and the realities of our material circumstances. We achieve our good and thrive when our inner desires find fulfillment in that unique configuration of external involvements that brings out our best and challenges us to keep striving without boring or overwhelming us—the fabled "goldilocks" zone where making progress on our goals is not too easy and not too hard but just right for the unique people we are in the specific places and times we find ourselves.

That our lives are so chancy and time-dependent significantly complicates the challenge of goal setting. None of us enjoys the luxury of choosing the inner or outer landscapes from which we venture forth. We're simply thrown into being and then at some point discover ourselves where we are, uniquely talented and flawed, always already shaped in advance by the personal and social circumstances that help and harm us on our way. History's legacies are generous to some groups of people and punishing to others. Our inner and outer geographies are rife with inequitably distributed opportunities and obstacles sorted by gender, race, orientation, dis/ability, age, class, nationality, and other modalities over which most of us have little to no control. The fates are fickle to all of us as individuals from day to day and even from minute to minute. In everything we do, from crib to crematorium, these indelible inflections of our individual and communal histories go before us, projecting the horizons of our being, understanding, and acting.

Maybe you're thinking, "Thanks, Captain Obvious, for these boilerplate philosophical musings about the uniqueness, complexity, contingency, and vulnerability of every human life. What's this got to do with going vegan, again?"

I couldn't agree more that it seems odd to have to remind ourselves of such pedestrian facts about our condition when it comes to going vegan. And yet, somehow, lots and lots of people (including me, at first) talk and act like they're dead convinced that the singular goal of going vegan *is* achieving instantaneous and perfect consistency in never eating or using animal products ever again, ever. In the popular cultural imaginary, what is at stake in adopting vegan aspirations and identifying as a vegan is nothing short of stopping something terrible once and for all and committing unwaveringly to perfection.

As entrenched as this common perception of going vegan may be, it makes absolutely no sense given what we know about the human condition. No human being is perfectly consistent. Not in their outward actions and certainly not inside. And thank goodness! Our inner ecologies are incalculably intricate systems of cognition, emotion, moral intuition, social desires, and physical embodiment. Our places and our people capriciously help or hinder us willy-nilly. Finding our best selves in this terrible beauty of a world is a perpetual work in progress. It's that much more difficult where our intimate foodways are concerned, especially considering that dietary change can be significantly more challenging for some of us than others.

If you're an adult making a living wage or better, you'll often have significant freedom to choose what you eat. If you're a kid, a young adult, an elderly person, a person with a disability, or you're incarcerated, you often will not.

If you're expecting a baby, you might face nutritional challenges associated with pregnancy and breastfeeding that others won't encounter. And dominant gender norms assure that stereotypes of alpha males gorging on meat and demure women smiling at salads will complicate matters for everyone.[1]

If you make a lot of money, you'll likely have access to the freshest farm-to-table produce, the latest greatest alt-proteins, and the most cutting-edge plant-based restaurants. If you make a low income, you probably won't enjoy such easy access and you're more likely to live in a food insecure neighborhood under conditions of food apartheid to boot (even though, counter to popular perception, you identify as vegetarian or vegan at more than twice the rate of upper-income people, according to a recent Gallup poll).[2]

If you're a city mouse, lifestyle divergences from traditional norms are likely celebrated or at least tolerated in your community and vegan culture may already have a foothold. If you're a country mouse, vegan community may be harder to find, in part because you're more likely to have friends and family whose cherished livelihoods and leisure activities include animal agriculture, hunting, and fishing.

If you're generally happy with your physical appearance and health, dietary change can feel like a welcome low-stakes challenge. If you have a more complex relationship to your body or have an eating disorder, adding rules and regulations around diet or reducing the range of foods you eat may be unwise until your relationship with food is on different terms.

If you're experienced in the kitchen, you can probably pivot to prepare inexpensive, delicious, plant-based meals with whole-food ingredients. If you rely on convenience foods or restaurants to meet your daily nutritional needs, it might be harder to keep costs down.

If you're part of a religious community whose fasting and feasting practices significantly shape your life, you may have a harder or easier time going vegan (depending on your tradition's approach) than your friends from other faith traditions or nonreligious friends who are neither constrained nor supported by their communities in this regard. As a Mennonite Christian who grew up eating animal products indiscriminately and couldn't vaguely imagine a palatable vegan diet, I initially felt a little jealous of Jains, Hindus, Jews, and Seventh-day Adventists whose dietary traditions reflected more explicit concern for other creatures, and Orthodox Christians whose fasting calendar is plant-based over half the year.

Even if dietary change is an absolute snap for you—and perhaps especially if it comes that easily—you may face a different set of challenges caused by the veneer of perfection at the surface. The temptation to self-righteousness. The inability to understand why others struggle. The deficit of empathy that often accompanies such lack of understanding. The illusion that striving is no longer necessary, because—poof!—no more animal products in your fridge. The occlusion of other important dimensions of going vegan, such as expanded consciousness of human oppression and the urgent need for environmental justice. The lapse into a flattened, judgmental, single-issue vegan*ism* that repels potential allies in adjacent social movements, emboldens adversaries, and unwittingly harms the cause of animal advocacy.[3]

No matter who you are, you're amazing in some ways, messed up in others, and a middling case overall. In our honest moments, we know this about ourselves. It's a mixed bag, baby. That's just the way it is.[4]

In view of our widely divergent circumstances and our mixed characters, setting the goal of perfect consistency in following a one-size-fits-all plan for going vegan seems unwise, demoralizing, and perhaps even cruel for creatures like us who must make our way in an unpredictable and so often unjust world. It should go without saying that such a goal is a ridiculous standard to set, especially if we hope to inspire enough of the planet's eight billion hungry beautiful humans to help us reach the tipping point toward a new vegan normal.

But the importance of customization in goal setting is not just a matter of compensating for our personal fragility. It's also a matter of unleashing the potential of our inimitable place-based and time-stamped passions, expertise, and influence to extend the abundance of a new vegan normal to everyone in our orbit who stands to benefit, whomever and wherever they are.

The flipside of understanding and accommodating our vegan fragility is experiencing the freedom to experiment with and eventually discover our vegan flow—that transcendent experience where diminishing anxiety, growing enthusiasm, and the ineluctable desire to meet our best selves just across the finish line of an achievable challenge coincide in what can feel like almost effortless thriving. Joy, even.

In dreaming about who you want to be in the world you want to see, it's easy to forget how much latitude you have beyond just what you're eating to discover what brings you vegan joy. Yes, dietary change is among the most symbolically powerful and practically effectual ways to model your desire to live toward a new vegan normal. Your goals should reflect this potency, and the adventure is often delicious, besides. But with a collective goal as capacious and shimmering as allowing abundant space for creaturely flourishing, you can rest assured that what you eat or do not eat on any given day is but one of many abundant opportunities to give expression to your aspirations.

Do you love to make your guests feel cherished and uplifted by your hospitality? Tremendous! We need home entertainers, chefs, and restaurateurs taking plant-based cuisine to new heights, not just in terms of creating delicious options for existing vegans but for delighting everyone with the abundance that awaits veg curiosity. And we need people showing up to all the block parties, barbecues, and birthdays with herbivorous dishes that are the first to disappear.

Are you gifted at helping people refine and integrate their intellectual, emotional, and moral capacities in learning new things? Marvelous! We need artists, teachers, professors, researchers, librarians, and intrepid family members and friends to showcase the potential of learning about the lives of other animals and the complexity and consequences of our food system so that more people can connect the dots across the most important environmental and moral issues of our age.

Are you someone whose expertise in agribusiness, farming, hunting, fishing, or trapping has given you insight into the appeal of these practices and a heart for the communities that depend on them? Superb! We need savvy agribusiness leaders and a new generation of farmers who see the opportunity of a transformed food system and can inspire their colleagues and industries to catch the vision too. And we need experienced empaths to blaze trails between orientations toward our fellow creatures that can seem completely sealed off from one another without the wisdom of those who have traveled the paths connecting them.

Do you excel at challenging people to strive for and maintain their physical health? Excellent! We need nurses, doctors, dieticians, trainers, and coaches who are educated about the power of plants to grow, strengthen, and heal our bodies and bold in their efforts to inspire patients and clients to reap these abundant rewards.

Do you feel called to walk with others toward spiritual fulfillment? Fantastic! We need bhikkus, gurus, imams, pandits, pastors, priests, and rabbis to push the boundaries of our spiritual awareness toward the many rich but often ignored resources in our sacred texts and traditions for illuminating an expansive vision of creaturely flourishing beyond the human/animal binary.

Do you love to inspire people to get out there and change the world? Right on! We need activists, lawyers, politicians, and philanthropists to pioneer approaches to social change that frame the pursuits of justice for human beings and justice for other creatures as mutually supporting goals that we can push toward simultaneously every time we sit down to eat.

Are you still figuring things out and unsure where to plug in? Totally fair. Find people and organizations that are doing work that makes your heart sing and support them with your treasure while you sort out whether, when, and where it makes sense to invest your time and talent.

Are you strong and silent? Bold and brash? Sleek and sporty? Stacking cash? Loosey-goosey? Buttoned up? Churchy? Skeptic? LEGO nut? Corporate normie? Wheatgrass pro? Henny sipper? Nat Light bro? Garth and Trisha? Jay and Bey? Always here for it? Just don't play? Partnered? Solo? Anti-marriage? Purple neon undercarriage? F-150? Beach all day? Slow foodie? Fast foodie? Don't wish to say? Perfect! Because whoever you are and however chill or zazzy your flow, there are many others on your wavelength who will need to feel seen and heard and loved for who they are before they can dare to imagine who they could be going vegan.

To make the world safe for a new vegan normal, we need all the people's passion and flow to model the beauty, abundance, and viability of the vision across the whole range of physical, social, emotional, intellectual, and moral desires that the call of human flourishing has gifted us. None of us needs to be perfectly consistent on every or even any of these fronts to be a shimmering piece in a gorgeous mosaic when the light falls just right at our peculiar place and time.

That our flow states can help us embrace our fragility without judgment is something we too often forget about our aspirational commitments. We usually don't aspire to these commitments any less, forgo working toward them as guiding ideals, or stop making significant progress toward them in some respects simply because we fail to achieve perfection. When we blow it, it's usually because there's some challenge in our immediate circumstances or some idiosyncratic struggle that makes it harder to be who we genuinely want to be in that situation. It's not because we've renounced the goal or ceased making progress on balance.

Especially where our biggest, most profoundly life-shaping aspirations are concerned—things like being a generous person, a supportive partner, a nurturing parent, a good Christ-follower, or a good Buddhist, say—we're usually comfortable both claiming the aspiration and acknowledging the need to allow ourselves generous breathing room for things to go well, badly, or just okay as circumstances allow. Except maybe in our most self-loathing moments, we typically don't say, "I just got angry. Guess I'm not a Buddhist after all." Or "I don't always love my enemies. So much for following Jesus." Or "I really messed up with my kid. Fuck parenting forever."

On the contrary, when we genuinely desire to make headway on these aspirations, our shortcomings often turn into occasions for refining our understanding of goals and abilities, improving tactics in problem areas, and perhaps most importantly, forgiving ourselves and going again. Sometimes we are at our most dazzling in precisely those moments when we fall short, give ourselves a break and own it, and just keep shining on in the other ways we were born to shine, serving thereby as vessels of grace for other people as desperate as we are to know whether they can love this beautiful life and strive to live it well despite their ineligibility for sainthood. Our imperfections can give us the gift of more compassionate self-knowledge and others the gift of permission to try, radiating the assurance that one can desire something deeply, claim it as an aspiration, and work toward it earnestly without needing, expecting, or even wanting to have it all at one go. As philosophers Tyler Doggett and Andy Egan observe,

"There's sometimes quite a bit to be said for getting things not quite right."[5]

Going vegan should be no different. When we're aspiring to something as bold, beautiful, and complex as allowing abundant space for creaturely flourishing across an all-species kinship, we can't afford to lose heart when we look down and see leather shoes, relax our commitments on a special occasion, roll flexitarian during a semester abroad or a season of loss or a stretch without a paycheck, or even find ourselves horking Port-A-Pit chicken in a strip-mall parking lot out of spite for a veg partner enjoying a smoother transition (hypothetically). In going vegan, each of us will negotiate our fragility and flow as we go, and there's no reason to give up the aspiration simply because we can't live as fully into it as we'd like to right away (or ever, for that matter). As a bonus, our patience with and kindness to ourselves produce a contagious delight in the adventure that is the most hospitable invitation we can offer to others on the threshold of discovering their inner vegan-in-waiting.

So please join me now in declaring ourselves liberated from the anxiety-inducing, enthusiasm-diminishing paradigm of defining our vegan aspirations by what we do *not* do. Sing hallelujah. Send the universe gratitude. Light a bundle of sage. Wipe your moist eyes in your animal companion's luxurious coat (unless they are human, in which case their shirt will suffice). Do what you do to mark deliverance from a burden. The fear that going vegan is beyond you is behind you, and the apprehension that remains is nervous energy preparing you to go out there and do your very best at something you love. Like butterflies before your show-stealing solo!

From now on, going vegan is no longer about stopping something terrible once and for all, but about starting something beautiful and aspiring to do better and better as circumstances allow, confidence increases, and momentum gathers. We're turning our collective aspiration from the narrow, stringent, scarcity-fearing goal of never eating or using animal products ever again (ever!) to the capacious, flexible, abundance-loving goal of always striving to make as generous a space for creaturely flourishing as we presently can. Space at our tables, yes, but space too in all the places where fierce and fragile minds, hearts, and bodies are striving to thrive, whoever they are. And let's affirm again and always that our individual goals for pulling weight as we live toward this collective aspiration are best discerned in view of a careful, compassionate inventory of our personal circumstances, especially those that—in our fragility—might tempt us to fear that our inevitable imperfections disqualify us from going vegan.

I can't tell you which goals to set. The best I can do is to pull a Socrates and strongly encourage you to "Know yourself!" as you set them. What would going vegan look like if the trail had been blazed just for you for the purpose of helping you to discover your most harmonious, ebullient, and engaged self? Not, mind you, the new and improved and ambitiously transformed Insta-self who can do anything and everything and fund it all with ad revenue. Let's bless and release that self, the dear heart!

I'm talking about your homey, homely self—the one with limited bandwidth and a little patch of ground who is nonetheless capable of remarkable resilience and great small things when there's a thoughtful, flexible plan and conditions cooperate. The

self that poet David Whyte so beautifully envisions when he
writes,

> Human beings do not find their essence through fulfillment or
> eventual arrival but by staying close to the way they like to travel,
> to the way they hold the conversation between the ground on which
> they stand and the horizon toward which they go. We are, in effect,
> always close, always close to the ultimate secret: that we are more
> real in our simple wish to find a way than any destination we could
> reach; the step between not understanding that and understanding
> that is as close as we get to happiness.[6]

My advice is to think of your goals for going vegan as simple
wishes to find a way to stay as close as you can to who you already
are. Nothing too big. Nothing too life-changing. Nothing too
permanent. It's much too soon to imagine where you might be
in your vegan journey at this time next year. What simple wishes
do you have right now to find your vegan way across your inner
ecology? In your family life? With your friendships? At work?
Out there in the world?

When you first get going, you may prefer to focus on just a few
of these simple wishes and defer getting too wishy too quickly
in any areas where you suspect that hoping for too much too
soon could induce anxiety or fear, and risk starving the seed of
your vegan desire before it can take root. Unless you have an
uncharacteristically supportive community of vegan-friendly
family, friends, and colleagues, it is often wise to focus first and
privately on the simple wish of amending your inner soil—
reflecting on your physical and emotional needs and shoring up

your intellectual and moral resources for making the most inspiring possible case to yourself before it comes time to engage with others. With tea or coffee, the Internet, the library, and a few new cookbooks, such experiments can be a joy.

This risk-averse, inspiration-hungry approach was key to my early success. I knew I had some inner work to do to manage the physical, intellectual, and emotional challenges of going vegan. But let's just say I was in no hurry to publish my fledgling thoughts in the world of professional philosophy—the audience than which none more critical can be conceived—and because many of my friends and family are opinionated intellectuals and not many of them were vegan at the time, I wasn't ready to make even simple wishes of them at first even if I suspected they'd be kind.

But I felt safe exploring this territory with curious, courageous students who had asked me to try. To my great good fortune, Susan loved a challenge in the kitchen. And I knew I couldn't live without a heart-stopping tiramisu.

These were my simple wishes. Teach an animal ethics class and see where it takes me. Eat a plant-based diet for three weeks and see how I feel. Find a way to make the world's most decadent vegan tiramisu. (Spoiler: Mission accomplished. See Appendix B.)[7]

I don't know what your simple wishes are, but I can tell you with great assurance that if you make them with your unique patterns of fragility and flow in mind and at heart, the experience of setting goals for your own vegan good can feel profusely liberating.

You can release any motivation-sapping pressure that may have gathered around the ideal of trying to be "the perfect vegan," both because the only ideal worth pursuing is your own and because your successes and failures alike simply push out the boundaries of what is possible for you, bringing you the joy and the challenge of a new personal ideal toward which to strive.

You can let your self-understanding lead the way, leveraging your strengths into progress that generates positive energy for coping with and compensating for weaknesses and buys you the time and confidence to live more fully into the vision as you go.

You can flow past judgmental fixation on your own or others' individual methods, failures, and successes toward a more holistic awareness of the collective progress we seek together. This one is especially gorgeous. Far from stringent ideals that always seem to find you cringing, just one moment of weakness away from failure, self-judgment, or jealousy of more "successful" others, your goals can liberate you to become who you most want to be in living toward a new vegan normal that we envision and enact together. In the wise words of pattrice jones, "Look for the best match between what you have to give and the many different things that need to be done."[8]

Maybe you'll be a hospitable foodie, gently opening minds and hearts with each delectable dinner party. Or a green entrepreneur, using creativity and business acumen to open markets for new and better products. Or a compassionate educator, leading students to scientific realities and spiritual awakenings that illuminate the promise of a vegan world. An abolitionist prophet, calling out evil and summoning forth the better angels of our nature. An incremental pragmatist, helping compromised institutions do just a little better. An artist advocate, provoking wonder about beautiful roads less traveled. A food justice activist, dismantling the intertwined oppressions of worker injustice, animal cruelty, and food apartheid. A companion rescuer, searching out forever homes for creatures who deserve to be loved. A holistic health evangelist. A climate champion. Or some strange and wonderful combination of these that only you can dream up. When you succeed, our collective burden is lightened. And when you fail, others are on the job. You can go again when you're ready, now with richer understanding of what's possible for you, and when, and why.

In setting goals for your own vegan good, to sum up, you can pursue the triple crown of ancient philosophical emancipation: the peace of mind that comes with taking the weight of the world off your shoulders, the independence to live in accordance with the knowledge of your good, and the cosmic consciousness to keep the bigger picture in mind as you strive to fulfill your own small part of the grand plan. Freedom from vain worries. Freedom to thrive on your own terms. And freedom to align your flourishing with the flourishing of the whole.

Self-knowledge can set you up to wish wisely in all these beautiful ways. But you'll need a little self-discipline to make your wishes come true.

CHAPTER 8

DISCIPLINE

SPIRITUAL EXERCISES FOR GOING VEGAN

IMAGINE A MODULAR ORIGAMI RAY GUN METICULOUSLY constructed from two sheets of printer paper. Now imagine every visible surface of the weapon (and some of the "top secret" underfolds besides) covered from barrel to grip in hand-drawn, assiduously annotated buttons and screens availing its brandisher of every conceivable tool for thriving in a pickle without breaking a sweat: "stun mode," "grappling hook," "transponder," "translator," "signal jammer," "bat hoard," "fresh underoos."

I was a nervous child. And because there wasn't a lot of latitude for anxious children in my era, I became obsessed with having a plan, a contingency plan, and a backup plan for the contingency plan in the very likely event of apocalypse or soiled pants. The joy I felt upon receiving my first Swiss Army knife is indescribable— a Wenger Matterhorn with thirteen tools and the width to make even the most flamboyant hedge fund manager's watch face blush.[1] With multiple blades, a mini-saw, a hex-head wrench, and much more at my immediate disposal, I fantasized that no bully, rogue tree branch, rusted bolt smaller than m5, or surprise bout of incontinence stood a chance against the confidence and calm I enjoyed with the Matterhorn hanging resolutely from my sagging belt. My days of having to parry the world's incursions with folded paper guns were over.

It turns out that giant knife sheaths are less impressive to potential dance dates than I had hoped. My infatuation with multi-tools was thus forced underground in late middle school and sublimated throughout four years of high school into my ever-burgeoning chest circumference and increasingly voracious appetite for entrepreneurial enterprises. To be the king of the weight room and a mixed-media T-shirt mogul (silkscreen *and* airbrush) was as far as my teen imagination could take me. Surely being ripped and rich would keep my anxiety at bay.

Upon graduating high school, my fantasy was to return to my ten-year reunion in a Bugatti, exit the vehicle, and set it on fire in a spectacular display of security unshakable enough to render million-dollar automobiles disposable. Less than two years later, thanks to the strange grace of initially unwelcome core curriculum requirements, I found myself a collegiate philosopher discovering that real security was to be found in facing life's complexities with honesty and resolve, relishing the loveliness of being alive in a world teeming with possibility, and striving within my limits to love and bless the whole of which I am but a minuscule part.

I consider it one of the greatest gifts I've received that philosophy was taught to me not as an abstract academic discipline but as a scintillating set of practical disciplines for living a beautiful life.[2] The pitch was irresistible. Through the daily practice of spiritual exercises that increased self-knowledge, expanded imagination, and most importantly, instilled transformational motivation for resilient future striving, one could move slowly but surely from the futile, self-consumed quest for ephemera like money, fame, and prestige to the joyful, world-healing pursuit of things that moths and rust can't devour, like truth, beauty, and goodness.

Philosophy was the origami ray gun multi-tool of the soul that I'd been dreaming of since childhood. For every imaginable existential threat, there was a discipline to help one persevere. And with a little creativity, you could get a regime of exercises working in concert to bring out your best, compensate for your worst, and even expand your range of possible flourishing simultaneously on all fronts.

For thirty years, this vision of philosophy as the lived pursuit of wisdom through the practice of spiritual exercises has powered me through every motivational challenge I've faced. It got me through graduate school, helped me find and keep a job in professional philosophy, has seen me through more than a quarter century of marriage, and finds me rising every morning to try yet again as a parent. For more than two decades, I've taken great pride in inviting students to discover for themselves the beauty of philosophy as a way of life. The dynamo of my pedagogy is the transformational power of spiritual exercises.

As for living out my vegan aspirations, the importance of these disciplines is impossible to overstate. Going vegan, as I have experienced it, just *is* the daily practice of an evolving program of experimental spiritual exercises. My experiments have consistently generated invigorating motivation to keep striving toward the ever-expanding vision of creaturely flourishing that first sparkled forth from a baby bulldog's eyes and continues to surprise and delight me over twenty years later.

The work of this chapter is to inspire you to construct your own program of spiritual exercises whose disciplined daily practice will both hasten you toward your vegan goals and generate a host of invigorating new possibilities to explore as your awareness of the uniqueness of your vegan good evolves and your confidence in its potential to bless the world grows ripe.[3] The central challenge is to walk the tightrope of doing the best we can without falling into the despair of life-negating perfectionism on the one side or succumbing to the temptation of self-excusing complacency on the other.

Like athletes (or mathletes!) in training, we'll discover that hitting the sweet spot of peak vegan striving is a matter of using a combination of exercises that strengthen our best abilities, identify and improve our weaknesses, and establish stretch goals that inspire us to push our limits without burning us out. Better get a nicer belt, because you'll soon be packing the custom vegan multi-tool than which none greater can be conceived.

Let's start by celebrating the elasticity of the adjective "spiritual" in "spiritual exercises." This word is a big tent that makes room for everything from sweet chariots of fire swinging low, to mountaintop meditations, to Tarot readings, to secular psychoanalysis.

Whether you're attuned by an interpretation as thick and rich as that of a traditional religious vision or as lean and pragmatic as a contemporary therapeutic approach, you can rest assured that what is at stake here is something familiar: the desire to bring our complex inner ecologies into liberating alignment for the purpose of delightful, leavening engagement with the world outside. What makes a given exercise "spiritual" in this context is not the peculiar details of your foundational assumptions about the world and what you're doing here, but the conscious intent to seek holistic flourishing by harmonizing your good with the good of the world.

You can also be confident that someone like you, somewhere in time, has made vigorous use of spiritual exercises to free themselves for a beautiful life of blessing the world. My favorite thing about sharing this approach to good living with students is how expansive and inclusive the possibilities are for finding your people. In my Philosophical Transformation seminar, we barely scratch the surface of what known human history has put forward in this genre. And yet we engage Jain, Daoist, Stoic, Judeo-Christian, and American transcendentalist visions of transformation via a slate of readings that spans twenty-six centuries, from Lao Tzu's Chu to St. Augustine's Roman Africa to Julian of Norwich's England to Gandhi's India to Simone Weil's France to Cornel West's America. The use of spiritual exercises is ubiquitous across times and traditions the world over.

As with most things that show up everywhere since time immemorial, one needn't care a whit about the history of philosophy intuitively to grasp how these exercises work. We all know how to breathe. We all know how to eat. And we all know that our flourishing depends on practicing certain behaviors over and over and over until they become habitual.

As much as we hated our parents for it (at least when we were babies), we can't learn to lift our huge noggins or roll over on our own without tummy time. We can't pass Spanish without flash cards or algebra without problem sets. We can't spit bars like RZA without nailing the breathwork. Or get a respectable golf handicap until our swings become automatic. Or put a decent dice on an onion until our knifework is on point. And we can't kill it in orchestra without mastering Simon Kovar's *24 Daily Exercises for Bassoon*. Everybody knows this. Learning basic life skills, much less achieving significant goals, takes a lot of practice.

If we're all familiar with the mechanics of using repetitive exercises to hone our skills and make headway on our goals, it's less common to apply this strategy to our most basic goal of all: doing well at managing the inner ecologies that enable us to be at our calm, confident, convivial best out there in the world no matter what we happen to be doing. Spiritual exercises are those disciplines we undertake with the express intention to harmonize our inner lives for the purpose of gearing our personal flourishing into the flourishing of the whole.

The fitness of this framework for clarifying what we hope to achieve in living out our vegan aspirations is exquisite. What makes going vegan so different from, say, getting good at bassoon or soccer or glassblowing is that it engages our whole inner system in a reorientation not just of how we see the world, but of how we desire to be in it. However popular it is to think of going vegan as a matter of practicing the single, stand-alone discipline of dietary change, we know better now.

Our relationship to food is much more complicated than the act of just putting random stuff in our pieholes. In a world where pig roasts are religious rituals, dead turkeys emanate gratitude, steak confers virility, wings are the life of the party, and chicken soup is a mother's love, it's naïve to hope that just swapping meat stuff with plant stuff will do the job all by itself. True, kindergarten ethics gives us everything we need to inspire curiosity and maybe even resolve from our inner vegan-in-waiting. And yes, the world of abundant creaturely flourishing that awaits our individual and collective efforts, from our own backyards to the arctic circle to the Amazon rainforest, is wildly beautiful and evocative of our deep desire to change. We've even had the good sense to set ourselves up for success by moderating this desire into simple wishes for making our way that honor the unique forms of fragility and flow that will characterize our new vegan normal.

But the reality on the ground is that the process of making our way even to the fulfillment of simple wishes involves finding the self-discipline to strive for transformation. To normalize vegan living, we must shed old habits of thinking, feeling, and socializing and supplant them with new ones across a wide variety of intermeshed existential fronts. Dietary change alone can't accomplish this feat. But with a custom program of spiritual exercises, we can dial in an intentional and varied set of practices that anticipates, accommodates, and eventually habituates our attitudes and actions across the physical, social, emotional, intellectual, and moral challenges that going vegan poses to us in different circumstances. Instead of having to depend on willpower, heroic resolve, and other unicorns to help us make this transition, we can custom build a vegan multi-tool with spiritual exercises for every occasion.

Consider the hidden complexities buried in the simple wish to have the closest thing possible to a stress-free Thanksgiving weekend. With an omnivorous extended family. Who loves you even more than they love to see vegans fail. If just barely. During your sixth month of going vegan.

Your mom does most of the cooking and is generally supportive of you. But she's also conflict-averse, nervous about departing too much from the traditional menu, and terrified of setting off her brother, your Uncle Keith, who is a pugnacious lawyer, avid hunter, and python breeder. Keith's daughter, your favorite cousin, Imani, is a graduate student in sociology with a passion for worker justice. She's veg-curious but reserved about making her interest public. Especially since Aunt Antonia (her mom, to whom she's very close) has become a vocal proponent of a meat-heavy training regimen to chase improved performance as a triathlete. Imani's brother Jaylen and your sister Sammy will spend the weekend rotating among the PlayStation 5, televised football games, and theological discussions over beer and buffalo wings with you and your dad—an electrician who always thought he'd end up a pastor and still reads and thinks like one. Jaylen and Sammy will regale you with bacon jokes and tempt you with wings (which won't be too difficult, alas). But it's your dad's concern that all this vegan stuff means you've rejected the family's religious heritage that looms largest in the pit of your stomach.

You love these people to pieces. But this event has all the makings of a shit show. Uncle Keith. Your mom's dread over balancing interests at dinner. Your only real ally having to protect both her parents. Jaylen and Sammy's bacon-snorting, wing-pushing antics. Your dad's suspicions of betrayal. All that risky business plus the unstable hybrid of enthusiasm and insecurity you feel as a newly aspiring vegan equals walking on broken glass all weekend between private and public meltdowns. At least you won't have to walk on eggshells now that you're going vegan. But in a worst-case scenario, an early, tear-streaked departure seems possible. Maybe even probable.

Not with spiritual exercises on the job![4] Instead of spending the month of November in dread over your simple wish for a lovely Thanksgiving, you decide to prepare. Using the spiritual exercise of attention—the continuous vigilant observation of your inner ecology's responses (or likely responses) to challenging circumstances outside—you take an inventory of your hopes and fears for the long holiday weekend. You immediately notice a tension between your mind and heart that could complicate both your social interactions and your physical well-being.

There's a strong intellectual desire to share your reasons for going vegan with the people you love. You want your mom to see how delicious and easy to prepare vegan holiday fare can be. You want Imani to know how deeply it resonates with her advocacy for worker justice. You want Antonia to discover the health risks of meat-heavy diets and the rewards of plant-powered athletic training. Most of all, you want your dad to understand that going vegan has invigorated and expanded your commitments to unconditional love and service to others that he has modeled since your earliest memories. You've taken these steps in large part *because* he trained you to practice what you preach.

But emotionally, you're not ready to risk making a big public show of your enthusiasm. You fear disapproval. And you have moral qualms, too, about making things hard on your mom and Imani. Even if you had the fortitude to handle Uncle Keith on blast with Jaylen and Sammy piling on, it wouldn't be fair to force your mom to endure her worst hospitality nightmare or your cousin to choose sides in a no-win situation. And you can't deny that parts of you are already anticipating the shame of too many beers leading to a wing binge, while other parts conspire to guzzle the very brews that will make the binge more likely. Part of you wants to just fly under the radar and pretend nothing's different. Clam up and eat whatever. It's just one long weekend.

As you attend to these emotional risks and note your inner dialogue, you discern that—tempting as it is—dissimulating is not intellectually, emotionally, or physically feasible. Pretending you're someone you're not, even to save the feelings of others, is at best unbecoming of cherished relationships and at worst an act of intellectual cowardice—dishonest both to your best self and to your loved ones. This kind of dishonesty is bound to result in unwanted emotional fallout for everyone, as your trust and intimacy with others and your own self-esteem suffer the predictable consequences of your reluctance to show them and yourself who you're striving to become.

All high-minded and stout-hearted considerations aside, hiding the truth will physically reduce you to a trembling, headachy omnishambles. Long days of eating around the edges, stealth snacking, and consuming foods you wish you hadn't are not going to power you through late nights of Scattergories (Cards

Against Humanity?), whisky-fueled ping-pong tournaments, and the umpteenth screening of *Planes, Trains and Automobiles*.[5]

Your hopes and fears are clarified. You hope to spend quality time with people you love in ways that are intellectually and emotionally true to yourself and respectful of them. You fear you'll either come on too strong, invite disapproval, and create conflict, or remain too timid, sacrifice intimacy, and let yourself down. The practice of attention has been fruitful.

Now it's time to take inventory of the other spiritual exercises in your arsenal and assemble a program to maximize the fulfillment of your hopes and minimize the likelihood that your fears diminish your resolve or sabotage your experience. In doing so, you'll want to choose exercises that work collectively to empower you in three complementary ways: (1) to think and act wisely when circumstances are under your control; (2) to respond graciously when circumstances are outside your control; and (3) to act and respond in mindful accord with the best interests of your community. Let's call these the powers of confidence, calm, and conviviality, respectively.

Your first challenge is to find a strategy for balancing your intellectual and emotional hopes authentically to share yourself with others with your social hope of doing so without causing emotional strain or even chaos for yourself and others. You discern that the safest way to strike this balance is to increase your power of confidence for the coming interactions with your mom, Imani, and your dad (which seem likely to go well if you approach them wisely); increase your power of calm for the coming interactions with Uncle Keith, Aunt Antonia, Jaylen, and Sammy (which seem unpredictable and potentially incendiary

unless you're on your guard); and increase your power of conviviality by thinking ahead about how to manage your planned
interactions with Mom, Imani, and Dad so that they're unlikely
to elicit stressful or hurtful interactions with the others. Nothing
ratchets anxiety higher at a family gathering than the selective
avoidance and abruptly halted interactions of ceding space to
unnamed elephants in every room.

Using the spiritual exercise of listening—seeking to learn and
empathize with the hopes, fears, and experiences of others—you
call your mom three weeks ahead of the event to talk about the
menu. She's incredibly relieved and touched by your thoughtful-
ness. You ask her how she envisions the event going and whether
there's anything you can do to help. She replies that she wants
to be as supportive as possible, but feels like it's a step too far to
take the turkey or bacon green beans almondine off the menu—
"Keith will sic Chumley [prized ball python] on me!" She asks
whether it would be okay if she plans to serve those items, while
using plant-based butter and soy milk to veganize all the other
sides. "If you tell your uncle he's eating vegan mashed potatoes
and creamed limas, we'll have words," she laughs, equal parts
reassured and apprehensive.

Using the spiritual exercise of taking on responsibilities—
making commitments that allow you to practice fulfilling your
expectations of yourself—you promise your mom that you'll
send her a list next week of the best products to use for these purposes. In the meanwhile, you pledge to experiment with recipes
for a delicious if unobtrusive vegan protein for yourself to add to
the feast, as well as an incredible dessert that everyone will love.
Here's your chance to perfect the tiramisu you've been working

on.[6] And you'll bring a variety of veg-friendly snacks, too, to take the pressure off your mom to do more than she can handle.

But if your mom loves advance planning, Imani and your dad will be stressed out by preliminary conversations featuring the v-word. Rather than giving them something to dread, you decide to discern how best to approach interactions with them catch-as-catch-can over the weekend, at least the interactions concerning your vegan journey. Using the spiritual exercise of research—investigating areas of inquiry pertinent to your own well-being and that of others with whom your flourishing is intermeshed—you begin looking into books and podcasts that might help you to frame your aspirations more confidently in terms that resonate with Imani and your dad.

You land on two simple wishes for sharing your aspirations with Imani. You'd like to be better prepared to discuss how going vegan aids the fight for worker justice. And you'd like to have a recommendation for learning more about plant-powered tri-athletes, given Imani's health concerns about her mom's meaty training regimen. This research will be a win-win-win: it will strengthen your own commitments, allow you to communicate them better to your cousin, and offer an indirect way to plant a seed of caring for your aunt without complicating the holiday.

For the vegan triathlete piece, you land on ultra-endurance athlete Rich Roll's celebrated classic *Finding Ultra*.[7] As a bonus, you discover Roll's scintillating podcast series in which he hosts conversations with everyone under the vegan sun on everything from life transformation through food (chef Babette Davis), to spiritual minimalism (Light Watkins), to the "meatless meat moonshot" (Bruce Friedrich), to Arnold Schwarzenegger

(Arnold Schwarzenegger).[8] Somehow it's midnight and your empowering research has given way to pure, unadulterated fun, reminding you that recreation is an important spiritual exercise, too, for finding joy and maintaining flow.

For the worker justice piece, you decide on the Reverend Dr. Christopher Carter's *The Spirit of Soul Food: Race, Faith & Food Justice*.[9] The second chapter, "Food Pyramid Scheme," offers the most concise account you've seen of how domestic and international food politics exacerbate existing problems for agricultural workers, including poverty, environmental injustice, food apartheid, and hunger, all of which disproportionately affect communities of color. And Carter's religious orientation makes this research a two-for-one, as the text and endnotes are full of references to work by theologians and philosophers who might be of interest to your dad (or at least helpful to you in meeting him where he is).

With the aid of the spiritual exercises of attention, listening, taking on responsibilities, research, and recreation, you feel confident in your preparedness to be yourself and enjoy your time with Mom, Imani, and Dad. You and your mom have an understanding and a concrete plan. You might continue casually to give some thought to strategies for sharing with your cousin and your dad that feel natural and socially low risk. Maybe one of your nice long walks with Imani will feel like the right time. Or a chat with Dad while others are preoccupied with video games and Keith's across town feeding Chumley. You experience a great sense of relief as it dawns on you that just feeling prepared for these interactions is liberating on its own even if they don't end up happening.

The next test is to find exercises to grow your calm for responding graciously if the going gets tough with Uncle Keith and company. Anticipating the need for increased patience with your uncle, you employ the spiritual exercise of remembering good things—calling to mind favorite memories of your time together and forming the intention to allow these fond feelings to shape your approach to the holiday.

You envision baby Chumley coiled atop Keith's bald head as you and Imani giggle from a shared beanbag. The full moon and a worn patch of grass oscillate between your sneakered feet on swing rides thrillingly higher than when your parents were supervising. You watch through split fingers your uncle's contagious joy at the terrifying miracle of python birth. A wave of warm, joyful empathy envelops you as your disgust with Keith the python breeder softens into curiosity about the inner vegan-in-waiting so clearly shining through the awed smile of Keith the Chumley lover.

You haven't realized you're in tears as you entertain a sparkling new query of yourself. "How can my presence this Thanksgiving leave abundant space for Keith the Chumley lover to be curious and delighted rather than ashamed and defensive?" You won't make any simple wishes for Keith to convert to vegan jerky or even sample your tiramisu without a flamboyant bout of faux dry heaving. But the hope of relating to him in ways that honor his inner vegan-in-waiting is calming, and taking the initial steps toward building that relationship feels like a heartening stretch goal.

Generous feelings toward your uncle will help. But you recognize a need, too, for generous feelings toward yourself, as you anticipate compression between the rock of your new aspirations and the hard place of your desire to fulfill the expectations of belonging to this clan. You need the radical self-acceptance to persevere in this pressure until your experiments create space enough for aspiring-you and belonging-you to flourish in the same ecology. Even if that process of tinkering finds you face down in a pile of wing bones after succumbing to Sammy's badgering or angrily (and worse, redundantly) calling Jaylen a "corpse-eating necrophagist" in a moment of exasperation after an ill-timed bacon joke.

Persevering in this pressure will require the powers of confidence, calm, and conviviality working in unison. You need to see that you are making progress toward your aspirations. You need to take shortcomings and even failures in stride, especially the ones that result from predictable falls into well-worn family grooves. And you need to pursue your aspirations in ways that make hospitable room for you and your loved ones to be who you are together.

This formidable job is reserved for the multi-tool of all multi-tools. Meditation. A spiritual exercise so customizable, transcultural, transdisciplinary, and historically ubiquitous that *The Oxford Handbook of Meditation* needed one thousand pages authored by a multicultural team of over forty experts in everything from neuroscience to medicine to rehabilitation psychology to religious studies just to get an introductory handle on the possibilities.[10]

Like a peaceful, contemplative John Wick choosing from an unlimited arsenal of meditative woo for the ultimate Thanksgiving showdown, you select intention meditation, loving-kindness meditation, and journaling meditation to create a three-layer flak jacket of conviviality, calm, and confidence.

With intention meditation—the spiritual exercise of setting an intention for how you will strive to show up for the day's challenges and returning to that intention for inspiration when needed—you keep your personal and interpersonal goals for the visit front of mind. With loving-kindness meditation— imagining yourself receiving lavish support and encouragement from a trusted friend or your highest, wisest self—you flood your brain with chemicals that make it easier both to take good risks and recover from the consequences of bad ones. And with journaling meditation—taking brief written stock of the day's successes, failures, lessons, and epiphanies and using them to shape the next day's intentions—you cultivate the confidence to build on strengths, shore up weaknesses, and launch promising new experiments.

We've focused on the value of these spiritual exercises for managing your outer family but notice their potency for improving relations across your inner family, too. Research can bring your intellectual commitment up to pace with your emotional investment. Loving-kindness can help moral-you to give physical-you a comforting hug instead of a shaming rebuke upon discovering a surreptitious mouthful of bacon green beans almondine. Attention can help you to adjudicate wisely whether intellect or emotion should be in the driver's seat for a particular exchange or when you should eat a snack to stabilize the ol' chemicals before a morally challenging interaction.

This account is idealized. Meltdowns can occur despite your best laid plans. Sometimes you'll be too tired or too busy to make the plans at all. Keith might wave taxidermy in your face and you might crumble seasoned tofu into the least accessible pocket of his knapsack in retaliation. Pumpkin cheesecake might mysteriously disappear in the dead of night when the risks of perceived inauthenticity and mocking ridicule are significantly reduced.

But with a little planning, practice, and luck, the odds that your simple wish for a lovely Thanksgiving comes true can significantly improve with a program of spiritual exercises behind you. As the little victories pile up and the range of circumstances to which you've applied these exercises expands, you'll accrue both the knowledge of what works best in like situations and the wisdom to improvise better in uncharted territory.

You'll have noticed that these exercises don't need to be vegan-specific to have transformative potential for your success at going vegan. That makes perfect sense now that we're tracking how profoundly our vegan commitments both challenge and potentially transform our inner ecologies and the complex relationships among their provinces. But one of the most beautiful perks of starting your vegan journey with a more holistic, less vegan-specific approach to your inner soil amendment is that the bumper crops of confidence, calm, and conviviality you reap through this work make the vegan-specific exercises that much easier to practice.

Suppose you take on the vegan spiritual exercise of learning to cook delicious plant-based meals to reduce cravings, save money on dining out, and improve the nutrient density of the food you're taking in. Won't that be significantly less burdensome with all the self-reflective and social benefits that come from having attention, listening, taking on responsibilities, research, recreation, remembering good things, and loving-kindness already working for you?

Imagine how much less stressful it will be to practice the exercise of building vegan community—finding other like-minded people to share the joys and burdens of going vegan—with these other practices already up and running, helping you to keep and strengthen existing relationships rather than exacerbating alienation and pushing you toward an increasingly segregated or lonely social experience. Taking the risk to make some new vegan friends is a lot more manageable when you're still friendly with the good folks you already know and love. The same is true for the exercises of vegan education and advocacy, modeling your behavior on vegan exemplars, and supporting vegan charities. The more confidence, calm, and conviviality you bring to your vegan-specific work, the more winsome and the less alienating that work is likely to be, both for you and for others.

This double effect of increasing our enthusiasm and diminishing our anxiety is a powerful generator of motivation to keep going vegan because it protects us from the two most demoralizing features of our experience—regret over past failures and fear of future ones. These motivation killers dim down the empowering possibilities of the present, swamping us in endless ruminations over a past we can't change and a future we can't control. But with an inner ecology trained on spiritual exercises designed to help us rise confidently to the challenge of the present moment, remain calm in the face of adversity, and act with the flourishing of the community in mind and at heart, we find ourselves emboldened to prioritize our deepest, most abiding desire to bless the world in striving to become our best selves.

As you assemble your program of spiritual exercises, you want this deep desire in the driver's seat and a custom interior specially designed to prioritize and accommodate your peculiar patterns of flow and fragility. Never forget that spiritual exercises are not obligatory practices that you've been shamed into reluctantly trying. They are powerful tools for transformation that you get to choose and refine for the express purpose of fulfilling your simple wishes to realize liberating progress toward the truth, beauty, and goodness of a new vegan normal. This is progress you passionately desire to make! So go after it!

Are you inclined to be a little too relaxed in your efforts? Then seek exercises that put your feet to the fire to challenge yourself. Are you inclined to self-ridicule the second you fall off the absolute highest standard of stringency? Then seek exercises that help you loosen up a bit. If you're like me, you might find that you have many inner parts that need different exercises at different times. Maybe some parts push too hard in some areas and some parts let you off too easy in others. Remember that the members of your inner family have different needs. Always seek to honor your unique mix of intellectual, emotional, moral, social, and physical excellences and limits and to cultivate harmony among them through a focus on bolstering strengths, compensating for weaknesses, and warding off predictable failures.

Ideally, your efforts will generate an inspiring synergy between regular small victories that build the confidence and experience necessary to stay energized, and harder-won challenges that build the resolve and resilience necessary to keep striving when the going gets tough. This process of refinement can be experimental and challenging—it takes practice to get your regime of exercises up and running, much less humming like a well-oiled machine.

But it shouldn't feel like drudgery. If it does, that's an indication that you haven't dialed into the right setup just yet and it's time to try a different configuration. For me, the process of tinkering with various exercises to keep my elevating chemistry internally harmonious and externally engaged in world-leavening work has always felt more like a life-giving hobby than a necessary evil. I even found a way to turn watching my favorite television show, *Twin Peaks*, into a spiritual exercise for converting alienation into resilient calm.[11]

If you're willing to get creative with the exercises you adopt and gamify things a little, going vegan can feel like building a wooden boat or tricking out a wicked awesome conversion van or cultivating a beautiful garden or curating the perfect spice cabinet or summiting a bunch of fourteeners or creating an absurdly nerdy website about your favorite TV show under a nom de guerre. It's just that you're the boat, the van, the garden, the cabinet, the mountain, the nerdy website.

The work is beautiful. The results are elevating too. But the real secret is to learn to love the work. Discipline can be a prelude to deep flow if we can just bring ourselves to start doing the reps.

I suspect you already know this.

I relearn the lesson at least four days a week on the elliptical runner. One minute, I'm a dour, self-loathing sad sack living in a failed future whose family is begging him to exercise. Nine minutes later, every fiber of my being is pulsating with the gospel truth of boygenius's "Not Strong Enough," and the scintillating montage I'm envisioning of my successful Senate campaign seems as inevitable as the oatmeal I'll eat after showering. Sometimes it's Public Enemy's "Fight the Power" and I'm galvanizing some nebulous but extremely inspiring movement. Usually, it's Kate Bush's "Running Up That Hill" and I'm hovering in a cemetery on the razor's edge of saving the world from a despotic wizard. The point is just that there is a pharmacy in my brain that desires my flourishing and richly rewards my efforts to try.

So let's try. Transformation awaits.

CHAPTER 9

TRANSFORMATION

GOOD VEGAN LIVING

I AM A CRIER. I CRY WHEN I'M SAD. I CRY WHEN I'M HAPPY. I cry when I'm angry. I cry when a work of art makes the dark places light or the light places dark or the middling places lovely. When a song on a show gets the feeling so right my neck and ears flush.[1] When forgiveness offers humiliation the possibility of self-love. When a word of comfort to a friend heals a part of me in hiding. When some indelible feeling from ages ago manifests from nowhere in a passing expression on my child's face. When my dour expectations are foiled by the joy of being wrong. I cry when the veil is thin—when the boundary becomes transparent between my desire for all to be well and the desires of everyone else to enter that same gorgeous space of open resonance.

Tears remind me how beautiful it feels to lose oneself momentarily in the grand mystery and yet how lucky I am to have the opportunity, in some miniscule yet urgent sense, still to be my own. To embody the enigma of being as only I can. To see uniquely the other broken, beautiful beings everywhere, so like and unlike me, through the gift of experiences no one else can have. To move to their aid with a mind, heart, hands, and feet tested by suffering, tempered by joy, equipped for special service by a life that is somehow both completely mine and yet also, in the moments of transcendence at its joyful outer limits, completely theirs, too.

As oceanic as these moments are, the fact that their harbingers are ducts in my eyes that pump out a heterogeneous mixture of mucus, water, and oil confirms that I am always and ever but a creature. A hungry beautiful animal with a simple wish to make my small way into the great way, armed with an annual supply of fifteen to thirty gallons of tears to keep me observant of when the veil between the small and the great is vanishingly thin. And to protect my corneas.

I don't claim to know the meaning of life. But in my experience, the joy of living comes from the hope of learning to love so abundantly that the veil is as thin as can be as often as can be. That the barriers routinely disintegrate between self and world, letting it be that we can see what is true of life, feast on its beauty, and live well from its abundance and from our own. This joy feels like receiving now, from forces invisible, a glimmer of everything all at once inflected and improved, if infinitesimally, by my silly little offerings of attention and acceptance.

The most astonishing thing about going vegan once you've been at it for a while is the way it normalizes thinning the veil across every aspect of our lives, allowing how we think, feel, experience, learn, eat, consume, advocate, and collaborate slowly but surely to shed selfishness and strident shortsightedness to susurrate in ever more profound resonance with everyone and everything. If we choose it, billions of simple wishes, pursued, achieved, and multiplied with the help of spiritual exercises, can generate billions of silly little offerings—each with leavening effects that, like yeast in a dough, can bring forth exponential expansion from the teamwork of tiny things. As simple wishes give way to silly little offerings, big things happen. When aspiration meets discipline, transformation follows. Miniscule as we are, going vegan can be transformational for us, for our fellow creatures, and for the common home we share.

The work of this chapter is to learn to identify and celebrate the practical effects of this holistic transformation as they manifest in good vegan living, harmonizing our inner desires and freeing us to channel our unique elevating chemistry into catalyzing collective desire to make the world a more beautiful place for everyone. If the guiding question of Chapter 7 was "How should we set goals in going vegan?" and Chapter 8 asked "How can spiritual exercises discipline our vegan striving?" our central query now is "How will going vegan transform our daily lives over time?" What does good vegan living look like and how do we know we're making progress, despite all the predictable frustrations and setbacks of being human?

It's tempting to hope for that one-in-a-million chance at instantaneous transformation—the fabled "conversion experience" through which all is made exhilaratingly and permanently new. But most of us will travel a different road on which transformation happens in fits and starts across a variety of fronts, progressing quickly on some, gradually on others, almost imperceptibly or even seemingly regressing in still others. The journey can feel so unpredictable and circuitous that progress can be difficult to see at all if one doesn't know exactly how to look for it.

Whether we're discerning the transformation of our inner ecologies or the wider world outside, hungry beautiful animals like us should always expect to see desire and limitation in constant negotiation with flourishing in the balance. Because our inner and outer circumstances are so complex and context dependent, and because they evolve—often dramatically—over time, we should expect the "progress" of transformation to crop up, disappear, and circle back in surprising and sometimes even counterintuitive ways that blur the lines between success and failure as we often construe them.

This is especially true on the outset of a transformational journey that contains as many inner and outer variables as going vegan. It might be that your intellectual and emotional provinces are making peace, while your social province continues to plot against them. Or maybe your intellect's increasing openness to listening to your emotions without immediately rationalizing them away is creating a new inner balance of power that feels unwelcome and unstable. Perhaps plant-based cooking is your new passion, but finding shoes and belts and bags that hit your sartorial sweet spot isn't going so well. Maybe the tables turn within the year, as the kitchen honeymoon ends badly but your wardrobe's back on point. It might be that your commitment to creating abundant space for creaturely flourishing is resplendent where pigs at the local sanctuary are concerned, but despondent in the face of squirrels in the attic or the ol' surprise millipede challenge. Maybe you feel publicly more at ease going vegan for health reasons even though you privately yearn to make joyful noise against food apartheid and industrial agriculture.

Transformation can be very much at work in and across these tensions. You've courageously introduced change into a complex system, and its unforeseen developments can and often do turn out to be as beautiful as their initial emergence is unsettling. If you try to force all the variables into immediate compliance, you're likely to mistake transformational growing pains for intractable dysfunctions and give up in despair. But with a little patience and curiosity, you can learn to tolerate and even relish these complex challenges, settling eventually into a new vegan normal that continues to evolve in the direction of your joy, if not always in the ways you'd predict. As ever, the healing wisdom of Adrienne Maree Brown is a balm:

> Transformation doesn't happen in a linear way, at least not one we can always track. It happens in cycles, convergences, explosions. If we release the framework of failure, we can realize that we are in iterative cycles, and we can keep asking ourselves—how do I learn from this?[2]

The best approach I've found to releasing the framework of failure is adopting the attunement of love. Nothing turns all challenges to the good like love, because love resonates now with the promise of fruition and inhabits the present as if all is already well. Love anticipates who we desire to be and accords that dignity and beauty to who we are now notwithstanding our present limitations, opening a safe and healing space to strive without shame, endure hardship, and repair to strive again. Love's superpower is dissolving the coagulants that thicken the veil between now and then, struggling and thriving, desire and fulfillment, our flourishing and that of every other.

Not everything I learned in Sunday school has survived the past four decades. But I've been kicking the tires of love for a good long time and tracking it through the wisdom literatures of other traditions, too. Love's attention seems perfectly attuned for discerning the strange and wonderful cycles, convergences, and explosions of transformation, abundantly tuning in, as it does, to the intricacies of our desires and limits and assiduously tuning out impediments to flourishing that distort what we want and obliterate boundaries we'd be wise to respect.[3]

Think about it.

Love is patient, so a difficult past, unstable present, and unpredictable future are endurable.[4]

Love is kind, so every struggle is met with caring and compassion.

Love doesn't envy, so the success of others can be desired, encouraged, and celebrated.

Love doesn't boast, so victories are held lightly, emanating warmth and inspiration without generating imperious expectations or anxiety over the likelihood of future success.

Love isn't proud, so it can keep generous company with almost anyone and join with others in laughing at its shortcomings and foibles.

Love doesn't dishonor others, so they feel liberated to try and unashamed to fail.

Love doesn't insist on its own way, so it can adapt to and even collaborate with different styles of striving, struggle, and flow without feeling threatened.

Love isn't easily angered, so no one must walk on broken glass (and even those who would otherwise still be walking on eggshells have nothing to fear).

Love keeps no record of wrongs, so the soil that nourishes inner and outer relationships is free from resentment's toxicity and enriched by the compost of experience.

Love does not delight in wrongdoing but rejoices in the truth, so it's doubly delighted to aggressively redress injustices that keep us wandering in darkness toward our demise, culpably ignorant of our own and others' true good.

Love never fails, because when the veil between desire and fulfillment is as vanishingly thin as it is through loving eyes primed to experience the present in hope of the most redemptive future, the framework of failure—that shameful gap in the scaffolding between our current position and the dizzying heights left to climb—simply collapses.

But let's not get carried away. Mister Rogers is correct that "love isn't a state of perfect caring. It is an active noun like struggle."[5] Love is perennially tested by hardships, losses, unmet challenges, unfinished business, less abundant plantings of simple wishes, and blighted harvests of silly little offerings. We can continue to call some of these baddies "failures" in the colloquial sense so as not to be too obtuse or cloying. But the point is just that success and failure as we typically think of them are not the parameters of love's purview. Love's goal is to become attuned to the most abundant ways of being present to ourselves and others in the hope of flourishing to whatever extent is possible in full acceptance of our limits. Right again, Mister Rogers:

> Listening is where love begins: listening to ourselves and then to our neighbors. To love someone is to strive to accept that person exactly the way [they are], right here and now: the lovely with the unlovely, the strong along with the fearful, the true mixed in with the façade, and of course, the only way we can do it is by accepting ourselves that way.[6]

In Mister Rogers' Neighborhood, Daniel Tiger, Prince Tuesday, Ana Platypus, and Officer Clemmons worked together to live by this wisdom.[7] Most of us and many of our neighbors, too, have been practicing some version of it since kindergarten, at least in our best moments. The thinner the veil on the inside, the thinner the veil on the outside. Attune. Attend. Accept.

This is the transformation that awaits going vegan: the journey from an orientation of scarcity, fear, and oppression in which we animalize, instrumentalize, and consume ourselves, others, and the world, into an orientation of abundance, joy, and liberation in which we become increasingly attuned to how best to attend to our flourishing and everyone else's, accepting our fragility but resolving to discover our flow—that peculiar elevating chemistry that frees us to leaven the world at large. In the shimmering words of the poet Czeslaw Milosz, "Whoever sees that way heals his heart, without knowing it, from various ills—a bird and a tree say to him: friend." This is love's desire: to live toward ourselves and the world so that we can all "stand in the glow of ripeness."[8]

For me, the cycles, convergences, and explosions of this transformational journey—the Wake Up Weekends, rib-smokey epiphanies, and goose-shitty bombs from the blue—have opened the way to gifts of discernment, confidence, resilience, and joy that I could never have imagined receiving and yet can no longer imagine living well without. Your cycles, convergences, and explosions will bear you along a different winding path (with luck, one appreciably less befouled by excrement).

But I'll wager that your path affords you similar cosmic gifts and that their leavening effects will be inflected and improved in ways that only your chemistry can catalyze. If you strive to make this journey in a spirit of self-love, traveling in such a way that your inner family has regular opportunities to feel as seen and cherished as your neediest, most beloved family member or friend, your adventures in going vegan are likely to shape you in the following ways. (I'll narrate the travelogue in the present progressive tense, given its perfect attunement to the ongoing work of transformation.)

Your powers of discernment are significantly increasing, deepening both your introspective capacity to be present to the complex desires and limits of your inner ecology, and your social capacities to maintain fulfilling relationships and serve your community. What initially seemed like the curse of going vegan—its ubiquitous ripple effects across your physical, social, emotional, intellectual, and moral selves—is turning out to be a great blessing, affording you the perfect opportunity to move toward the balanced, holistic way of life you've always wanted but never knew how to get. In retrospect, it seems obvious: consuming energy and attentively caring about others—sustaining your own flourishing and that of your community—are as foundational to doing well as it gets. It makes perfect sense that cultivating careful daily attention at that intersection would pay big existential dividends.

Before going vegan, you were much less attentive to the complex synergy that powers or drains your inner family and inspires or curtails your engagement with the world. Because you had no basis for comparison, you never realized how fracturing of your well-being and frustrating of your deepest desires the status quo really was. But now you're witnessing the power of going vegan for unifying and energizing the different parts of who you are. You're feeling the physical uplift in your body. You're experiencing the exhilaration of aligned and authentic collaboration among your intellectual, emotional, and moral selves. You're amazed by the growth in your relationships and the clever strategies you're discovering for making new ways normal, just a few simple wishes, spiritual exercises, and silly little offerings at a time.

Your ascending discernment is creating a boom in confidence. You're surprised how complicated you are, but also delighted and proud. It turns out that containing multitudes can generate effusive generosity. The more intimately you understand your complex inner family, the more easily you can attend with hospitality to other complicated creatures. You increasingly know who you are, what you believe, how you feel, and what you want, and making your decisions by light of this self-knowledge means you're both much less susceptible to self-doubt and much more receptive to constructive criticism. By now, you're familiar with most of the cycles, triggers, and feedback loops of going vegan. The new ones that crop up intermittently are increasingly less taxing to negotiate. On the inside and the outside, you know who you can trust, who needs a little grace, and who requires very special handling (with fleece gloves, if no longer kid gloves).

The most amazing thing about your growing confidence is that it isn't tied to the perfect exercise of willpower or anything like it. You're discovering that going vegan is about attunement and acceptance, not achievement. It's about carefully listening to the others in your inner and outer midst, striving to receive them for exactly who they are, and being open to discovering how your humble presence can leaven them, even if that's as simple as allowing more space. Within an orientation of scarcity, confidence often manifests as an increase in power to dominate or a rigorous drive for perfection. But your confidence is coming from waxing abundance—not greater power or perfection, but deeper attunement to where your flow is most needed and when. You increasingly trust and accept yourself, so there's no need to constantly try to prove your worth or overcompensate for weakness. Your community receives the abundance of this inner shift as increased humility and generosity.

It's not like you always get things right. Far from it. But that's okay because your burgeoning confidence is supercharging your resilience. Your inner ecology is becoming a more functional ecosystem, capable of dazzling feats of self-repair that increasingly don't even register as your system automatically takes care of work that used to feel grueling. The effects of this shift are especially clear when you consider the evolution of your orientation toward aggressive detractors—a change that was barely perceptible as it unfolded but feels almost shocking in retrospect. The meat bullies, bacon jesters, protein police, and even the skeptical needlers were fearsome at first, enraging as your resolution grew, pitiable as their juvenile public ignorance began tugging at your empathy, and now possibly lovable as their inner vegans-in-waiting peer curiously back at you from behind crumbling fortifications.

These resilient powers of self-repair are rooted in your increasing patience and caring for the parts of you that continue to struggle. It's clearer to you with every passing challenge why it was so difficult to be resilient within the rigid confines of scarcity: the minute life took you outside the rules (as life inevitably does), you found yourself lost, confused, bewildered, ashamed, despairing, or all of the above. It was impossible to trust yourself when you were perpetually living one weak moment away from having to give up or start over. But now the challenges feel like opportunities to explore rewarding inner and outer collaborations between your discerning magic and whatever surprises your inner family or the world outside have in store.

As failures increasingly morph into learning experiences, the veil between now-you and aspiring-you grows ever thinner, your skin grows ever thicker, and your flow states are more difficult to interrupt. Things are generally going better, but you're much closer to flourishing even when they aren't. It's easier to embrace yourself in the fullness of your aspirations and less tempting to reduce yourself to your present level of rectitude. Some of your most exhilarating adventures in going vegan are happening precisely when the rules fall away. When you enjoy a meal you wouldn't have chosen at a new friend's home without a twinge of apprehension that your commitment is faltering. When you delight in watching your child enjoy a birthday cupcake you wouldn't have served or don an outfit you wouldn't typically have worn as an attendant in your friend's wedding, knowing that scarcity from you in moments like these can be a slow poison to another's inner vegan-in-waiting.

It's not that your resilience is turning you into a scofflaw. On the contrary, it's your discipline to and increasing facility with spiritual exercises that have brought you to a place where the music is beautiful when the universe decides to use you as an instrument. You're putting in the work so that when the mission gets bigger than the rules can contain, you're free to let the cosmos take over, releasing the playbook so that the purpose for which you learned the plays in the first place can be more lavishly served. Like when all twenty-four of Simon Kovar's *Daily Exercises* finally give way to the most sublime performance of Mozart's Bassoon Concerto in B-flat Major, K. 191 ever to grace human ears. This is where the veil is at its thinnest. Where disciplined self-love and capacious love of the world are so aligned and so abundant that, in the twinkling of a watering eye, the miniscule gift of your silly little offering is raised to the power of everything.

This experience lives beyond description. Joy is the state of being in which we prepare to undergo it and return from it elated, invigorated for continued service.

I can't tell you about your joy. That's for you to know and for the world to find out.

I can tell you that going vegan, if not by far the only source of my joy, has been one of the most abundant contributors, catalyzing daily the elevating chemistry that thins the veil and pulls me into everything's embrace, within and without. What could be more uplifting more often than a way of life that normalizes acts of intentional caring from moment to modest moment—at the table, at the dresser, in the neighborhood, in the yard—even as it attunes us for service to the fullness of time? Not even Taylor Swift.

Today's world would have us believe that going vegan is a journey into abstention, deprivation, self-judgment, exclusion, scarcity.

But we know better now.

The veil has grown thin enough to catch sight of tomorrow's world shimmering behind it. A world where the truth is incandescent that our joy cannot be full (nor our flourishing even sustained) in a state of indifference to the flourishing of our fellow creatures and our shared home. A world where the beauty of inner healing, communal justice, all-species kinship, and planetary restoration is the sparkling of our pursuit of this truth. A world where the goodness of enjoying the fullest abundance our creaturely limits can allow is the birthright of all hungry beautiful animals.

We have it within us to live toward tomorrow's world today that our joy may be full.

ACKNOWLEDGMENTS

I hope *Hungry Beautiful Animals* reads like a work of gratitude, because the twenty years of self-discovery, community-building, and world-expanding collaboration that gave rise to it are among the greatest blessings of my life. I'm going to take my time in thanking all of you, hoping against hope that this enthusiastic expression of gratitude for your contributions is as delightful to read as it was to write (and not rather an occasion ripe for the use of Dave Chappelle's "Wrap It Up" box).

I'll start with you, dear reader. I wrote this book in the humble hope that some of what I've learned in going vegan might be helpful to you in the quest to live your truest, most beautiful, best life. Thank you for reading this book and for sharing it with anyone you think might be leavened by it. Do let me know what worked and didn't work and feel free to reach out with questions or follow-ups. I do sincerely hope that the pros outweighed the cons for you, even if a career in philosophy has persuaded me that there are few more excellent gifts than constructive criticism.

Giles Anderson (my agent) and Kate Adams (his associate) excel at helping scholars become writers. With their expert guidance, I learned how to envision, organize, write, and sell an expert nonfiction proposal. Let my appreciation to them equal the distance between the efforts I produced with and without their help. That's a *lot* of gratitude.

TJ Kelleher (my editor) created the ultimate space of abundance in which to write a book: presence, time, emotional investment, and beautiful encouragement that helped me realize I could do it. I started from an anxious place of deep scarcity and ended up feeling joyful, first for a few days after each of our meetings but then more consistently until that spirit just took over the project. TJ says that his job is to make something very difficult a bit easier to do. But he made the experience of writing this book a fully joyful one for me.

Basic Books got all the details right. Thanks so much to Lara Heimert (my publisher) for believing in this project and keeping it on schedule, to Emma Berry for editorial guidance with Chapters 3 and 4, to Kristen Kim for managing the editorial process moving into production, to Melissa Veronesi (my production editor) and Lillian Duggan (my copy editor) for eagle-eyed attention to small things that make a big difference, to Liz Wetzel and Jessica Breen and team for their excellent work on publicity and marketing, and to Chin-Yee Lai and Ann Kirchner in art direction and design for helping me communicate my vision winsomely to readers before they've even opened the book.

For my author photo on the book jacket, I'm indebted to the wonderful Michael Newsted, who was serendipitously visiting Grand Rapids from Los Angeles just days before the photo was due. As the official photographer of Wake Up Weekend back in the day, he took many of the snaps that helped me reconstruct elements of the narrative for Chapter 4, so Michael's inimitable photographic warmth and energy have variously elevated this project.

In the late stages of the writing process, when shambling across the finish line seemed likelier than an invigorated final sprint, the Karuna Foundation awarded me a matching challenge grant for a campaign of public scholarship to support the book's release, and Michael Beckley and Ana Echemendia made a generous lead gift to leverage the match. By enabling me to imagine the world in which *Hungry Beautiful Animals* was ready for prime time, these partners helped me find my stride to finish strong. Many thanks to them, and to the valued partners who have joined us since, including Justice for Animals Fund, Dave and Yvonne Bishop, Tom and Trinda Bishop, Andrew Chignell, Joel Farran, and Jim and Jane Halteman.

The Better Food Foundation has been essential to the life of this book from day one. Thanks to Jennifer Channin, Aaron Gross, and Unny Nambudiripad for everything from help with framing the project for grant proposals, to connecting me with potentially interested supporters, to funding course releases to make time for me to write this book, to partnering with me on a campaign of public scholarship to promote *Hungry Beautiful Animals*.

Calvin University, my vocational home for over twenty years, has steadfastly supported my work in animal and food ethics. I am grateful for grant support from the Calvin Research Fellowship program, the William Harry Jellema Chair in Christian Philosophy, and the Writing Co-op in the Calvin Center for Christian Scholarship. Kevin Timpe, my department chair, colleague, and friend, encouraged me to explore every avenue for support and worked unstintingly to enable me to take the opportunities that came. Many thanks to Dean Benita Wolters-Fredlund, Dean David Wunder, and Provost Noah Toly for their support of the grants and research leaves required to keep this project on track.

I am especially thankful to my colleagues in the philosophy department: Corrie Bakker, David Billings, Kevin Corcoran, Rebecca Konyndyk DeYoung, Joe Shin, James K. A. Smith, Jeff Snapper, and Kevin Timpe. This department has created an atmosphere where books written to promote flourishing beyond the walls of academe are not only allowed but encouraged and celebrated. It's hard to imagine that *Hungry Beautiful Animals* would have made it through the woods without the trail blazed by books like Kevin Corcoran's *Church in the Present Tense*, Rebecca Konyndyk DeYoung's *Glittering Vices*, James K. A. Smith's *You Are What You Love*, and Kevin Timpe's *Disability and Inclusive Communities*. My colleagues care deeply about the flourishing of the world and have shown me what it looks like to do philosophy as a form of service to others. Their friendship, collegiality, and general brilliance have been wellsprings of inspiration, motivation, and delight for me since 2003.

Another Calvin colleague paved the way for *Hungry Beautiful Animals* in a more literal sense—my friend and writing mentor Kristin Kobes DuMez, who got me an agent, doggedly encouraged me to work up a proposal, and helped me navigate every step of the very new terrain of turning academic training to trade publishing purposes. Without Kristin's encouragement and advocacy, it's unlikely I would have gotten this opportunity much less survived to see it through.

My students at Calvin are owed a huge measure of credit for inspiring the vision and strategy shared in this book and for the enthusiasm and confidence I have built in road testing this approach with them for the past two decades. In 2004, Amelia Hicks—now a philosophy professor at Kansas State—asked me to teach a class on animal ethics. I taught Peaceable Kingdom for the first time in January 2005, and the good folks from that very special seminar founded the Calvin Students for Compassionate Living (SCL) just months later. The enthusiasm of that group—Bethany Bertapelle, Jordan Carr-DeVries, Mary Carr-DeVries, Amelia Hicks, Sarah Bodbyl Roels, and Emily (Schreur) Turcotte, among others—left an indelible impression on me, and inspired us all to try to be the change we wanted to see.

With the help of SCL and Calvin alumna and visionary animal advocate Gracia Fay Ellwood, we founded Wake Up Weekend and the Animals and the Kingdom of God Lecture Series, both of which had a profound shaping effect on the vision of this book. Over the years, many SCL cochairs including Briella Cumings, Beth Doty, Andrea Krudy, and Noah Praamsma have inspired me with their advocacy work, and for many the work continues! In April of 2024, Noah—now Noah Praamsma, MS, RDN—guest lectured on plant-based nutrition to a new crop of Peaceable Kingdom students from his station as a nutrition education coordinator for the Physicians Committee for Responsible Medicine. Insofar as there is no richer pleasure for an educator than to see the student become the teacher, this was the best gift for my twentieth anniversary of teaching animal ethics I could have hoped for. You too can learn more from Noah in Appendix A of this book.

I'm grateful to all my students for the opportunity to teach and for the annual reminders of the power of philosophy as a way of life. Members of my Spring 2023 Philosophical Transformation seminar deserve special mention for providing inspiration before an important deadline (thanks, Sara Brown, Weston Fields, Rachel Gabor, Aidan Hillman, George Holmes, Cody Husted, Tianrong Lin, Maria Poortenga, Diego Rivera, Jack Rogers, Anya Rop, Josiah Ryan, Yohan Shin, Raegan Visker, and Gabriel Wood).

I'm deeply appreciative of my teachers, too. Bruce Ellis Benson's pedagogy during my college years and Stephen H. Watson's direction when I was a graduate student combined indelibly to impress upon me the importance of aesthetics for understanding and pursuing the good life. My abiding hope that being moved by the world's beauty can also make us more authentic disciples of truth and goodness is a legacy of their influence.

I was thirty years old before the urgency and beauty of the animal question dawned on me, and so my teachers in the ways of cultivating animal consciousness and going vegan thankfully never had to encounter my pre-vegan insouciance in a classroom.

Canine professors Gus (2003–2015), Charlie (?–2015), Daisy, and Cooper Halteman have offered daily opportunities to expand my consciousness and have been skilled diplomats at negotiating treaties across the provinces of my inner ecology to open abundant space for the pigs, orcas, geese, rabbits, robins, raccoons, opossums, ants, aphids, bees, and paper wasps responsible for my continuing education. I am grateful to Dr. Richelle Smith, Gus's veterinarian, for pulling back the curtain on the congenital difficulties of being a bulldog and igniting my empathy for other-than-human creatures.

My good friend and fellow philosopher Nathan Nobis got the pedagogical ball rolling for me, daring me to teach a class in animal ethics and providing a treasure trove of resources for doing so when I finally agreed to take up the challenge.

Philosopher and vegan advocate Mylan Engel Jr. gave me early opportunities to present and publish work in the field.

Andrew Linzey welcomed me into fellowship at the Oxford Centre for Animal Ethics and encouraged me to stay at the challenging work of engaging religious audiences, a mission he has pioneered for fifty years to make it possible for the rest of us.

Matthew Scully found some of my lectures online, sent them to influential friends, and has been a generous booster of my efforts ever since. His many accessible and beautifully written works on justice for animals have gifted me powerful teaching tools and inspired me to stretch beyond the confines of my academic comfort zone.

Christine Gutleben gave me an opportunity to publish my first work in animal ethics in the Humane Society of the United States's Faith Outreach series. Without her vision for bringing *Compassionate Eating as Care of Creation* into the world, it's hard to imagine how *Hungry Beautiful Animals* could have happened.

Bryant Terry taught me to see going vegan as a beautiful opportunity rather than a looming obligation. Chapter 4 begins to express the debt of gratitude I feel for this gift.

Carol J. Adams has vastly expanded my understanding of human/animal studies, helped me bring a much more holistic vision of justice to my teaching and scholarship, and offered generous mentoring, support, and friendship, especially on the rigors and rewards of writing books for wider audiences. She also has a vegan recipe library than which none more delectable can be conceived and a contagious enthusiasm for cuisine and hospitality that makes vegan living as joyful as can be.

The initial idea for *Hungry Beautiful Animals* came out of the Wake Up Weekend experiment to try to give participants a gorgeous window into a vegan world where they couldn't turn around without finding yet another feast for the stomach, eyes, mind, or heart. So many activists and scholar-advocates made repeated if not annual visits to Grand Rapids from wherever they hailed, often out of the goodness of their dumb ol' hearts because we were running things on a shoestring. Thanks so much to Nekeisha Alayna Alexis, Kolene Allen, Harold Brown, Charlie Camosy, Ryan Cappelletti, Brett Colley, Lexi Croswell, Ben DeVries, Brianne Donaldson, Jon Dunn, Adam Durand, Juan Garcia, Noah Gittell, Erika Jane, Nicole Renee Matthews, Sarah McMinn, Laura and Steven McMullen, Laura Mulder, Lisa Oliver King, Gail Philbin, Matt Poole, Michael and Megan DeMaagd Rodriguez, Milo Runkle, Matthew Russell, Paul Shapiro, Kolin Smith, Annie Smolinski, Christin Smolinski, Lena Spadacene, Cindy and Jody Talbert (of the inimitable Brick Road Pizza), Bryant Terry, and Karen Tracey. I've already expressed appreciation for my chief coconspirators Adam Wolpa and Michelle Loyd-Paige in Chapter 4, but I can't thank them enough.

Many colleges, universities, churches, and nonprofit organizations helped me to write the book you're reading by hosting me for presentations and giving me feedback. For invaluable help, many thanks to my gracious hosts and audiences at the American Academy of Religion Animals and Religion group, the American Philosophical Association Central Division Meeting, Andrews University, Calvin University, Church of the Servant

(Grand Rapids, MI), Davidson College, Eastern Avenue Christian Reformed Church (Grand Rapids, MI), Ferrysburg Community Church (Ferrysburg, MI), Free Methodist Church of Santa Barbara (CA), The Good Food Institute, Goshen College, Grand Valley State University, Houghton College, the Jackson Family Center for Ethics and Values at Coastal Carolina University, Love Thy Neighborhood (Louisville, KY), Michigan State University, Morehouse College, Northwest Nazarene University, Plant Based Roots (Grand Rapids, MI), Princeton University, Saint Mary's College (Notre Dame, IN), St. Christopher's Episcopal Church (Chatham, MA), St. Cloud State University, St. Joseph's College of Maine, St. Peter Claver Catholic Worker (South Bend, IN), Trinity Reformed Church (Grand Rapids, MI), University of North Texas, University of Notre Dame, University of Vermont, Westminster Presbyterian Church (Grand Rapids, MI), Wheaton College (Wheaton, IL), and Young Harris College.

Many generous people have helped me with the development of this book by agreeing to read drafts, corroborating memories and experiences, or offering guidance and support during the writing process in their special areas of expertise. Thanks to Jonathan Balcombe, Jessica Banaszek, Joanna Boer, Sophie Canadé, Melanie Challenger, Jennifer Channin, Andrew Chignell, David Clough, Anna Daining, Tyler Doggett, Lucy Engelman, Bruce Friedrich, Cassie Hagedorn, Dara Homer, Steve Kaufman, Lisa Kemmerer, Syl Ko, Amy Lovejoy, Michelle Loyd-Paige, Lori Marino, Noelle Mayhew, Bonnie Nadzam, Elizabeth Niemczyk, Ruth Bell Olsson, Rhonda M. Roorda, James K. A. Smith, Gail Spach, Anne Sullivan, Jonathan Swindle, Patricia Swindle, and Bryant Terry for their help in these regards. Special thanks to

Carol J. Adams and Jonathan Balcombe for indispensable input on how to manage writing a book for wider audiences, to David Clough and Aaron Gross for scheduled monthly advice and support, to Andrew Chignell and Tyler Doggett for randomly checking in always at precisely the right time, to Noelle Mayhew for excellent suggestions for the endnotes and appendices, and to Christina Bierdeman for introducing me to Internal Family Systems therapy and helping me to keep my inner family flourishing during the great adventure of writing a book.

Megan Halteman Zwart deserves extra special mention and an abundance of credit for being both an excellent philosopher whose collaboration and input have profoundly shaped this book and an excellent sister who was right all along about going veg (and even forgave me for all the bacon jibes if not for convincing her that a Hugga Bunch doll was all she was getting for Christmas '86). Our shared experience of siblinghood and the ideas we developed together in various cowriting endeavors are both grounding energies of this work, so Meg's sparkling presence is everywhere.

Many other generous people have helped me with the development of this book by being supportive friends to me and to our family while I was writing it. Much gratitude to Auntie Ana; Bridie, Bill, and Maeve Bereza; Wiebe and Joanna Boer; Kim Bradshaw; Jessica Brady; Jim Cooper; Ashleigh, Matt, Greta, and Sig Draft; Joyce, Rick, Hazel, Sam, and Gus Franklin; Cassie, Josh, Soren, and Nadia Hagedorn; Maranda Hanna; Gail, Mike, and Eleanor Long; Michelle Loyd-Paige and Darrell Paige; Michael, Megan, and Lewis DeMaagd Rodriguez; and Heather, Thad, Elliott, and Felix Salter. Andrew Chignell deserves special mention for well-timed visits to Grand Rapids and daily comic relief, Martin Lane for providing countless hours of healing retreat from writing fatigue through conversation over long walks and/or well-crafted libations, and Tyler Gaul for constant friendly reminders to stay hydrated and to write and live from abundance rather than scarcity.

I love my family and owe them everything. All the values that animate the vision of this book, but especially the idea that caring service to others is what makes life beautiful, were modeled for me in inspiring, indelible ways by Jim and Jane Halteman, my parents. Win and Jan McCausland, my parents-in-law, have shown me nothing but love and total support; how many vegan authors can say that their in-laws invited them to present work in progress at their church? From all-inclusive vegan Thanksgivings and plant-based birthday tasting menus with Meg, Jeff, Lee, and James, to socially distanced vegan donuts in the garage and hot sauce acquisition expeditions to Jungle Jim's with Doug, Julie, Ethan, and Evelyn, our terrific family makes it easy as vegan pie to feel loved for who we are and stay abundantly well fed.

The gratitude I feel to Susan, Andrew, and Eleanor for their support, encouragement, and patience (unto long-suffering, I fear) throughout the writing process is inexpressible. They all know how to bring out my best even in challenging times. As the closest members of my outer family, the joy of living with them each day is the elevating chemistry that keeps my inner family up and running, beloved and delighted, ready to serve.

Matthew C. Halteman
Grand Rapids, MI
August 2024

APPENDIX A

RESOURCES FOR EXPLORING PLANT-BASED NUTRITION

Though I have a strong hunch backed by a lot of reading that two decades on a plant-based diet has contributed generously to my physical flourishing, mental health, and discounted life insurance rates, I am not credentialed to offer nutritional advice. For that reason, and because the territory is exceedingly well-mapped by many excellent folks with better credentials, I do not offer coverage of the nutritional case for going vegan apart from noting in a variety of places that the existing case is very strong.

Even so, because concerns about the nutritional adequacy of a plant-based diet are among the main obstacles to moving forward for many people who are otherwise intrigued by the promise of going vegan, I am including some introductory resources here to help folks on their way to a solid layperson's education in plant-based nutrition. Instead of trusting myself with this task, I solicited the help of someone eminently more qualified—Noah Praamsma, MS, RDN.

As a nutrition education coordinator of the Physician's Committee for Responsible Medicine, Noah's job is to help folks like us understand the power of plant-based nutrition as a tool of preventive medicine. You can read about Noah's impressive credentials at www.pcrm.org/about-us/staff/noah-praamsma. You can also take my word as his friend and former professor that there's no one I'd trust more with my education on these matters. We're in very good hands! Having said that, please remember that personal research even in cutting-edge resources is not a substitute for medical advice, so if you're planning significant dietary changes, please consult with your physician to help you make the transition in the most holistic, healthful way possible given your specific circumstances.

What follows are Noah's suggestions for getting the lowdown on how a whole-food, plant-based diet can help us on our way.

The health benefits of a whole-food, plant-based diet are wide reaching, and a consensus among researchers, clinicians, and the public is quickly growing around its potency to achieve a variety of health goals. The Academy of Nutrition and Dietetics summarizes some of these benefits in its statement on vegetarian and vegan diets:

> It is the position of the Academy of Nutrition and Dietetics that appropriately planned vegetarian, including vegan, diets are healthful, nutritionally adequate, and may provide health benefits for the prevention and treatment of certain diseases. These diets are appropriate for all stages of the life cycle, including pregnancy, lactation, infancy, childhood, adolescence, older adulthood, and for athletes.

Plant-based diets are more environmentally sustainable than diets rich in animal products because they use fewer natural resources and are associated with much less environmental damage. Vegetarians and vegans are at reduced risk of certain health conditions, including ischemic heart disease, type 2 diabetes, hypertension, certain types of cancer, and obesity. Low intake of saturated fat and high intakes of vegetables, fruits, whole grains, legumes, soy products, nuts, and seeds (all rich in fiber and phytochemicals) are characteristics of vegetarian and vegan diets that produce lower total and low-density lipoprotein cholesterol levels and better serum glucose control. These factors contribute to reduction of chronic disease. Vegans need reliable sources of vitamin B-12, such as fortified foods or supplements.[1]

Much of the progress we've made since 2000 in understanding these benefits must be credited to foundational figures in the field whose research and publications have given those who want to eat compassionately not only moral substance, but an incredibly strong nutritional argument as well. These include Dr. Dean Ornish (*Program for Reversing Heart Disease* and his research with the Lifestyle Heart Trial), Dr. Neal Barnard (*Program for Reversing Diabetes* as well as many other books and research articles), T. Colin Campbell (*The China Study*), John Robbins (*Diet for a New America*), Dr. Michael Greger (*How Not to Die* and other books on weight loss and aging), Dr. Caldwell Esselstyn (landmark research on cholesterol and heart disease), Dr. John McDougall (*The Starch Solution* and founder of the McDougall Program), Dr. Michael Klaper

(*Vegan Nutrition: Pure and Simple*), Dan Buettner (*The Blue Zones*), and others.

More recently, we've witnessed an explosion of written resources on topics pertinent to vegan nutrition. Breast cancer surgeon Dr. Kristi Funk's book, *Breasts: The Owner's Manual,* equips women to employ plant-based eating for prevention and dealing with diagnoses. Dr. Will Bulsiewicz digs into the fascinating world of gut health in *Fiber Fueled*. Registered dietitian Brenda Davis offers a radically comprehensive guide to eating healthfully on a vegan diet in *Becoming Vegan: The Complete Reference to Plant-Based Nutrition*. Bariatric surgeon Dr. Garth Davis's *Proteinaholic* dives into the problematic nature of America's obsession with protein. And athletes looking to up their game with the most powerful foods for physical performance can find helpful books and podcasts from Rich Roll, Brendan Brazier, and Rip Esselstyn.

On the digital side, the ever-burgeoning library of videos on Dr. Greger's NutritionFacts.org is the discerning layperson's go-to resource for everything from acne to pork tapeworms. The Physicians Committee for Responsible Medicine, a nonprofit with a nearly fifty-year track record of nutrition education and advocacy, distributes a wide range of resources. In addition to their website, they produce *The Exam Room*, a top-rated podcast that covers an expansive range of health topics with the leading voices in nutrition science and practice with twice-weekly episodes. Their 21-Day Vegan Kickstart app and Food for Life programs offer delicious recipe plans and both in-person and online cooking classes.

Finally, documentary recommendations are something of a currency in the plant-based community. *Forks over Knives* is an excellent starting point. Others include *What the Health*, *The Game Changers*, *Diet Fiction*, *The Invisible Vegan*, *Eating You Alive*, *Food Choices*, and *PlantPure Nation*, many of which present uniquely compelling perspectives on a plant-based diet.

APPENDIX B

DECADENT CASHEW COCONUT CREAM TIRAMISU (VEGAN)

Apologies in advance that this recipe is somewhat involved. The perfect results take a little effort to achieve, but HOLY SMOKES is it worth it. And though I call this recipe "cashew coconut" tiramisu, the result of using a combination of cashews and coconut instead of mascarpone cheese and eggs does not result in a dessert that tastes like cashews or coconut. Those ingredients in this case serve more for texture than for taste, and the resulting dessert tastes just like the decadent coffee, custard, and sponge cake dream you've always loved!

LADYFINGERS

1. Make a 9×13 single layer of your favorite vegan vanilla cake. I make one batch of Isa Chandra Moskowitz's classic golden vanilla cupcake batter, pour it into a greased 9×13 baking dish, and bake for 22 minutes until the edges are pulling away from the pan and a toothpick comes out of the center clean. Here's that recipe: www .veganpeace.com/recipe_pages/recipes/GoldenVanilla Cupcakes.htm.
2. Cool completely.
3. Cut the cake into 1×3×1.25-inch ladyfingers and then cut each ladyfinger in half horizontally to yield double the number of ladyfingers. (If you are an experienced baker and can remove the full layer and cut it in half at one go with a really sharp knife, then do that before cutting the ladyfingers; I have had more success with the cake staying intact by cutting the fingers from a single layer and then cutting the resulting fingers in half.)

4. Set the ladyfingers aside for a couple hours in open air to let some of the moisture dry out.

COFFEE HOOCH SAUCE

In a flat dish that will accommodate dipping an entire ladyfinger, mix four tablespoons brewed espresso or strong coffee, three tablespoons coffee liqueur, three tablespoons light rum, and three tablespoons dark rum. Purists might prefer marsala wine or cognac, but I like rum better in combination with the cashew and coconut elements.

CASHEW COCONUT CREAM

1. In a Vitamix or powerful blender, blend 2 cups cashews, 1 cup soy milk, and 3 tablespoons B-grade maple syrup until completely smooth (test cream between thumb and forefinger to assure there is no grit whatsoever). Set aside. (Note: If you do not have a Vitamix or equally powerful blender, it is best to soak the cashews for a few hours in water to soften them up and make them easier to blend until perfectly smooth.)
2. Remove into a separate bowl the hardened coconut cream from two very well-chilled cans of full-fat coconut cream (the same brand you might use for a curry—in a chilled can, about ⅔ of the can will be a solid but still creamy opaque white substance and about ⅓ will be coconut water with little flecks of cream). USE ONLY THE SOLID COCONUT CREAM and discard the water.

3. Beat the coconut cream to peaks with 2 teaspoons of vanilla. Don't worry too much if it is not completely stiff (like a full-on whipped cream), as the mixture will set into the ladyfingers and form a perfect texture in the refrigerator overnight.

4. Gently fold the cashew cream into the coconut cream until the mixture is a uniform color and texture, but don't beat it or get too overzealous. Easy does it!

ASSEMBLY

1. Choose a serving dish that reflects the aesthetics you want for serving. Do you want to do it "trifle style"? Then use a glass bowl and build it like a trifle. Do you want to be able to cut square pieces to plate individually? Then choose a 9×13 or something similar. Do you want to do individual servings in crème brûlée ramekins or parfait cups? Go for it! The above elements can be combined delightfully in whatever way you like. I prefer square slices that can be plated, so I usually do a 9×13 assembly.

2. Dip ladyfingers in coffee booze so that they become about half-saturated and arrange them into a layer in the pan/bowl/ramekin/dish; if you have a few that get totally submerged, that's OK, but too many like that can lead to standing liquor at the bottom of the pan, which can affect service and texture. Also, leave some room between fingers for the cream to seep in and fill the gaps.

3. I like three layers of ladyfingers, so pour about ⅓ of your cashew coconut cream onto the first layer and smooth it over the entire layer. (Obviously, you'll need to adjust your approach if you're doing individual ramekins or parfait cups, but let common sense be your guide.)

4. Put about 5–6 tablespoons of dark cocoa into a sifter or strainer and tap the side evenly to distribute generously over the entire layer so that no cream shows through.

5. Repeat steps 2–4 until you have three layers of each: ladyfingers, cream, cocoa.

6. Grate an entire 3-ounce bar (or more!) of premium vegan dark chocolate over the final layer of cocoa to cover the entire dish in a generous, well-distributed layer of chocolate shavings.

7. Cover tightly with foil (to avoid the cake and cream absorbing unwelcome flavors and smells that might be in the fridge) and refrigerate for at least 24 hours. It's positively delicious after 24, but even better at 48— this is one of those recipes that is unimaginably good to begin with, but somehow just keeps improving with time.

DAZZLE YOUR FRIENDS AND FAMILY!

NOTES

Introduction: Hungry Beautiful Animals

1. Yuval Noah Harari, *Sapiens: A Brief History of Humankind* (New York: Harper Perennial, 2014), 12.

2. The profusion of Oreo flavors that has graced the world since my dear friend Sophie Canadé informed me that Oreos were vegan in 1998 is a phenomenon that I'm not sure whether to be elated or appalled about despite being elated about it. In 2019, Maximilian Schramm composed a "Complete List of All Oreo Flavors" some eighty-five varieties long including such alluring curiosities as "Cherry Cola," "Pistachio Creme," "Marshmallow Moon Cookies," and "Hot & Spicy Cinnamon." Peruse his findings at your own risk, as my engagement with his work resulted in multiple research excursions to the grocery during which considerably more energy was stored than expended. See https://medium.com/@mail_81120/85-oreo-flavors-the-complete-list-of-all-oreo-flavors-38ecee49d165.

3. J. Poore and T. Nemecek, "Reducing Food's Environmental Impacts through Producers and Consumers," *Science* 360, no. 6392 (June 1, 2018): 987–992, www.science.org/doi/10.1126/science.aaq0216.

4. Xiaoming Xu et al., "Global Greenhouse Gas Emissions from Animal-Based Foods Are Twice Those of Plant-Based Foods," *Nature Food* 2 (August 14, 2021), www.fao.org/3/cb7033en/cb7033en.pdf; and Elysia Lucas, Miao Guo, and Gonzalo Guillén-Gosálbez, "Low-Carbon Diets Can Reduce Global Ecological and Health Costs," *Nature Food* 4 (May 15, 2023), 394–406, https://doi.org/10.1038/s43016-023-00749-2.

5. See Michael Greger, M.D., *How Not to Die: Discover the Foods Scientifically Proven to Prevent and Reverse Disease* (New York: Flatiron, 2015); and David Robinson Simon, *Meatonomics: How the Rigged Economics of Meat and Dairy Make You Consume Too Much, and How to Eat Better, Live Longer, and Spend*

Smarter (San Francisco: Conari, 2013). Check out Appendix A of this book to discover some excellent resources for exploring the wide-ranging health benefits of a whole food, plant-based diet.

6. Leah Garcés, "COVID-19 Exposes Animal Agriculture's Vulnerability," *Agric Human Values* 37, no. 3 (May 14, 2020): 621–622, https://doi.org/10.1007/s10460-020-10099-5. A recent joint report from the Brooks McCormick Jr. Animal Law & Policy Program at Harvard Law School and the Center for Environmental and Animal Protection at New York University puts the risks of zoonotic disease creation and transmission caused by animal agriculture into harrowing perspective. See "Animal Markets and Zoonotic Disease in the United States," July 2023, https://animal.law.harvard.edu/wp-content/uploads/Animal-Markets-and-Zoonotic-Disease-in-the-United-States.pdf. "The Risk Is Staggering," says the *New York Times* (Emily Anthes, "'The Risk Is Staggering,' Report Says of Disease from U.S. Animal Industries," July 7, 2023, www.nytimes.com/2023/07/06/health/animals-agriculture-disease-spillover.html).

7. The Editors, "To Fight Antimicrobial Resistance, Start with Farm Animals," *Scientific American*, March 1, 2023, www.scientificamerican.com/article/to-fight-antimicrobial-resistance-start-with-farm-animals.

8. Almost 70 percent of American households have one or more companion animals as a part of the family. Americans spend over $100 billion a year making them feel at home. Globally, more than 840 million dogs and cats cohabitate with human beings. Thirty-seven million millennials live with companion animals. My favorite companion animal statistic? I'm glad you asked: "Over 1.5 million households have over 2.2 million bunnies in their homes." You're welcome! For these and many more data points that vividly capture our wholehearted commitment to the animals we call family, check out TheZebra.com's informative aggregation of key information from a wide variety of sources: www.thezebra.com/resources/research/pet-ownership-statistics. It initially seemed odd to me that a website touting itself as a "one-stop shop for insurance comparison" would be featuring such a thorough and well-sourced set of statistics on who companion animals are, where they live, and how much one must expect to pay monthly to be a good guardian. Then I stumbled over this statistic: "Only 2% of Americans admit to having pet insurance." Mystery solved!

9. Oxfam, "No Relief: Denial of Bathroom Breaks in the Poultry Industry," Oxfam America, 2013–2106, https://s3.amazonaws.com/oxfam-us/www/static/media/files/No_Relief_Embargo.pdf.

10. John Rossi and Samual A. Garner, "Industrial Farm Animal Production: A Comprehensive Moral Critique," *Journal of Agricultural and Environmental Ethics* 27, no. 2 (March 16, 2014).

11. I've shared some of these biographical details previously using similar language in "Eating toward Shalom: Why Food Ethics Matters for the 21st-Century Church," *Banner*, February 19, 2018, www.thebanner.org/features/2018/02 /eating-toward-shalom-why-food-ethics-matters-for-the-21st-century-church. I appreciate their permission to repurpose that material here.

12. My realization of this truth came more from my own lived experience with shame and the debilitating perfectionism that resulted from it than from book learning. But there's plenty of social science out there in support of the view that shame is not typically a driver of positive change. Brené Brown's *Atlas of the Heart: Mapping Meaningful Connection and the Language of Human Experience* is an accessible entry point for reflecting on the advantages of self-compassion over shame, especially Chapter 8, "Places We Go When We Fall Short: Shame, Self-Compassion, Perfectionism, Guilt, Humiliation, Embarrassment" (New York: Random House, 2021, 132–50).

13. If you're not familiar with Bryant Terry's work and you have some birthday or holiday money left to spend, visit his website to get the lay of the land (www.bryant-terry.com/about) and then do yourself a favor and just splurge on as many titles as you can manage. *Vegan Soul Kitchen: Fresh, Healthy, and Creative African-American Cuisine* (New York: Da Capo, 2009) and the James Beard Award–Winning *Afro-Vegan: Farm-Fresh African, Caribbean & Southern Flavors* (New York: Ten Speed, 2014) are among the most beloved cookbooks in our home, but we've got 'em all and you can't go wrong with *The Inspired Vegan* (New York: Da Capo, 2012) or *Vegetable Kingdom: The Abundant World of Vegan Recipes* (New York: Ten Speed, 2020) either. Outside the vegan space, Terry's skill and grace in bringing plant-based sensibilities winsomely into the wider culinary world are on full display in his luxuriously curated, James Beard Award–nominated *Black Food: Stories, Art, and Recipes from across the African Diaspora* (New York: 4 Color, 2021). Perfectly described as "a visual and spiritual feast with contributions from more than 100 Black cultural luminaries," *Black Food* is the kind of book you'll be tempted to buy two copies of so that you can keep your coffee table copy pristine and trash up your kitchen copy with reckless abandon. The good ones always end up grease-spattered, flour-dusted, syrup-smeared rags within a decade!

14. Farhad Manjoo, "Stop Mocking Vegans," *New York Times*, August 28, 2019, www.nytimes.com/2019/08/28/opinion/vegan-food.html.

15. Though deep engagement with the urgently important topics of the ethics of zoos and aquariums and the use of animals in commercial and scientific research lies beyond the scope of this book, I have found that the cases against animal captivity for these purposes are ironclad, and that one can arrive at this

conclusion from a wide variety of perspectives. Lori Gruen's *The Ethics of Captivity* is an excellent place to start for overviews of various problem areas authored by some of the world's leading experts (New York: Oxford, 2014). Peter Singer's definitive classic *Animal Liberation Now* makes the consequentialist case against animal testing in Chapter 2, "Tools for Research" (New York: Harper Perennial, 2023). See also Jeremy R. Garrett's *The Ethics of Animal Research: Exploring the Controversy* (Cambridge, MA: MIT Press, 2012).

16. If you've never experienced the inimitable elevating chemistry of being part of a fandom, you should consider becoming a fanatical supporter of the Arsenal Football Club—North London's most winsome practitioner of the beautiful game as it is played in the English Premier League. Intrigued? Read Nick Hornby's *Fever Pitch* (New York: Riverhead, 1992) for a primer on what it means to be a Gooner (i.e., an Arsenal supporter) and Charles Watts's *Revolution: The Rise of Arteta's Arsenal* (London: HarperCollins, 2023) for insight into why now is the perfect time to join our ranks. Then learn our new anthem (www.youtube.com/watch?v=X3ZDwnGqLY4), curse the existence of our bitter rivals, Tottenham Hotspur, and check out the most recent merch drops (www.arsenal.com). As a bonus, one of our attacking midfielders is an animal advocate whose philanthropic portfolio includes a donkey sanctuary (https://kaihavertz-stiftung.de/projekte/#1). *COME ON YOU GUNNERS!*

17. Keeanga-Yamahtta Taylor, "Are We at the Start of a New Protest Movement?," *New York Times*, April 13, 2020.

18. From my earliest work in animal ethics, I've always thought of going vegan as an aspirational rather than a perfectionistic pursuit (see, for instance, in Matthew C. Halteman, *Compassionate Eating as Care of Creation* [Washington, DC: Humane Society of the United States Faith Outreach, 2008]). But I think it was reading Lori Gruen and Robert C. Jones's terrific "Veganism as an Aspiration" (in Ben Bramble and Bob Fischer, *The Moral Complexities of Eating Meat* [Oxford, UK: Oxford University Press, 2015], 153–171) that really sold me on the idea of framing the practice explicitly in these terms.

Chapter 1: Vegan or Bust

1. "Gus Snoring Lullaby" was composed and arranged by Jim Cooper—Detholz! front man, Chicago freak rock titan, and sometime bassist for the legendary Van Dyke Parks. Listen here: https://soundcloud.com/Hallameat/Gus-snoring-lullaby. Watch Detholz! cover Kool & the Gang's "Celebration" here: www.youtube.com/watch?v=FPql21wtehI.

2. Judson Brewer, *Unwinding Anxiety: New Science Shows How to Break the Cycles of Worry and Fear to Heal Your Mind* (New York: Avery, 2021), 159.

3. Kathleen D. Dannemiller and Robert W. Jacobs, "Changing the Way Organizations Change: A Revolution of Common Sense," *Journal of Applied Behavioral Science* 28, no. 4 (December 1992): 480–498, https://doi:10.1177/002188 6392284003.

4. Pope Francis, *Encyclical Letter Laudato Si' of the Holy Father Francis on Care for Our Common Home*, Chapter One, paragraph 19, www.vatican.va/content/francesco/en/encyclicals/documents/papa-francesco_20150524_enciclica-laudato-si.html.

5. For a classic articulation of the abolitionist case against animal exploitation that argues that sentient beings are persons and thus morally impermissible to treat as property for human use, see Gary L. Francione's *Animals as Persons: Essays on the Abolition of Animal Exploitation* (New York: Columbia University Press, 2009).

6. For a compelling overview of the myriad ways that the "agricultural sprawl" of our animal-based food system is failing us and the transformational promise of moving toward a plant- and cell-based food system, see George Monbiot, *Regenesis: Feeding the World Without Devouring the Planet* (New York: Penguin, 2022).

7. The term "food apartheid" was coined by Karen Washington, the New York–based community organizer, farmer, and food justice advocate. For an accessible introduction to her work and a helpful primer on the idea of food apartheid, see Anna Brones, "Karen Washington: It's Not a Food Desert, It's Food Apartheid," Guernica, May 7, 2018, www.guernicamag.com/karen-washington-its-not-a-food-desert-its-food-apartheid/. To learn more about the four decades (and counting!) of Washington's transformational work that have earned her a James Beard Leadership Award and many other accolades, see www.karenthefarmer.com/about.

8. Elysia Lucas, Miao Guo, and Gonzalo Guillén-Gosálbez, "Low-Carbon Diets Can Reduce Global Ecological and Health Costs," *Nature Food* 4 (2023), 394–406, https://doi.org/10.1038/s43016-023-00749-2. From the abstract: "We find that, globally, approximately US$2 of production-related external costs were embedded in every dollar of food expenditure in 2018—corresponding to US$14.0 trillion of externalities. A dietary shift away from animal-sourced foods could greatly reduce these 'hidden' costs, saving up to US$7.3 trillion worth of production-related health burden and ecosystem degradation while curbing carbon emissions. By comparing the health effects of dietary change from the consumption versus the production of food, we also show that omitting the latter means underestimating the benefits of more plant-based diets. Our analysis reveals the substantial potential of dietary change, particularly in high and

upper-middle-income countries, to deliver socio-economic benefits while mitigating climate change."

9. Some of the material in these last few paragraphs is adapted from my *Compassionate Eating as Care of Creation* (Washington, DC: Humane Society of the United States Faith Outreach, 2008). I own the copyright.

10. My love for Gus swamped by far the financial stresses caused by his biological disadvantages, but I should have been a much more vigilant future guardian. Before you welcome a bulldog into your life, please carefully consider both what supporting bulldog breeders means to the lives of the creatures who must live with these bodies, and the question of whether you can bear the costs of making life as good as it can be for creatures selectively bred for these burdensome traits.

If you decide you're up for the challenge, please strongly consider going the rescue route to make life beautiful for a bulldog who needs your help! Learn more about the breed-specific problems bulldogs face in Meera Pal's "English Bulldog Common Health Issues," *Forbes*, March 29, 2023, www.forbes.com/advisor /pet-insurance/pet-care/english-bulldog-common-health-issues. If sharing life with a bulldog still seems a good idea, set a bookmark at Bulldog Rescue Network to learn who needs help in your area: www.rescuebulldogs.org/.

11. I am of two minds about whether to recommend that people subject themselves to the gory details of animal suffering in the industrial agricultural system. On the one hand, some people do seem to find it necessary to see the abjection of these situations for themselves to believe it is really happening, much less to be moved to empathy and resolved to change.

On the other hand, subjecting oneself to this level of suffering and sadness can feel debilitating. These descriptions and images are hard to "unsee," and for some, they leave impressions that are more demoralizing than enlightening. In addition, as I discuss in Chapter 5, the abjection of animals in confinement is often so extreme that it is difficult even to see, much less empathize with, animals as individuals—their subjectivity is completely swallowed in a sea of suffering that, ironically, can make it harder for some to imagine the flourishing of individuals as a real possibility. My advice is to think carefully about your threshold of tolerance for processing these types of images before you elect to subject yourself to them. Consider galvanizing your resolve, instead, by reflecting on the dignity of the lives these animals could be living if they were given the chance, with the help of Isa Leshko's *Allowed to Grow Old: Portraits of Elderly Animals from Farm Sanctuaries* (Chicago: University of Chicago Press, 2019).

If you need to "see to believe," the 2018 documentary film *Dominion* offers a comprehensive, if relentless, overview: www.dominionmovement.com/watch.

As someone who is inclined to skeptical first impressions and doesn't appreciate being emotionally manipulated, I find it helpful to juxtapose the footage in these documentaries with footage put out by the industries themselves. For this purpose, the videos on offer from the Glass Walls project with Temple Grandin are a helpful resource: www.youtube.com/playlist?list=PLkBbso1kwZ3bZTq N5MBLqHWGpRqPCH7gK.

If these are images you do not care to see, but still feel that knowing the details of animals' concrete circumstances is important to your journey, you can read all about them in "Down on the Factory Farm," Chapter 3 of Peter Singer's *Animal Liberation Now* (New York: Harper Perennial, 2023), 107–174. If you're concerned that the plight of animals is sensationalized in accounts like these and too dependent on worst-case scenarios to amount to a strong critique of the system at large, I invite you to consider the argument to the contrary I offer in Matthew C. Halteman, "Varieties of Harm to Animals in Industrial Farming," *Journal of Animal Ethics* 1, no. 2 (Fall 2011): 122–131, available online at https://philpapers .org/archive/HALVOH.pdf.

12. Elizabeth Gamillo, "More Than 50 Billion Tons of Topsoil Have Eroded in the Midwest," *Smithsonian*, April 19, 2022, www.smithsonianmag.com /smart-news/57-billion-tons-of-top-soil-have-eroded-in-the-midwest-in-the-last -160-years-180979936/.

13. *Philosophy Comes to Dinner: Arguments about the Ethics of Eating* (Andrew Chignell, Terence Cuneo, and Matthew C. Halteman, eds. [New York: Routledge, 2016]) was even dedicated to Gus, whose stately visage in profile appears in a photograph beneath words of gratitude in the front matter.

14. As a professional philosopher who got into this business in part because my life was changed forever by this riveting realization when I first encountered it as a college student, I can't resist recommending the two works by the late great German philosopher Hans-Georg Gadamer that turned me on to it. Truth in advertising, though: if wrestling with academic philosophy is not your thing, maybe skip these. But if you're up for an imagination-expanding adventure even at the cost of wading through a little turgid prose, feast your mind on Gadamer! Try "Man and Language" first in *Philosophical Hermeneutics* (Berkeley, CA: University of California Press, 1976). If you enjoy that, check out the ol' magnum opus, *Truth and Method* (New York: Crossroad, 1975). If you're not into it, you can repurpose this six-hundred-page behemoth as a doorstop or just let it emanate sophistication from your most prominent bookshelf.

15. James Baldwin, *The Devil Finds Work*, 1976, as cited in Ezra Klein's *Why We're Polarized* (New York: Avid Reader, 2020), 106.

Chapter 2: Anything but Vegan

1. This cookbook is an absolute treasure. Susan and I have our own dog-eared copy strewn with notes on successful vegan substitutions where necessary. Doris Janzen Longacre, *More-with-Less: Recipes and Suggestions by Mennonites on How to Eat Better and Consume Less of the World's Limited Food Resources* (Goshen, IN: Herald Press, 2011, updated).

2. Ezra Klein (citing Kahan), *Why We're Polarized* (New York: Avid Reader, 2020), 96.

3. Megan Halteman Zwart and I describe these two challenges as the "malaises of imagination and will" in "Philosophy as Therapy for Recovering (Unrestrained) Omnivores," Andrew Chignell, Terence Cuneo, and Matthew C. Halteman, eds., *Philosophy Comes to Dinner: Arguments about the Ethics of Eating* (New York: Routledge, 2016), 129–148.

4. Adam Grant, *Think Again: The Power of Knowing What You Don't Know* (New York: Viking, 2021), 31.

Chapter 3: The Vegan Imagination

1. Mylan Engel Jr.'s classic article "The Immorality of Eating Meat" was my first exposure to a "common sense" approach to making the vegan case that proceeds from beliefs, values, and feelings most people already have rather than from controversial views about animals or complex philosophical theories. See Louis P. Pojman, *The Moral Life: An Introductory Reader in Ethics and Literature* (New York: Oxford University Press, 2000), 856–890, https://philpapers.org/archive/ENGTIO-16.pdf.

Mylan Engel Jr. and Kathie Jenni develop this approach in further detail in *The Philosophy of Animal Rights: A Brief Introduction for Students and Teachers* (New York: Lantern, 2010). My own *Compassionate Eating as Care of Creation* (Washington, DC: Humane Society of the United States Faith Outreach, 2008) develops a similar approach from within a Christian perspective. Each of these works has inspired and informed my account of kindergarten ethics here in its own way.

2. My development of the idea that most of us are vegans-in-waiting owes a great deal to Carol J. Adams's treatment of "blocked vegetarians" in *Living Among Meat Eaters: The Vegetarian's Survival Handbook* (New York: Lantern, 2001).

3. James McWilliams's "Loving Animals to Death" (*American Scholar*, March 11, 2014, https://theamericanscholar.org/loving-animals-to-death) is top of mind here. I have a bit more to say about it in Chapter 3 note 6 below.

4. Don't miss Jonathan Safran Foer's excellent "Why We Must Cut Out Meat and Dairy Before Dinner to Save the Planet" for a good read and a humanizing

airport burger confessional. See the *Guardian*, September 28, 2019, at www
.theguardian.com/books/2019/sep/28/meat-of-the-matter-the-inconvenient
-truth-about-what-we-eat.

5. It wasn't for a lack of trying and it's not that I set out to be dismissive. On
the contrary, I was desperate for high-welfare animal products to work out and
regularly begged Susan to reconsider occupying that space. When those efforts
fell short, I devoured every neo-agrarian source of potential inspiration I could
find in hopes of salvaging the prospect. Wendell Berry's *The Unsettling of America: Culture & Agriculture* (New York: Random House, 1982). Michael Pollan's
The Omnivore's Dilemma: A Natural History of Four Meals (New York: Penguin,
2006). Barbara Kingsolver's *Animal, Vegetable, Miracle: A Year of Food Life* (New
York: Harper Perennial, 2007). Norman Wirzba's *Food & Faith: A Theology of
Eating* (New York: Cambridge University Press, 2011).

But none of these, and none of the many others, had anything I found compelling to say about the fundamental question that seemed (and still seems)
decisive to me: How do you respectfully (not to mention justly) slaughter animals whose creaturely dignity you openly acknowledge (even celebrate!) without degrading them, especially when you have many other nourishing options
to choose from? More pointedly, how can Joel Salatin write a book titled *The
Marvelous Pigness of Pigs: Respecting and Caring for All God's Creation* (New
York: FaithWords, 2016) and then advocate killing them for profit well before
the prime of their lives—indeed, when just 1/30th to 1/40th of their natural potential for "marvelous pigness" is behind them? Is it that this mysterious
essence "pigness" catastrophically implodes at seven months, and so compassion
demands that we put them out of their misery at five to six months, before they
have an inkling of the coming horror—coincidentally at just the time they've
reached optimal market weight? It just doesn't check out. We know better
than this.

6. One of the most compelling treatments I've seen of this paradox at the heart
of the agrarian vision is James McWilliams's "Loving Animals to Death: How Can
We Raise Them Humanely and Then Butcher Them?" (*American Scholar*, March
11, 2014, https://theamericanscholar.org/loving-animals-to-death/). McWilliams chronicles the moving story of small-scale pig farmer Bob Comis's personal
experience with loving animals to death, an experience Comis self-describes as
"unethical" and that eventually drove him out of the pig business and into produce farming. McWilliams exquisitely captures the paradox of "humane farming"
on which Comis's resolve finally foundered in one of the most memorable sen-
tences I've read: "How can a movement claim to care so deeply about farm animals
that it wants to restructure all of animal agriculture to ensure their happiness but,

at the same time, turn those same animals into an $11 appetizer plate of fried pig head?"

I continue to wonder whether a solution to this paradox is forthcoming. The best attempted explanation I've seen so far—"'Eat Responsibly': Agrarianism and Meat"—is one that I commissioned myself from the excellent philosopher Benjamin J. Bruxvoort Lipscomb for the volume *Philosophy Comes to Dinner: Arguments about the Ethics of Eating,* Andrew Chignell, Terence Cuneo, and Matthew C. Halteman, eds. (New York: Routledge, 2016), 56–72. It's a great read and I recommend it. But I'm not convinced.

7. I've already noted the influence of Carol J. Adams's *Living Among Meat Eaters: The Vegetarian's Survival Handbook* (New York: Lantern, 2001) on my notion of being a "vegan-in-waiting." As I was writing this book, Adams and Bloomsbury gifted the world a revised and updated edition of this classic, now with the new subtitle: *The Vegetarian and Vegan Survival Guide* (New York: Bloomsbury, 2022). If you're looking for additional expert help with unblocking your vegan-in-waiting, add this essential reading to your library!

8. Alejandro Jodorowsky and Marianne Costa, *The Way of Tarot: The Spiritual Teacher in the Cards* (Rochester, VT: Destiny), 248.

Chapter 4: Human Beings

1. This recipe is an absolute beauty, too, for practicing your chiffonade technique, which is helpfully explained in the instructions. Bon appétit! See Bryant Terry, "Citrus Collards with Raisins Redux," *Epicurious*, April 16, 2009, www.epicurious.com/recipes/food/views/citrus-collards-with-raisins-redux-352451.

2. David Whyte, *Consolations: The Solace, Nourishment and Underlying Meaning of Everyday Words* (Langley, WA: Many Rivers, 2015), 25.

3. I think the notion of an "inner family" is a helpful metaphor for reflecting on the different parts of the self and the complex relationships and group dynamics across the multitudes we all contain (as Walt Whitman might put it). But it's more than just a helpful metaphor for those who, like me, practice Internal Family Systems therapy (IFS) in pursuit of good mental health and daily flourishing. Given the transformational impact of this therapeutic practice on my own life—among many other happy outcomes, it inspired my inner family to cooperate on writing this book!—I am delighted to share resources with those who may wish to learn more.

For a charming, helpful, and very accessible illustrated introduction to Internal Family Systems therapy, see Tom Holmes, Ph.D., Lauri Holmes, MSW, and Sharon Eckstein, MFA, *Parts Work: An Illustrated Guide to Your Inner Life* (Kalamazoo, MI: Winged Heart, 2007).

If you're nerdy enough to read the (fascinating) therapist's manual, check out Richard C. Schwartz and Martha Sweezy, *Internal Family Systems Therapy, Second Edition* (New York: Guilford, 2019).

For something in between, check out Richard C. Schwartz, *No Bad Parts: Healing Trauma and Restoring Wholeness with the Internal Family Systems Model* (Louisville, CO: Sounds True, 2021); or Richard C. Schwartz, *Introduction to Internal Family Systems* (Louisville, CO: Sounds True, 2023). Many thanks to Christina Bierdeman, LMSW, for introducing me to this powerful tool for pursuing wellness.

4. Thich Nhat Hanh, *How to Relax* (Berkeley, CA: Parallax, 2015).

5. "Flourishing" is an imperfect English translation of the ancient Greek philosopher Aristotle's conception of *eudaimonia*—the particularly robust form of capacity-fulfilling happiness that Aristotle identifies as the ultimate end of human existence—the one thing we pursue for its own sake (rather than as a means to some other end). Will Buckingham's "Aristotle on Flourishing" is an eight-minute read that can help you decide if you want to go all the way back to the source, Aristotle's famed *Nicomachean Ethics* (Chicago: University of Chicago Press, 2012). See www.lookingforwisdom.com/aristotle-on-flourishing. If eight minutes is too much to ask, BBC Radio 4 has produced a charming two-minute explainer, also titled "Aristotle on 'Flourishing,'" that is available here: www.youtube.com/watch?v=j_7deR0idvs.

6. The philosopher Megan Halteman Zwart first called my attention to the strategic value of curiosity for overcoming defensiveness. To learn more about how curiosity is a natural antidote to defensiveness, helping one notice and respond to feelings that naturally occur when engaging new ideas, see Megan Halteman Zwart, "Can Developing Virtues Improve Dialogue Across Political Difference?," *Journal of the Scholarship of Teaching and Learning* 21, no. 4 (December 2021): 239–254, https://scholarworks.iu.edu/journals/index.php/josotl/article/view/32699/37286. For advice on how to practice the skill of asking curious questions to grow one's own curiosity and invite productive engagement, see Megan Halteman Zwart, "Intellectual Hospitality as a Guiding Virtue in Campus Conversations on Abortion," *Journal of Moral Theology* 12, no. 1 (January 2, 2023): 139–144, https://jmt.scholasticahq.com/article/66251-intellectual-hospitality-as-a-guiding-virtue-in-campus-conversations-on-abortion.

7. The qualifier "If we're not careful" is important here, as I think that philosophical arguments for going vegan (and about the ethics of eating more broadly) can have important uses, including shoring up our own intellectual confidence, defending our views from critics, learning how careful thinking can clarify complex issues, and convincing people to take the ethics of eating more seriously (even

if arguments are often less effective when it comes to helping people undertake and habituate new dietary practices). I coedited a book to sharpen our argumentative tool kits to these ends. If you want to burnish your skills in any of these ways, check out Andrew Chignell, Terence Cuneo, and Matthew C. Halteman, eds., *Philosophy Comes to Dinner: Arguments about the Ethics of Eating* (New York: Routledge, 2016).

8. Two invaluable resources for understanding this problem are Christopher Carter, *The Spirit of Soul Food: Race, Faith, & Food Justice* (Urbana, IL: University of Illinois University Press, 2021), especially Chapter 2: "Food Pyramid Scheme," 57–86; and Aph Ko, "Vegans of Color and Respectability Politics: When Eurocentric Veganism Is Used to Rehabilitate Minorities," in Aph Ko and Syl Ko, *Aphro-ism: Essays on Pop Culture, Feminism, and Black Veganism from Two Sisters* (New York: Lantern, 2017), 76–81.

9. I discuss this trend in some detail in Matthew C. Halteman, "We Are All Noah: Tom Regan's Olive Branch to Religious Animal Ethics," *Between the Species* 21, no. 1 (Spring 2018): 151–177, https://digitalcommons.calpoly.edu/cgi/viewcontent.cgi?article=2152&context=bts.

10. Peter Singer, *Animal Liberation Now: The Definitive Classic Renewed* (New York: Harper Perennial, 2023), 208–243.

11. In pursuit of this exciting counternarrative, I've devoted much of my teaching and writing over the past twenty years to clarifying how beautifully the practices of dietary change and food systems reform resonate with the Judeo-Christian vision. In doing so, I've tried to write in ways that will speak to the concerns of the many people I know who really want to do what is right but have genuine faith-based concerns that dietary change (and especially going vegan) sits ill with their religious beliefs and practices. I've also taken great care to leave plenty of space for divergences of individual conscience about what, specifically, dietary change as a religious discipleship practice should look like. If you or your friends or family experience these sorts of challenges, your inner vegans-in-waiting might find it liberating to explore some of what I've written for Christian audiences (and about religious food ethics more broadly). I've organized these briefly annotated recommendations into the order I might find most helpful were I new to the issue and starting from a place of general skepticism, but feel free to mix and match as interest dictates.

For a brief overview of why the church should take food systems reform seriously, see "Eating toward Shalom: Why Food Ethics Matters for the 21st-Century Church," Banner, February 19, 2018, www.thebanner.org/features/2018/02/eating-toward-shalom-why-food-ethics-matters-for-the-21st-century-church.

To follow the journey of a (hypothetical) Christian college student into deeper animal consciousness, check out Matthew C. Halteman and Megan Halteman

Zwart, "Reimagining Our Kinship with Animals," in David Paul Warners and Matthew Kuperus Heun, eds., *Beyond Stewardship: New Approaches to Creation Care* (Grand Rapids, MI: Calvin University Press, 2019), 121–134, https://phil papers.org/archive/HALQSR.pdf.

To learn more about the promise of dietary change as a Christian spiritual exercise, see *Compassionate Eating as Care of Creation* (Washington, DC: Humane Society of the United States Faith Outreach, 2008), https://philpapers .org/archive/HALLTT.pdf.

Are you looking to convince a pastor or theologically sophisticated family or friends that attention to food systems reform is essential to the integrity of the church's mission? See Matthew C. Halteman, "Knowing the Standard American Diet by Its Fruits: Is Unrestrained Omnivorism Spiritually Beneficial?" in *Interpretation* 67, no. 4 (2013): 383–395, https://philpapers.org/archive/HALKTS .pdf. For many other helpful resources to get your pastor more interested, check out the Christian social justice organization CreatureKind (for Animals, Peoples, and the Earth): www.becreaturekind.org/.

For a window into life as a Christian vegan, see Matthew C. Halteman, "Imagining Creation as a Christian Vegan," Sarx, https://sarx.org.uk/articles /christianity-and-animals/imagining-creation-as-a-christian-vegan-matthew-c -halteman.

My interest in engaging Christian communities on these issues was inspired in significant part by scholar-advocate Roberta Kalechofsky's pioneering work in Jewish communities; see *Judaism & Animal Rights: Classical and Contemporary Responses* (Marblehead, MA: Micah Publications, 2002). I've also learned an enormous amount from Aaron S. Gross (*The Question of the Animal and Religion: Theoretical Stakes, Practical Implications* [New York: Columbia University Press, 2015]) and Rabbi Dr. Shmuly Yanklowitz (*The Jewish Vegan* [Shamayim V'Aretz Institute, 2015]), whose unique and inspiring approaches to religious advocacy for animals and food justice indelibly impressed upon me how crucial it is to maintain an unwaveringly holistic vision of justice in doing this work. Finally, Jonathan Safran Foer's compelling efforts to weave his Jewish heritage and personal experience through a scintillating engagement with contemporary food ethics in *Eating Animals* (New York: Little, Brown, 2009) inspired me to bring my own religious heritage and personal experience to bear in *Hungry Beautiful Animals*.

Beyond my own humble offerings to Christian animal and food ethics, I'm thrilled to report that there's an excellent and ever-burgeoning literature by experts writing accessibly from a variety of perspectives. For an introductory overview of the issues at stake, see Tripp York and Andy Alexis-Baker, eds., *A Faith Embracing All Creatures: Addressing Commonly Asked Questions about Christian*

Care for Animals (Eugene, OR: Cascade, 2012). From a Catholic perspective, see Charles C. Camosy, *For Love of Animals: Christian Ethics, Consistent Action* (Cincinnati, OH: Franciscan Media, 2013). From an evangelical Christian perspective, see Sarah Withrow King, *Vegangelical: How Caring for Animals Can Shape Your Faith* (Grand Rapids, MI: Zondervan, 2016). From a Quaker perspective, see Gracia Fay Ellwood, *Taking the Adventure: Faith and Our Kinship with Animals* (Eugene, OR: Wipf and Stock, 2014). For a holistic perspective on going vegan as an act of justice and a spiritual exercise for decolonizing Christianity, see Christopher Carter's *The Spirit of Soul Food: Race, Faith, & Food Justice* (Urbana, IL: University of Illinois Press, 2021). I'll have more to say about this excellent book in Chapter 8.

For more on Christian theology and the animal question, check out Andrew Linzey's pioneering *Christianity and the Rights of Animals* (New York: Crossroad, 1987); David L. Clough's bar-setting two-volume series *On Animals, Volume 1: Systematic Theology* and *Volume 2: Theological Ethics* (London: T&T Clark, 2012 and 2019, respectively); and Karla Mendoza Arana and Aline Silva's (eds.) groundbreaking gift to the church, *A CreatureKind Lectionary for All Creation: For Animals, Peoples and the Earth*, www.becreaturekind.org /the-creaturekind-lectionary.

Finally, for a brief, broader philosophical perspective on food ethics and religion, see Tyler Doggett and Matthew C. Halteman, "Introduction to Part 6: Food and Religion," in Anne Barnhill, Mark Budolfson, and Tyler Doggett, eds., *Food, Ethics, and Society: An Introductory Text with Readings* (Oxford, UK: Oxford University Press, 2016), 275–292. For a book-length treatment, see Lisa Kemmerer, *Animals and World Religions* (New York: Oxford University Press, 2011).

12. For a window into Wolpa's approach to provoking curiosity and heightened consciousness of the beauty of a vegan world, see Adam Wolpa, "Seeing Meat Without Animals: Attitudes for the Future," in *The Future of Meat without Animals*, Brianne Donaldson and Christopher Carter, eds. (New York: Rowman & Littlefield, 2016).

13. A. Breeze Harper, ed., *Sistah Vegan: Black Female Vegans Speak on Food, Identity, Health, and Society* (New York: Lantern, 2010).

14. Harper, *Sistah Vegan*, xix.

15. Michelle R. Loyd-Paige, "Thinking and Eating at the Same Time: Reflections of a Sistah Vegan," in Harper, *Sistah Vegan*, 1–7, 1–2.

16. On women's reproductive rights, see Carol J. Adams, "Abortion and Animals: Keeping Women in the Equation," in *The Carol J. Adams Reader: Writings and Conversations 1995–2015* (New York: Bloomsbury, 2016), 287–292;

on effective altruism, see Carol J. Adams, Alice Crary, and Lori Gruen, eds., *The Good It Promises, The Harm It Does: Critical Essays on Effective Altruism* (Oxford, UK: Oxford University Press, 2023). Adams is best known for her feminist vegan classic *The Sexual Politics of Meat: A Feminist-Vegetarian Critical Theory* (New York: Continuum, 1990).

17. On euthanasia, see Peter Singer, *Practical Ethics* (Cambridge, UK: Cambridge University Press, 1980); on effective altruism, see Singer, *The Most Good You Can Do: How Effective Altruism Is Changing Ideas about Living Ethically* (New Haven, CT: Yale University Press, 2015). Singer is best known for the classic *Animal Liberation* (New York: HarperCollins, 1975).

18. Matthew Scully, "Pro-Life, Pro-Animal: The Conscience of a Pro-Life, Vegan Conservative," *National Review*, October 7, 2013. Scully is best known for his classic book-length critique of industrial animal agriculture, *Dominion: The Power of Man, The Suffering of Animals, and the Call to Mercy* (New York: St. Martin's, 2002). Don't miss Scully's newest book, *Fear Factories: Arguments about Innocent Creatures and Merciless People* (Troutdale, OR: Arezzo, 2023), which collects forty-five essays penned and published over the past three decades in some twenty different newspapers and magazines.

19. Loyd-Paige, "Thinking and Eating," in Harper, *Sistah Vegan*, 1–7. See also Loyd-Paige and Michelle D. Williams, *Diversity Playbook: Recommendations and Guidance for Christian Organizations* (Abilene, TX: ACU Press, 2021).

20. Adrienne Maree Brown, *Emergent Strategy: Shaping Change, Changing Worlds* (Chico, CA: AK Press, 2017), 119.

21. In describing how approaches to advocacy that are in apparent tension at the surface can be in powerful subterranean synergy, pattrice jones captures this messy beauty well: "What I believe, based on extensive study (and practice!) of activism, is that significant social change is most likely to occur when a variety of people approach the same problem from a variety of angles using a variety of tactics—ideally, although not necessarily, in cooperation with each other. That makes sense: Big problems tend to be complex situations in which social, cultural, economic, and material factors all play causal roles. It will rarely be the case that a single intervention can make a big difference. Even comparatively smaller problems, such as the need for a simple change at the local level, will be easier to solve if agitators are marching in the streets while insiders are simultaneously proposing practical solutions behind closed doors." pattrice jones, "Queer Eye on the EA Guys," in Adams, Crary, and Gruen, *The Good It Promises*, 123.

22. Brown, *Emergent Strategy*, 119.

23. Whyte, *Consolations*, 103.

Chapter 5: Animals

1. I'm deeply grateful to Lori Marino for several conversations about the inner and social worlds of dolphins and whales that helped me find the courage to try this little experiment in writing from a very different perspective. If you want to see the transformational potential of passionate scholar-advocacy at work in the world, look no further than Lori Marino's Whale Sanctuary Project: https://whalesanctuaryproject.org/.

2. Isa Leshko, *Allowed to Grow Old: Portraits of Elderly Animals from Farm Sanctuaries* (Chicago: University of Chicago Press, 2019).

3. I first came across the term "animal consciousness" and the idea that it comes in degrees and can result, after a certain point, in a "change in perception" that revolutionizes our moral world in Tom Regan's 2004 classic *Empty Cages: Facing the Challenge of Animal Rights* (New York: Rowman & Littlefield, 2004). Even after two decades, Regan's account of how the onset of animal consciousness can change us is among the most memorable and popular readings I teach. See Chapter 2: "How Did You Get That Way?" pp. 21–34. For a compelling documentary film on the onset of animal consciousness, check out Tribe of Heart's *The Witness* (directed by Jenny Stein), which tells the story of Eddie Lama, a hardscrabble Bronx contractor whose unlikely experience fostering cats turns him into a passionate animal advocate.

4. For a book-length exploration of this controversial comparison, see Charles Patterson, *Eternal Treblinka: Our Treatment of Animals and the Holocaust* (New York: Lantern, 2002).

5. Ozick's words serve as the epigraph for Jewish scholar-advocate Roberta Kalechofsky's excellent *Animal Suffering and The Holocaust: The Problem with Comparisons* (Marblehead, MA: Micah, 2003), 5.

6. Aph Ko and Syl Ko, *Aphro-ism: Essays on Pop Culture, Feminism, and Black Veganism from Two Sisters* (New York: Lantern, 2017).

7. This idea is woven throughout the essays by both authors in *Aphro-ism*, but receives a more sustained treatment in Aph Ko, *Racism as Zoological Witchcraft: A Guide to Getting Out* (New York: Lantern, 2019), especially Chapter 3, "Moving from Intersectionality to Multidimensional Liberation Theory," 73–95.

8. Syl Ko, "Addressing Racism Requires Addressing the Situation of Animals," in Ko and Ko, *Aphro-ism*, pp. 44–49. I'm relying heavily on Julie Gueraseva's helpful framing of the general project of *Aphro-ism* here. Gueraseva, "Interview with Aph Ko and Syl Ko: The Writers and Activists on the Entanglements of Race, Species and Gender," *Laika*, http://laikamagazine.com/interview-aph-ko-and-syl-ko/. For more in-depth treatments, see Syl Ko, "By 'Human,' Everybody Just

Means 'White,'" in Ko and Ko, *Aphro-ism*, 21–27; and Syl Ko, "Addressing Racism"; and Aph Ko, *Racism as Zoological Witchcraft*, especially pp. 39–72.

9. Syl Ko, "Addressing Racism," 45.

10. Another helpful resource for rethinking the human/animal binary is Melanie Challenger's *How to Be Animal: A New History of What It Means to Be Human* (New York: Penguin, 2021). Challenger offers a bracing perspective on how human reluctance to accept our biological status as animals has affected our history as a species and how embracing our animal being could improve our collective future.

11. Syl Ko, "Addressing Racism," 47.

12. Syl Ko and Aph Ko, "Why Black Veganism Is More Than Just Being Black and Vegan," in Ko and Ko, *Aphro-ism*, 50–55, 55.

13. I am drawing here on Aph Ko's claim that "white supremacy's grammar system is consumption." Aph Ko, *Racism as Zoological Witchcraft*, 17.

14. I came across this framing of creaturely experience as "fierce but fragile" in a lovely essay by Lorena Slager Wenzel and I've latched onto it. Lorena Slager Wenzel, "Scorpion Hearts Club," January 4, 2023, https://medium.com/@lorislagerwenzel/scorpion-hearts-club-7a2641b139cf.

15. I love the way the philosopher Martha C. Nussbaum characterizes our sense of wonder as "an epistemic faculty oriented to dignity: it says to us, 'This is not just some rubbish, something I can use any way I like. This is a being who must be treated as an end.'" Nussbaum, *Justice for Animals: Our Collective Responsibility* (New York: Simon & Schuster, 2022), 96. For more on how the concept of dignity can be applied beyond the realm of human experience, check out *Animal Dignity: Philosophical Reflections on Non-Human Existence*, Melanie Challenger, ed., (London: Bloomsbury Academic, 2023).

16. Jennifer Ackerman, *The Genius of Birds* (New York: Penguin, 2016).

17. Jonathan Balcombe, *What a Fish Knows: The Lives of Our Underwater Cousins* (New York: Scientific American/Farrar, Straus and Giroux, 2016).

18. Michael Tye, *Tense Bees and Shell-Shocked Crabs: Are Animals Conscious?* (New York: Oxford, 2017).

19. Carl Safina, *Becoming Wild: How Animal Cultures Raise Families, Create Beauty, and Achieve Peace* (New York: Henry Holt, 2020).

20. Ed Yong, *An Immense World: How Animal Senses Reveal the Hidden Realms Around Us* (New York: Random House, 2022).

Chapter 6: Earthlings

1. For helpful contemporary takes on the culture/nature binary and its racialized entanglements with the human/animal binary, see Aph Ko, *Racism as*

Zoological Witchcraft: A Guide to Getting Out (New York: Lantern, 2019), especially 99–106 ("How Nature Became the Playground for White Supremacy"); and Christopher Carter, "Race, Animals, and a New Vision of the Beloved Community," in Dave Aftandilian, Barbara R. Ambros, and Aaron S. Gross, eds., *Animals and Religion*, (New York: Routledge, 2024).

2. Particularly influential titles were Marti Kheel's *Nature Ethics: An Ecofeminist Perspective* (New York: Roman & Littlefield, 2008); Frances Moore Lappé's classic *Diet for a Small Planet* (New York: Ballentine, 2021); and the legendary "Slices of Paradise/Pieces of Shit" chapter in Jonathan Safran Foer's *New York Times* bestselling *Eating Animals* (New York: Little, Brown, 2009), 149–199. For a one-stop shop of helpful essays written from various ecofeminist vantage points, see Carol J. Adams and Lori Gruen's classic *Ecofeminism: Feminist Intersections with Other Animals & the Earth*, Second Edition (London: Bloomsbury Academic, 2022).

3. Aph Ko's wisdom is ringing in my ears here: "Going vegan (as a diet) is merely a natural byproduct of a larger conceptual shift—it's not the main point." Aph Ko, *Racism as Zoological Witchcraft*, 117.

4. Martha Nussbaum, *Justice for Animals: Our Collective Responsibility* (New York: Simon & Schuster, 2022), 56.

5. Nussbaum, *Justice for Animals*, 107. I'm taking cues here from Nussbaum's extension of her "capabilities approach" to seeking justice for human beings into the realm of seeking justice for animals. Says Nussbaum, "Human beings are vulnerable, sentient animals, each trying to achieve a good life amid dangers and obstacles. Justice is about promoting the opportunity of each to flourish in accordance with the person's own choice, through the use of laws that both enable and restrain. . . . Why on earth would such an approach to the lives of other animals not be appropriate, for similar reasons? They too are vulnerable sentient animals. They too live amid a staggering, and today increasing, number of dangers and obstacles, many of them of our making. They too have an inherent dignity that inspires respect and wonder. The fact that the dignity of a dolphin or an elephant is not precisely the same as human dignity—and that the dignity of an elephant is different from that of a dolphin—does not mean that there is not dignity. There, that vague property that means, basically, deserving of end-like treatment rather than means-like use," 95–96.

6. Paige Embry, *Our Native Bees: North America's Endangered Pollinators and the Fight to Save Them* (New York: Timber, 2018).

7. There are many wonderful books about the lives of bees and the inestimable importance of their life projects for the rest of us. The book cited above, Embry's *Our Native Bees*, is a particularly engaging one.

8. I don't think we need philosophers' permission to develop these bonds of physical proximity and emotional depth with other creatures and experience them as friendship-like, but I often appreciate what they have to say about the possibilities and limits of cultivating friendship with members of other species. See Nussbaum, *Justice for Animals*, Chapter 11, "The Capabilities of Friendship," 255–278.

9. Syl Ko with Lindgren Johnson, *Re-Centering the Human*, Mooni Perry in collaboration with the Um Museum (Korea) for the exhibition #Coroseum AndChaosOnTheTable, www.mooniperry.com/text/re-centering-the-human -syl-ko-and-lindgren-johnson/view/4921017/1/4921097.

10. Starre Vartan, "How Wildlife Bridges over Highways Make Animals—and People—Safer," *National Geographic*, April 16, 2019, www.nationalgeographic .com/animals/article/wildlife-overpasses-underpasses-make-animals-people -safer.

11. George Monbiot, *Regenesis: Feeding the World Without Devouring the Planet* (New York: Penguin, 2022). See also Paul Shapiro, *Clean Meat: How Growing Meat Without Animals Will Revolutionize Dinner and the World* (New York: Gallery, 2018).

12. Monbiot, *Regenesis*, 189. The United Nations Environment Programme sees the potential of alternative proteins to be a part of the solution, too. See "What's Cooking? An Assessment of Potential Impacts of Selected Novel Alternatives to Conventional Animal Products," December 2023, www.unep.org/resources/whats -cooking-assessment-potential-impacts-selected-novel-alternatives-conventional.

Chapter 7: Aspiration

1. The genre-defining classic on these matters is Carol J. Adams's *The Sexual Politics of Meat: A Feminist-Vegetarian Critical Theory* (New York: Continuum, 1990). For a helpful shorter treatment of some of the problems raised by the gendered character of eating practices, see Christina Van Dyke, "Manly Meat and Gendered Eating: Correcting Imbalance and Seeking Virtue," in Andrew Chignell, Terence Cuneo, and Matthew C. Halteman, eds., *Philosophy Comes to Dinner: Arguments about the Ethics of Eating* (New York: Routledge, 2016), 39–55.

2. Gallup's latest Consumption Habits poll found that low-income adults were among the subgroups most likely to identify as vegetarian or vegan. See Jeffrey M. Jones, "In U.S., 4% Identify as Vegetarian, 1% as Vegan," Gallup News, August 24, 2023, https://news.gallup.com/poll/510038/identify-vegetarian-vegan.aspx. As Tabitha Brown describes in a brief video (www.youtube.com/watch?v =ooPRPqlEOwU), you never had to be rich to go vegan if you built your diet on staple foods rather than processed foods. But it's easier than ever to go vegan on

the cheap with resources like Toni Okamoto's beautiful and fun *Plant-Based on a Budget Quick & Easy* (Dallas: BenBella, 2023). Visit her website at https://plant basedonabudget.com/.

3. In my experience, few vegan practices are more liberating or more necessary than expanding the horizons of our collective vegan vision toward common ground with other communities and social movements. I've already mentioned some helpful resources for engaging the (not mutually exclusive) perspectives of, among others, American conservatives (Chapter 4, note 18), Black vegans (Chapter 4, note 13; throughout Chapter 5; and Chapter 6, note 1), ecofeminists (Chapter 6, note 2), feminist vegans (Chapter 7, note 1), and religious (especially Judeo-Christian) food ethicists (Chapter 4, note 10). Two additional anthologies that have expanded my vegan horizons are *Veganism in an Oppressive World: A Vegans of Color Community Project*, Julia Feliz Brueck, ed. (Monee, IL: Sanctuary, 2017), and *Earth, Animal, and Disability Liberation: The Rise of the Eco-Ability Movement*, Anthony J. Nocella II, Judy K. C. Bentley, and Janet M. Duncan, eds. (New York: Peter Lang, 2012). For those interested in the latter topic, Sunaura Taylor's *Beasts of Burden: Animal and Disability Liberation* (New York: New Press, 2017) is an absolute must-read. I am anxiously awaiting the opportunity to read her new book, *Disabled Ecologies: Lessons from a Wounded Desert* (Berkeley: University of California, 2024), which—alas!—I cannot do before this book goes to press.

4. That human character is a mixed bag is something most of us will intuit at some point from an honest reckoning with our everyday experience, even if we tend to overestimate our virtue when asked. But it turns out there is significant empirical evidence that human character is generally decidedly mixed, too. See Christian B. Miller, *The Character Gap: How Good Are We?* (New York: Oxford University Press, 2017). For a helpful summary of the book's conclusions, see Massimo Pigliucci, "*The Character Gap* by Christian B. Miller," *Philosophy Now*, June/July 2020, https://philosophynow.org/issues/138/The _Character_Gap_by_Christian_B_Miller.

5. For a terrific essay on some of the ways that falling short of our dietary ideals can sometimes help us, see Tyler Doggett and Andy Egan, "Non-Ideal Food Choices," in Chignell, Cuneo, Halteman, *Philosophy Comes to Dinner*, 109–128.

6. David Whyte, *Consolations: The Solace, Nourishment and Underlying Meaning of Everyday Words* (Langley, WA: Many Rivers, 2015), 40–41.

7. See Appendix B for a vegan tiramisu recipe that will blow your mind and dazzle your friends and family. If you're like me, you'll be sneaking down at two a.m. to pilfer it out from under them while they sleep!

8. pattrice jones, "Queer Eye for the EA Guys," in Carol J. Adams, Alice Crary, and Lori Gruen, eds., *The Good It Promises, The Harm It Does: Critical Essays on Effective Altruism* (Oxford, UK: Oxford University Press, 2023).

Chapter 8: Discipline

1. Still, my beloved Matterhorn was but a pale simulacrum of my dream Swiss Army knife, the magisterial Wenger 16999 Giant. I could've kicked anxiety to the curb forever with this leviathan at my side, even if wearing the requisite sheath would have rendered me homebound. Behold the glory here: www.amazon.com /Wenger-16999-Swiss-Knife-Giant/dp/B001DZTJRQ.

2. There are too many excellent on-ramps to the journey into philosophy as a way of life to map them all here, but I can't resist sharing a few of the ones that have profited me most.

As an introduction to the tradition (especially as it unfolds in the West), Pierre Hadot's *Philosophy as a Way of Life* excels as a series of standalone essays that you can dip into and out of as interest dictates. Don't miss, especially, "Philosophy as a Way of Life" and "Spiritual Exercises" (Oxford, UK: Blackwell, 1995).

A classic popular treatment is Karl Jaspers's *Socrates, Buddha, Confucius, Jesus: The Paradigmatic Individuals*—a brief and accessible text that, if now a bit dated, does a winsome job of capturing the appeal of this approach to the love of wisdom across Eastern, Western, and Middle Eastern philosophical and religious traditions (New York: Harcourt Brace, 1962).

Martha C. Nussbaum's *The Therapy of Desire: Theory and Practice in Hellenistic Ethics* is more demanding of the reader but incredibly rewarding for those who wish to become true students of this approach (Princeton, NJ: Princeton University Press, 1994).

As for texts that show philosophy as a way of life in action, my top five favorites are Lao Tzu's *The Way of Life* (New York: Perigee, 1994); Gandhi's *An Autobiography: The Story of My Experiments with Truth* (Boston: Beacon, 1993); Henry David Thoreau's *Walden* (New York: Norton, 1966); Simone Weil's *Late Philosophical Writings* (Notre Dame, IN: University of Notre Dame Press, 2015); and Cornel West's *Democracy Matters: Winning the Fight Against Imperialism* (New York: Penguin, 2004).

3. Megan Halteman Zwart and I have explored the value of spiritual exercises for habituating dietary change in two previous publications. See Halteman and Halteman Zwart, "Philosophy as Therapy for Recovering (Unrestrained) Omnivores," in Andrew Chignell, Terence Cuneo, and Matthew C. Halteman, eds., *Philosophy Comes to Dinner: Arguments about the Ethics of Eating* (New York: Routledge, 2016), 129–148; and Halteman and Halteman Zwart, "Reimagining

Our Kinship with Animals," in David Paul Warners and Matthew Kuperus Heun, eds., *Beyond Stewardship: New Approaches to Creation Care* (Grand Rapids, MI: Calvin University Press, 2019), 121–134.

4. In sketching this account of spiritual exercises to fulfill your simple wish for a lovely Thanksgiving weekend, I'm taking inspiration from the list Pierre Hadot offers in "Spiritual Exercises," *Philosophy as a Way of Life* (Oxford, UK: Blackwell, 1995), 81–125, 84–85.

5. One of the sure signs that Susan and I were destined for each other was the discovery that both of our families religiously watched John Hughes's 1987 screwball road comedy, *Planes, Trains, and Automobiles*, every Thanksgiving. If your family hasn't instituted this tradition yet, there's no time like the present to lighten your holiday load by watching Del Griffith (the late great John Candy) and Neal Page (Steve Martin) madcap their way from New York to Chicago in diverted planes, exploding trains, buses full of spit-swapping exhibitionists, and incinerated cars, just in time for Thanksgiving! And if you already enjoy this tradition, be advised that a new 4K release of the film was gifted to the world in 2022 that includes over an hour of unreleased footage from the fabled four-hour director's cut that never saw the light of day. Read all about it in Anthony Breznican's "*Planes, Trains and Automobiles*: Watch the Long-Lost Sing-Along Scene," *Vanity Fair*, November 22, 2022, www.vanityfair.com/hollywood/2022/11/planes-trains-automobiles-deleted-scene.

6. Don't forget about Appendix B! I've got you covered!

7. Rich Roll, *Finding Ultra: Rejecting Middle Age, Becoming One of the World's Fittest Men, and Discovering Myself* (New York: Crown Archetype, 2012).

8. The Rich Roll Podcast is a treasure trove of resources for anyone interested in wellness. If you're going vegan, it's an absolute must. Check it out at www.richroll.com/all-episodes/.

9. Christopher Carter, *The Spirit of Soul Food: Race, Faith, & Food Justice* (Urbana, IL: University of Illinois Press, 2021).

10. This book is an incredible resource, but with a retail price of $165 and a heft pushing five pounds, you'll want to bulk up that grip strength before contacting your local librarian to get a place in the queue. Miguel Farias, David Brazier, and Mansur Lalljee, *The Oxford Handbook of Meditation* (Oxford, UK: Oxford University Press, 2022).

11. You can read the essay in which I attempt this bizarre feat, "The Roadhouse and Mindful Alienation: On Fearlessly Losing Hope in *Twin Peaks*' House Away from Home," in *Supernatural Studies: Twin Peaks Special Edition*, guest edited by Frank Boulègue and Marisa C. Hayes, forthcoming in Spring/Summer 2024. You can also go to YouTube and watch me present this talk (featuring my mad skills

in Photoshop and PowerPoint) to attendees of the It Is in Our House Now: *Twin Peaks: The Return* Online Conference: www.youtube.com/watch?v=CTJYH jrChco&t=10909s. If you haven't already done so, you will want to experience the world of *Twin Peaks* first; that's one two-hour pilot episode, twenty-nine hours of network television programming, a two-hour feature film, three adjacent novels, and an eighteen-episode limited series on Showtime (that aired as a "third season" of the show just twenty-six years after the second season ended). Otherwise known as THE BEST 50+ HOURS OF YOUR LIFE!!!

Chapter 9: Transformation

1. The gold standard in recent history is Devi and Paxton's (aka "Daxton's") first kiss in season 1, episode 8 of *Never Have I Ever* as Cannons' sublime "Fire for You" kicks into gear: www.youtube.com/watch?v=ShJdUWVkn4w. Further back, there's Dawson and Joey ("DJo") daring to hold hands during the pilot episode of *Dawson's Creek* in the healing embrace of Heather Nova's "London Rain": www.youtube.com/watch?v=umg4Qm9kgLY.

2. Adrienne Maree Brown, *Emergent Strategy: Shaping Change, Changing Worlds* (Chico, CA: AK Press, 2017), 105.

3. I didn't realize it at first, but in speaking of "love's attention," I'm pretty sure Martha C. Nussbaum's *Love's Knowledge: Essays on Philosophy and Literature* (Oxford, UK: Oxford University Press, 1992) is running in the background in some sort of twisted four-corded braid with Reiner Schürmann's *Wandering Joy: Meister Eckhart's Mystical Philosophy* (Great Barrington, MA: Lindisfarne, 2001), Hans-Georg Gadamer's *Truth and Method* (New York: Crossroad, 1992), and Pierre Hadot's *The Present Alone Is Our Happiness* (Stanford, CA: Stanford University Press, 2009). Some books so capture our imaginations that they become like conditions of possibility for everything we say. It can be difficult to remember to cite them!

4. And speaking of books so influential you forget to cite them: If you've ever been to a Christian wedding, some of the following might sound familiar. I'm riffing on the classic passage on love from St. Paul's First Letter to the Corinthians, Chapter 13. Because I'm more about the spirit of the law than the letter of the law in situations like this one, and because I'm generally not one for proof-texting, I'm opportunistically toggling back and forth from the New Revised Standard Version and the New International Version translations as it serves my rhetorical purposes. My sincere apologies, Youth-minister-who's-name-I've-forgotten-at-a-church-I -visited-with-a-friend-once-who-tried-to-translation-shame-me-when-I-was-six.

5. Fred Rogers, *The World According to Mister Rogers: Important Things to Remember* (New York: Hachette, 2019), 53.

6. Rogers, *World According to Mister Rogers*, 93, 95.

7. One of my top one hundred favorite things ever is that Ana Platypus's first name is an abbreviation of the binomial name of her species, *Ornitho-rhynchus anatinus*. Remember that song? Watch it here: www.facebook.com/watch/?v=1682948175095265. Handyman Negri's got a nice vibrato. When my kids were small and avidly watching *Daniel Tiger's Neighborhood* (animated second-gen *Mister Rogers*, if you haven't had the pleasure), I went to this video to try to cleanse my mind of Daniel's infernally earwormy advice in "Stop & Go Potty" to "flush and wash and be on your way!" Readers who may have heard me mumbling the Latin for "platypus" from roughly 2012–2018 now understand.

8. Czeslaw Milosz, from "Love" in the series "The World," *The Collected Poems: 1931–1987* (Hopewell, NJ: Ecco Press, 1988), 50. Fun side note: Susan and I elected to have this poem read (along with its companions "Faith" and "Hope") at our wedding ceremony in lieu of subjecting attendees to yet another reading of 1 Corinthians 13. The greatest of these three poems is definitely "Love."

Appendix A

1. Vesanto Melina, Winston Craig, and Susan Levin, "Position of the Academy of Nutrition and Dietetics: Vegetarian Diets," *Journal of the Academy of Nutrition and Dietetics* 116, no. 12 (December 2016), https://pubmed.ncbi.nlm.nih.gov/27886704/.

INDEX

domesticated animals, 121, 122, 127, 140

Dominion (documentary), 256n11

Donaldson, Brianne, 264n12

donkey sanctuary, 254n16

"Don't Stop Believin'" (Journey), 99

earth/environment, 145–165
  climate change, 3–4, 5, 13, 31, 146
  conflicts of interest and, 160–161, 162
  flourishing, 146, 151, 154, 155, 157, 159, 162, 164, 165
  as home, 146, 154
  innovations and, 163–164
  interdependence in, 154–155
  nonintervention in, 157–160
  persistence of suffering and death in, 158–159

Earth, Animal, and Disability Liberation: The Rise of the Eco-Ability Movement (Nocella, Bentley, Duncan, eds.), 270n3

"'Eat Responsibly': Agrarianism and Meat" (Lipscomb), 260n6

eating disorders, 177

Eating Animals (Foer), 263n11

"Eating Toward Shalom: Why Food Ethics Matters for the 21st-Century Church" (Halteman), 253n11

Eating You Alive (documentary), 243

EAT-Lancet Commission on Food, Planet, and Health, 4

Egan, Andy, 183–184, 270n5

egg-laying chickens, 44

Ellwood, Gracia Fay, 231, 264n11

Emergent Strategy: Shaping Change, Changing Worlds (Brown), 113, 114, 217, 265n20

emotional province
  conflicts in, 129, 130, 131, 132
  spiritual exercises and, 200–201, 207
  transformation and, 216, 222

Empty Cages: Facing the Challenge of Animal Rights (Regan), 266n6

Engel, Mylan, Jr., 258n1

English bulldogs, 27, 41, 256n10
  See also Bulldog Rescue Network

environment. *See* earth/environment

environmental consciousness, 155

environmental justice, 154

environmental morality, 159–160

Esselstyn, Caldwell, 241

Esselstyn, Rip, 242

Ethics of Animal Research, The: Exploring the Controversy (Garrett), 254n15

Ethics of Captivity, The (Gruen), 254n15

eudaimonia, 261n5

Exam Room, The (podcast), 242

factory farms. *See* concentrated animal feeding operations

fairness, 74, 78, 82, 84
  author's experience of, 86
  in blocked *vs.* aspiring vegans, 88
  characteristics of, 75–76
  vegan-in-waiting and, 83–84

fast food, 36

Fear Factories: Arguments about Innocent Creatures and Merciless People (Scully), 265n18

Index

feed companies (role in industrial animal agriculture), 34
fertilizers, 34, 157
Fiber Fueled (Bulsiewicz), 242
"Fight the Power" (Public Enemy), 212
Finding Ultra (Roll), 203
"Fire for You" (Cannons), 273n1
flexitarianism, 184
flourishing
  animal, 121, 122, 125, 139, 140, 141, 142–143
  Aristotelian origin of term, 261n5
  aspiration and, 171, 173, 174, 182, 184, 185
  earthly, 146, 151, 154, 155, 157, 159, 162, 164, 165
  human, 93, 95, 99, 100, 103, 111, 112, 114, 117–118
  self-understanding and, 173
  spiritual exercises and, 193, 194, 195, 196, 203, 209
  transformation and, 220, 224, 226
flow, 179, 182, 184, 187
  spiritual exercises and, 197, 210, 211
  transformation and, 220, 224
Foer, Jonathan Safran, 258n4, 263n11
Food and Agricultural Organization of the United Nations, 4
Food & Faith (Wirzba), 259n5
food apartheid, 36, 104, 108, 177, 189, 217, 255n7
Food Choices (documentary), 243
food deserts, 36, 104
Food for Life, 242
foodways, 92, 101
  author's dependence on, 59
  as customs and habits, 52
  defined, 50
  difficulty of overcoming, 57, 176

as lifeways, 94–95
shaping forces behind, 61–62
wisdom of ancient, 97
Forks over Knives (documentary), 243
fragility, 182, 184, 185, 187
  spiritual exercises and, 197, 210
  transformation and, 220
Francione, Gary, 255n5
Francis, Pope, 31, 84
free-living animals, 121, 122, 140, 142, 151
Friedrich, Bruce, 203
Funk, Kristi, 242
Future of Meat without Animals, The (Carter and Donaldson, eds.), 264n12

Gadamer, Hans-Georg, 257n14
Game Changers, The (documentary), 243
Gandhi, Mohandas, 195, 271n2
Garrett, Jeremy R., 254n15
geese, 136–139, 140, 141, 142, 151, 155, 170, 221
gender norms, 177, 269n1
generosity, 222, 223
generous feelings, 205–206
Genius of Birds, The (Ackerman), 139
Glass Walls Project (documentary), 257n11
goals
  author's approach to, 187
  complications to setting, 175–176
  customization of, 173, 179
  how to set, 185–186
  setting realistic, 171
  as simple wishes (*see* simple wishes)

new vegan normal (*continued*)
  spiritual exercises and, 210
  status of animals in, 121
  transformation and, 217
  Wake Up Weekend and, 100
New York Times, 10, 38
Night (Wiesel), 130
No Bad Parts (Schwartz), 261n3
nonintervention, 157–160
"No Relief: Denial of Bathroom
    Breaks in the Poultry Industry"
    (Oxfam), 252n9
"Not Strong Enough" (boygenius), 211
Nova, Heather, 273n1
Nussbaum, Martha C., 151, 152,
    267n15, 268n5, 271n2, 273n3
NutritionFacts.org, 242

oil companies (role in industrial
    animal agriculture), 34
Okamoto, Toni, 269–270n2
orcas, 3, 119–121
Oreos, 3, 251n2
Ornish, Dean, 241
Ornithorhynchus anatinus, 274n7
  See also Ana Platypus
Orthodox Christians, 178
*Our Native Bees: North America's
    Endangered Pollinators and the
    Fight to Save Them* (Embry),
    268nn6,7
Oxfam, 5
*Oxford Handbook of Meditation,
    The*, 206
Ozick, Cynthia, 132, 266n5

Parks, Rosa, 94
Parts Work (Holmes, Holmes, and
    Eckstein), 260n3

perfectionism, 176, 179, 182–183,
    187–188
  as the enemy of the good, 174
  kindergarten ethics in lieu of, 74
  self-righteousness stemming
    from, 178
  spirituality in lieu of, 194
  transformation in lieu of, 223
pesticides, 34, 157
pets, statistics on, 252n8
  See also companion animals
pharmaceutical companies
    (role in industrial animal
    agriculture), 34
Philosophical Transformation
    (author's seminar), 195
philosophy
  author's profession, 7, 103,
    192–193, 195
  the transcendentals in, 15
  as a way of life, 271n2
Philosophy as a Way of Life
    (Hadot), 271n2
"Philosophy as Therapy for Recovering
    (Unrestrained) Omnivores"
    (Halteman and Halteman
    Zwart), 258n3
*Philosophy Comes to Dinner:
    Arguments about the Ethics of
    Eating* (Chignell, Cuneo, and
    Halteman, eds.), 48, 257n13,
    261–262n7
Philosophy of Animal Rights (Engel
    and Jenni), 258n1
Physicians Committee for Responsible
    Medicine, 240, 242
physicians, consulting with, 240
pig roast (Mennonite church), 51–55,
    59–60, 130

Index

Yale University, 9–10

Yanklowitz, Shmuly, 263n11

Yong, Ed, 139

York, Tripp, 263n11

TheZebra.com, 252n8

zoonotic viruses, 4, 252n6

zoos, ethics of, 253n15

Zwart, Megan Halteman, 258n3, 261n6, 271–272n3

Matthew C. Halteman is professor of philosophy at Calvin University in Grand Rapids, Michigan, and fellow in the Oxford Centre for Animal Ethics, UK. He is the author of *Compassionate Eating as Care of Creation* and coeditor of *Philosophy Comes to Dinner: Arguments about the Ethics of Eating*. He lives in Grand Rapids.